AMY

MY SEARCH FOR
HER KILLER

AMY

MY SEARCH FOR HER KILLER

*Secrets & Suspects in
the Unsolved Murder of
Amy Mihaljevic*

James Renner

GRAY & COMPANY, PUBLISHERS
CLEVELAND

Gray & Company, Publishers
www.grayco.com

Library of Congress Cataloging-in-Publication Data
Renner, James
Amy : my search for her killer / by James Renner.
p. cm.
1. Mihaljevic, Amy. 2. Murder—Ohio—Cleveland—Case studies.
3. Murder victims—Ohio—Cleveland—Case studies.
I. Title.
HV6534.C55R46 2006
364.152'3092—dc22
2006027885

ISBN: 978-1-938441-40-0

Printed in the United States of America

This book is dedicated to a few women I love dearly:
To my mother, Connie;
To my sisters, Jessica, Joline, Barbara, and Emma;
To my wife, Julie;
And to Amy, my first crush.

Tyger! Tyger! burning bright
In the forests of the night
What immortal hand or eye
Could frame thy fearful symmetry?

—WILLIAM BLAKE

Contents

AMY

MY SEARCH FOR
HER KILLER

CHAPTER ONE

Taken

I FELL IN LOVE with Amy Mihaljevic not long before her body was discovered lying facedown in an Ashland County wheat field. I fell for her the first time I saw that school photo Northeast Ohio TV stations flashed at the beginning of every newscast in the weeks following her kidnapping in the autumn of 1989—the photo with the side-saddle ponytail. First love in the heart of an eleven-year-old boy is consuming. One look at that brown-eyed girl and I knew that, if she had gone to my school, she would have been the one I passed notes to behind Miss Kline's back.

But Amy didn't go to my school. She went to Bay Middle, which was somewhere on another planet, far from the sub-suburban cow town where I lived with my father. I had a vague notion, though, that Bay Village was somewhere near my mother's apartment in Rocky River. When I visited Mom every other weekend, I looked for Amy's face in the crowds at Westgate Mall, hoping to find her wandering the aisles at Waldenbooks—as if she'd simply been lost there the whole time. I would be the one to lead her home.

Throughout the last part of October and the whole of November 1989, local newscasts began their six o'clock coverage with updates on the investigation. It was my routine to come home from school and turn on the TV to see if there were any new developments, to see if she'd finally been found. I watched closely. I learned to pronounce that difficult last name—"Mah-*hal*-leh-vick." I memorized the face of her abductor from the police-artist sketches and searched for him in crowds.

With time, the reports became less frequent. A brief news segment in December covered her eleventh birthday party, which her family celebrated without her. Then the reports dropped off altogether. But I knew she was alive. She had to be. I was supposed to meet the girl in that photo. Maybe at a high-school football game five years in the future. Or in college. She would be found, and I would get to tell her that I never stopped looking for her.

On Thursday, February 8, 1990, I came home and flipped on the television. I sat cross-legged in front of it, and when the tube finally warmed up, her face was on the screen. It was that fifth-grade class picture again. I turned the volume up and listened as my innocence died.

Dead.

Murdered.

Dumped.

The news anchors cut to aerial pictures of County Road 1181 in Ashland County. Men in dark trench coats milled about a wheat field, tiny black specs in a sea of brown. The image was strangely ethereal, like the final glimpse of earth seen by a detached soul. It was here, they said, that Amy's body had been found. A jogger had spotted what looked like a large doll lying on the frozen ground during a morning run. That patch of road they kept showing looked as far from the civilized cul-de-sacs of Bay Village as anyone could get. I didn't see a single house in the background. Just a ragged field stretching to the horizon. It looked desolate. It looked unkind.

Police and FBI were guarded with information, but there were some details. We learned Amy was stabbed in the neck and hit on the head with a blunt instrument. No word on time of death. She was found fully clothed, but no one was sure what exactly that meant, yet. The composite sketches of her abductor appeared again, under an urgent voice-over. The news anchor couldn't stress one fact enough— further tests were being conducted to determine if she had been sexually assaulted.

I swallowed the information like a diluted poison, feeling it burn away a kind of protective inner coating that had once made me feel safe. Years later, when I tried my first cigarette at Seven Ranges Boy Scout Camp, I would remember this feeling—like healthy tissue being singed by flames. Still, I couldn't stop listening to the details. I couldn't stop the words from forming scenarios in my head—silent films that obeyed all the new facts and ended with Amy's body in that field.

I would not be the one who would find her and bring her back to her mother. That was a fantasy I could no longer indulge. Sitting there, staring into the smiling eyes of a girl now dead, I began to entertain a different dream. Adrenaline lit up my senses, making them detailed and fine. Now I pictured myself tracking down her killer, following him back to his lair. I saw myself knocking on his door, a snub-nosed revolver tucked under the waistband of my raggedy jeans. When he answered, I filled him with hot lead. I'd become an eleven-year-old vigilante.

"Jimmy?"

My dad, home from work, interrupted this macabre daydream.

"She's dead," I offered as a greeting.

"I know, I heard it on the radio," he said. He came and sat next to me. He was bulky with muscle, a bushy beard shadowing his face, towering over me at five feet, eight inches. Most days, I didn't see him until just before bedtime. He owned a fledgling construction business with his brother and often worked late pounding two-by-fours or laying shingle after the crew had already gone home. That day, he was home very early.

I quickly noted the affable expression on his face. His eyes were open wide and he was forcing a smile. I knew better than to trust that mock casualness. Then, as now, when my father adopts a look of non-concern it can only mean there's some trouble that he's still riddling out a way to break to me.

At first, I interpreted this as concern for my emotional state. He must have noticed how closely I had followed the case since October. But there was another reason he was home early, and what he said next linked me to Amy in a way that, as the coming years would reveal, not even her death could sever. Her death was about to become a part of me.

"I need you to know something," my dad said. "I've been getting . . . some death threats."

Inside a scrawny chest, my heart skipped a beat. "What? Somebody wants to kill you?"

My dad snapped off the television. Amy's image shrank away to a speck of white in the center of the screen.

"No. Somebody wants to kill *you*."

I didn't know what to say. Was he joking? The fear in his eyes told me he definitely was not.

"Remember that guy I fired a couple months ago?"

"Yeah."

My dad nodded his head.

"Why is he mad at *me*?"

"He's not," my dad said. "He's mad at me. He's really, really mad at me. And he's crazy. That's why I fired him. He's not all there in the head. He left a note for me the other day. It said he was going to come after you. You or your sister."

I thought of Joline, only four years old. I thought of Amy. I thought of two men I could hate.

"He's all talk," my dad continued. "He's a coward, really. Okay? I don't think he's really going to try anything."

Liar, I thought. *I know you're lying. Why else would you be telling me this?*

He looked at me with a mixture of caution and shame. "Do you know what to do if you're ever abducted?"

I hadn't watched three months of reports on a kidnapping without learning a little. "Make a lot of noise," I said. "I should scream for help and try to get away. I should kick him in the nuts?"

My dad laughed a little at that, which was good. It washed away some of the fear from his eyes. But he had reason to worry—especially as his business grew. There would be nights, years later, when we faced off against other enemies as they broke into our house. On those nights my dad carried a baseball bat. I carried a bowling pin. This was only the first day I realized such danger was possible. He wanted me to be prepared, as if he could sense the future.

"Good," he said. "But what about if you find yourself back at their house and they tie you up or handcuff you to a couch?"

I tried to imagine such a thing.

"They said on the radio that they were going to do an autopsy on that girl, Amy," my dad said. "I tried to think why they would want to do that after three months. I tried to think what kind of clues they were hoping to find. And then I thought if she was real smart they might find everything they needed."

"What do you mean?" I asked.

My dad paused, perhaps searching for a way to put into words the idea he'd been running through his mind on the way home. Finally, he looked me directly in the eyes. No sign of fear anymore, only cold resolve. "If you ever find yourself in that situation, here's what I want you to do. I want you to put everything you can into your mouth. Pull out pieces of the carpet. Bits of the couch. Hairs you might find lying on the floor. Knickknacks that you can reach. Anything. I want you to swallow it all down. As much as you can. That way, if this happens—if what happened to Amy Mihaljevic happens to you—when they do the autopsy, we can find out who did it." He leaned forward. I smelled a hint of Old Spice.

"And then I'll know who I should kill."

CHAPTER TWO

The Rookie

I NEVER WANTED to be a journalist. The word conjures images of sharp-featured men in fedoras holding spiral notepads, asking the new widow who just fled a burning house what it feels like to lose her husband and three children. I wanted to be a screenwriter, a Hollywood director. But I got tired of waiting tables at Rock Bottom Brewery in the Flats one day and figured I should try to make use of my Kent State English degree by writing freelance stories for local newspapers and magazines. At the time, *Cleveland Scene* magazine offered as much as $2,500 for a single article. That's more than I made in two months at the brew pub.

Every Wednesday afternoon for two years I would pick up the latest issue of *Scene* and read it cover to cover. I studied the format. I taught myself the style of a couple of the best writers. I honed my craft and waited for a unique idea.

In November 2003, I submitted to *Scene* a profile of Bill Watterson, the creator of *Calvin and Hobbes*, who lives a reclusive life in Chagrin Falls. *Scene* took a chance on it and me. That article led to more, and soon I was working as the magazine's full-time mail sorter. When I was promoted to staff writer in December 2004, I needed stories to pitch. My first thought was Amy.

Many years had passed since her body was found in that Ashland County field. Although that fifth-grade class photo was still vivid in my mind, I had forgotten many of the details about her case. Wanting to refresh my memory before pitching the story, I contacted the Bay Village police department; thankfully, a detective agreed to meet with me.

Although my mother lived in Rocky River for a number of years and I had visited her on rotating weekends and summers throughout my teens, I never actually set foot in Bay Village until February 9,

2005. Turning off I-90 onto Crocker-Bassett, I felt an odd quiver in the pit of my stomach. It was a little like the fuzzy-headed feeling of déjà vu, that sense of being outside yourself, but not quite. I had experienced this once before, on a brief visit to Bangor, Maine. I spent that trip touring a number of sites resident author Stephen King described vividly in his novels. Actually walking across the Penobscot River on a stone bridge that was featured in *It*, I felt as if I had crossed into King's imagination. It was the location where the evil clown's first victim turned up. I remembered reading that passage in the fourth grade. By the time the police found the guy, a fish had eaten part of the man's penis. I didn't look over the edge to see if the clown was still there.

Driving into Bay Village I felt the same way. I had come to know the town in two-dimensional images when I was eleven years old—seeing it on newscasts, reading about the community in newspapers—but the story of Amy's abduction remained removed from me, abstract, until this moment. I had been able to consider it the same way I could consider a particularly scary King novel: spooky, but safely separate from my reality. Now I could feel myself entering the story. I was becoming a character of my own, appearing for a brief cameo in Amy's epilogue.

There are no rundown houses on the main roads leading into Bay Village. Mostly there are only two-story Cape Cods or Colonials, vinyl-sided with well-kept lawns. These are homes I associate with bankers and lawyers, but maybe that's because I come from middle-class rural dirt roads where double-wides are the norm. To me, Bay Village looked like the towns featured in John Hughes movies—a *Home Alone, Sixteen Candles* kind of place.

At the corner of Lincoln and Bassett, I waited while a crossing guard led a gaggle of students across the street, kids born after Amy died. They probably knew her name vaguely as something invoked during sleepovers, words whispered into bathroom mirrors at thirty seconds before midnight. The middle-schoolers were dressed conservatively. I would be surprised if any understand what a hand-me-down is. There was not a single black child among them. Bay Village, unlike Lakewood and Rocky River, had not really integrated. I'm not saying it was a racist town. It merely hadn't had the chance to find out where it stood on that issue yet.

Farther on, I turned right onto Wolf Road. Little Red Riding Hood came to mind. Amy, too, had met a wolf in human clothing somewhere near here, only she had not emerged unscathed from the beast's belly. No heroic woodsman appeared at the last moment to cut her out.

Past Bay Middle School was the town center, then in the throes of a major construction project. The bridge on Wolf was open only to eastbound travelers. The police station was inside the town hall at the corner of Wolf and Dover Center. The town hall itself could have been set dressing from some Mark Twain tale. The large brick building with its steeply slanting roof was the oldest I'd seen in Bay Village, a reminder to the seventies architecture of the shopping plaza across the street that things were once beautiful. Lake Erie blended with the winter horizon on the other side of the baseball diamond behind the parking lot. I pulled into a visitor's space and walked inside.

At the end of a hallway I reached a bulletproof glass window.

"I'm here to see Detective Lieutenant Mark Spaetzel," I said to the uniformed cop behind the glass.

I felt nervous then. In a moment, the lone detective still assigned to Amy's case would step through that heavy metal door next to the glass partition and see me for the fraud I was. Some journalist. A kid, really. Still young enough for a trace of acne. Not tall. A small paunch above belted jeans. Dressed like a metrosexual on a budget. Carrying a battered leather satchel that screamed, *Please, take me seriously. See, I'm a writer!*

Trying to seem at ease, I bent over a display case filled with bongs and pipes confiscated from drug busts. I tried to look interested but not so interested that the cop behind the glass would think I was surveying goods. On a separate shelf was an open ledger—the officers' logbook from the evening in 1954 that Doctor Sam Sheppard was charged with murdering his wife.

"Mr. Renner?"

Detective Spaetzel—that's "*Spet*-zel," like "pretzel"—held the door open. He was younger than I expected, the first hints of gray playing at his temples. Most of his hair was still jet black and cut short, parted smartly to one side. He had a welcoming smile and alert eyes, seemingly unjaded by the grim details of the case to which he has devoted his care.

I shook his outstretched hand.

"Come on inside," he said. He ushered me into the narrow confines of the police department's detective bureau, down a hall to his cramped office. "He did it, you know."

"What?"

"Sam Sheppard. He killed his wife. We know that for sure."

Sheppard was actually acquitted of the crime after a highly publicized retrial by Cuyahoga County's best prosecutors in 1966. By then, he had already served ten years in prison, following an initial flawed conviction. Several books have been written on this case, each pointing to other men as the real murderer of Marilyn Sheppard. *The Wrong Man* implies that the Sheppards' window washer, Richard Eberling, did it. *Tailspin* points the finger at a "bushy-haired" air force major. My own mother, who worked briefly in a Lakewood Hospital mental ward, claims she knows "the true story," told to her by a patient one stormy night. I came to learn that people in Bay Village will ask a stranger "Who did it?" as a sort of litmus test. Any answer will do, but people get a little fussy if you don't have any opinion at all. The case casts a shadow over Bay Village, and its residents don't like their darkness ignored.

"Is that true?" I asked.

"Yes, but I can't tell you anything more. The doctor killed his wife," he said. Spaetzel motioned for me to step into his office.

I had imaged it would look like some film noir set: papers piled high on a well-worn desk, a second suit hanging on a coat rack for those occasions he worked through the night, a bottle of Jameson in the top drawer of his desk—all this behind a frosted-glass door marked HOMICIDE. The reality was anticlimactic.

Everything on his desk was in its proper place. There were a couple reports, but these were stacked neatly on top of each other and pushed to one side. No extra suit. Wooden door, not glass. And, this man did not have the look of a heavy drinker. He was more like a soccer coach, or an English teacher.

I knew better than to fall for this mild-mannered front. Spaetzel had earned a reputation as a sharp, cunning detective in 2001, when he solved a strange homicide that took place not far from Sam Sheppard's old house on Lake Road. A roofer was found shot to death behind his residence. Based on a scrap of paper found near the body, upon which was written a fake name, Spaetzel was able to track down the killer. His investigative skills helped put the murderer behind bars for life.

Hanging to the right side of Spaetzel's desk was the "missing" poster I remembered so clearly. Amy's face was blown up ten times the size of a normal flyer photo and laminated to heavy foam board. It was the first time I had seen this picture for many years. I had remembered her ponytail on the wrong side; I thought it had been hanging to her right.

I noticed something else about that photo. The way Amy's head was tilted, it didn't look posed. It looked like an insecure gesture, a shy girl's unconscious reaction to attention. But, then, maybe I was just looking too hard for minute evidence of her personality.

The door shut behind us and Spaetzel took a seat behind his desk. I sat in a chair to one side of him, facing the poster. I set my satchel on the floor and withdrew a legal notepad and a blue pen.

"Are you a fan of *The Wizard of Oz*?" I asked, pointing to a bright yellow brick mounted on a shelf behind him.

The detective smiled. "No. I got that for completing the FBI training course at Quantico."

"Oh. Were you in the FBI?"

"No. Just did a little training out there."

My eyes drifted to the window behind Spaetzel. Outside, a car drove down Wolf Road, sending a fishtail of snow in its wake before turning into a plaza across the street.

"So, what can I help you with?" he said.

"I want to write a story about Amy Mihaljevic. I think I remember most of the story, but I was hoping you could fill in holes before I pitch the idea to my editors."

"Why do you want to write a story about Amy?"

For a moment, I didn't say anything. This was a question I had anticipated, and I figured I had two choices: one, give this detective an easy answer, something like "I'm a fan of *Unsolved Mysteries* and I'm looking for unsolved cases in the Cleveland area to write about"; or two, share the story of how my father taught me to get the best out of my own autopsy. I took another look in Spaetzel's eyes and made a decision. This man needed something personal.

"I was the same age as Amy, and although I didn't live in Bay Village at the time, I followed the case on TV. The day her body was found, my dad came home and sat me down and gave me some advice . . . "

Spaetzel's eyes grew wide as I continued. By the end, he was laughing.

"Your father's a smart man," he said at last. He leaned back in his chair, his hands clasped behind his head. "What do you want to know?"

"Well, I want to get my bearings first. Can you tell me where she was abducted so I can visit the site before I head back to the office?"

"Sure." Spaetzel swiveled his chair and pointed out the window, toward the parking lot across the street. "Right about there."

"Across from the police station?"

He nodded.

"In broad daylight?"

He nodded again.

"Oh my God."

"Yeah. We took it kind of personally."

"You were working then? I thought you'd be too young."

He smiled and leaned back in his chair again. "I was a rookie at that time. It was my job to go to the school and talk to students about child safety."

"That's ironic."

"It gets better. I spoke to Amy's class that day."

The hairs on the back of my neck shot up. A cool rush filled my body. How *awful*. During the next year I discovered many horrific coincidences related to Amy's case, but this turned out to be the worst, the most tragic irony of them all.

Can it be mere happenstance that the last detective still working Amy's case actually warned her about talking to strangers the day she disappeared? That kind of stuff keeps me up at night. Some people might think it was some higher power giving Spaetzel a chance to save her. Other people, and I'm afraid I fall into this category, see this coincidence as a device God might use to imprison the detective, something to make the case so personal he cannot rest until the mystery is solved. Spaetzel was drafted that day into a battle he didn't choose to lead.

When the goose bumps settled, I asked him to walk me through Amy's last day. I didn't need a second-by-second account. The article hadn't been approved yet. I just needed a refresher, and I didn't want it to come from some old newspaper clipping.

Most of what Spaetzel told me that day I had heard before, as had most Northeast Ohioans. But there were some new details and at least one bit of information he probably shouldn't have shared.

The week before she disappeared, a man called Amy at home. The call came after school while her parents were still at work. Class ended for fifth-graders at Bay Middle an hour before the older grades that year, around 2 p.m. That usually found Amy home alone for an hour before her brother, Jason, who was in the seventh grade, got there.

I work with your mother, the man said to Amy. *She just got a promotion. If you'd like, I can meet you after school and help you pick out a present for her. You can have a present, too. Just don't tell anyone about this. Let's not ruin the surprise.*

Amy's mother, Margaret, worked for *Tradin' Times* in 1989, selling classified ads for the Westlake-based barter magazine. She went from part time to full time that year but had not been promoted.

The ruse worked almost perfectly; Amy disobeyed the man by blabbing to her friends. She told them she was meeting this man on Friday. She lied to her mother, telling Margaret she had to stay late that day for choir tryouts.

Shortly after 2 p.m. on October 27, Amy was spotted walking with classmates toward the Baskin-Robbins located in the shopping plaza a quarter mile down Wolf Road.

An eyewitness remembers watching Amy twirl around a pole outside the ice cream shop at around 2:45 p.m. The witness recalls hearing a man's voice calling for Amy.

When Jason Mihaljevic returned home shortly after 3 p.m., he called Margaret at work to let her know Amy wasn't there. Worried,

Margaret started packing her things to leave. Then the phone rang again. It was Amy.

Where have you been? Margaret asked.

Choir tryouts, Amy answered.

Margaret assumed Amy was calling from home. The conversation was brief. Amy sounded like she wanted to get off the phone. Feeling unnerved, Margaret left work and drove to the family's house in Bay Village. When she arrived, Jason told her Amy had not come home.

Amy was reported missing that evening, and by sunup, the FBI was working the case; kidnapping is assumed to be a federal crime because most victims end up across state lines.

For the next 104 days, Bay Village police worked hand in hand with the Cleveland FBI office, Police Chief William Gareau coordinating his officers under the direction of Detective Lieutenant Jim Tompkins. They, in turn, assisted SAC (Special Agent in Charge) Bill Brannon and his point man Dick Wrenn, who organized the FBI's presence in Bay Village.

A command center was set up in the town hall—two, actually: an FBI post in the basement and an army of volunteers on the second floor. The volunteers were led by Howard Kimball, a local man who ran the Bay Village Youth Cabin during happier times. Kimball's assistants copied hundreds of thousands of flyers, first of Amy's school photo and then, once the sketch artist was done, a composite of her abductor based on the testimony of two secret witnesses. Kimball's office was referred to as the "Amy Center" by the town folk.

Some eighteen thousand interviews were conducted by FBI and police. Inch by inch they searched the woods behind the horse farm where Amy took riding lessons. About twenty suspects were closely monitored. All but one took a lie detector test. The lone holdout was a local attorney.

One suspect who seemed promising for a time was a young man with the last name of Strunak. He lived in Fairview Park and volunteered at the Amy Center. To many, Strunak seemed too interested in the case. After police discovered Strunak had a criminal history, he was asked to leave.

The search became a hunt for a killer when Amy's body was discovered in February 1990.

Fiber samples recovered at the dump site were sent to an FBI lab for analysis. Results were inconclusive. A few days after Amy's body was found, Strunak committed suicide. An FBI agent named Robert Ressler felt so strongly that Strunak was the killer that he later identified him in a chapter for his book on serial killers, *Whoever Fights Monsters*.

In 1999, as the ten-year anniversary of the recovery of Amy's body approached, the FBI released a few new clues in an article that appeared in *Cleveland Magazine*. Whoever had murdered Amy had likely taken a few souvenirs from her. Missing items that should have been with her body included green horse-head earrings, a white nylon windbreaker, leather boots that laced up the front, and a black binder with "Best in Class" written on a gold snap on the cover.

No one was ever arrested or charged with her murder. Prosecutors never even convened a grand jury.

At the time of my interview with Detective Spaetzel, Amy's case file was sealed in an old photographic darkroom. The lead sheets and interviews rested inside four maroon filing cabinets. The remaining forensic evidence was stored in locked cabinets.

"Do you think it was Strunak?" I asked when Spaetzel had finished his account.

"No," he said. "I think it's someone else. I think he's still out there."

That would not be the last time I sat in Spaetzel's office, not by a long shot. However, there would come a day when he refused to give me any more information, possibly at the behest of retired FBI agents.

By the time I left Bay Village that day, I knew I had my story. No paper had yet named a suspect in the Amy Mihaljevic case. I already had one—Strunak. I wondered if I had it in me to find the other nineteen?

But before I pitched the idea to my editors, there was one other person I wanted to speak with, someone who knew Amy outside of case files and evidence bags, the person who launched the search for the missing girl: Jason, Amy's brother.

CHAPTER THREE

Amy's Brother

JASON MIHALJEVIC DROVE a bus for Kent State while I worked for the university's student newspaper and television station. There must have been times I sat less than three feet away from him as he took me from the underclassmen's parking lot to Dunbar Hall, where I lived, or from a fiction-writing class at Satterfield over to Music and Speech for drama. But we never met. I never knew how close I was to a member of Amy's family. If I had known, we might have become friends, because when we finally did meet in February of 2005, I liked him from the start.

Jason and his wife lived on a side street in Ravenna full of modest ranches and low-rent split-levels. It wasn't the large colonial in which he grew up in Bay, but it wasn't bad, either. By the time I got there the sun had just set and I could only see outlines of objects in different shades of gray. I couldn't tell what kind of condition the place was in, but none of the gutters hung loose and the siding seemed to be in good repair. I parked my car, an inconspicuous compact the color of guacamole, across the street, gathered my satchel, and walked to a side door.

There were lights on in the house, so I knew somebody was home. I hesitated for just a moment. A knock on a person's door at night, one they're not expecting, never sits well with people. It's a hurdle you don't have to overcome if you can call them first, but the number I'd found listed in the phone book under Jason's name was out of service. The truth is, no one likes visitors anymore—certainly not visitors who carry notepads. But what choice did I have? Either Jason was going to talk to me or not.

I rapped a fist against the door three times. I heard movement from the other side, the creak of feet on hard floors. The door opened and a woman's face appeared. Jason's wife. She had reddish hair and a warm, inviting face with large eyes.

"Hello?" she said.

"Uh, hi. I was hoping . . . does Jason Mihaljevic live here?"

The woman's eyes scanned my body, eventually landing on the satchel. *Salesman*, she seemed to be thinking. "Can I ask what this is regarding?" Her tone wasn't snippy, but it was getting there in a hurry.

"I want to talk to him about Amy."

The name took the woman aback. It was a name she knew well, obviously. I wondered how Jason talked about Amy with his wife. What did he allow himself to remember when no one else was around? "Oh," she said. "I'll get him. Hold on."

She closed the door, but I could hear muffled voices from the other side. My heart sank. I thought for sure his wife would be the one to return, lingering in my company just long enough to tell me to get the hell off the property. But when the door opened again, Jason stood before me.

I had hoped he would look enough like Amy for me to see her in his face. If they share features, though, I didn't see them in the yellow light cast by the kitchen. His face was round. He was stocky—thick, but not fat. His eyes were kind, but the smile his mouth formed was insincere. Not that I blamed him. If our situations were reversed, I wouldn't have even tried to smile.

"Can I help you?" he said.

"I'd like to write an article about your sister, Amy." Of course, what he heard probably sounded like some prolonged nervous stutter. "I was hoping we could sit down sometime and talk about her. Whatever you feel comfortable sharing, anyway. I just want to get a better idea of what she was like before I get started on this."

Jason stepped outside and shut the door behind him.

"I see," he said.

At the time, I thought it was odd how formally he and his wife spoke. They both had that aloof way of speaking that I associate with people who have read a library full of books. People don't usually say stuff like "what is this regarding" or "I see" unless they're pretending to be someone they are not. And I could tell he wasn't pretending.

"Sorry to surprise you like this," I said. "I tried to call."

"I disconnected our phones last month. We switched to cell phones. It's cheaper."

"I see."

"So, you want to talk about Amy? Why now all of a sudden?"

"It was the soonest I could do it. I've only been working as a writer for a couple months. It's just something I've always wanted to learn more about if I had the chance. Maybe shed some new light on it . . . or at least get her name out there again."

"Okay," he said. "I can do that. But my wife and I are busy tonight. And, I'd rather not do it here. What are you doing tomorrow?"

The next day, I arrived early at the Borders bookstore in Cuyahoga Falls, where we had arranged to meet, but Jason was already there, sitting at a table in the café, facing the entrance. He waved as I came in, and he smiled. This time it seemed sincere. I approached him and shook his hand.

Sitting down next to him, I was again struck by that odd feeling of stepping into a novel. The fabric of the reality between us felt tinged with electricity—unstable and unsafe.

Jason got right to the point: "Why do you want to write about my sister?"

I did not hesitate either. I launched into the story of the day Amy was recovered, and the conversation with my father. I thought that if Jason could see how personal this story was to me, maybe he would feel more comfortable with me. Like Spaetzel, Jason was too smart to pacify with some cut-and-dried answer.

At one point, my eyes welled a little. I was surprised to find I was actually growing angry. The more I told that story, the more I realized what an effect it had on me. And yet I was so removed from the tragedy. I can't fathom the effect Amy's death had on her brother. How had it altered the course of his life? The answer floated out of the mist: *at least enough to bring him here.*

"It was October 27, a Friday," he said when I was done. "I was in seventh grade, and I should've been there, in that plaza, when she was abducted."

"What do you mean?"

"I had a coupon in my pocket for a free birthday cone for Baskin-Robbins," Jason said. "I'd had it for a while, but I was going to use it that day. I had it with me. And, when I got out of school at three, I started walking in the direction of the Bay Village shopping plaza. But then I saw a group of older boys that picked on me. I went home instead, so they wouldn't pick on me. If they hadn't been there, I would've been at Baskin-Robbins with Amy."

He had lived with this guilt for fifteen years. He thought that if he'd only been stronger, or less fat, less pick-on-able, maybe he could have saved his sister.

"Would it have changed things?" he asked. "I don't know. They can't figure out the timing. She might have already been taken. But maybe not."

Jason took a sip from his drink

"What was she like?"

"Amy? She was a little spitfire. We had just started to become friends. She was very popular at school. Very outgoing. She had a couple close friends. The Kristens. Kristen Bonham or Balas or something. And Kristen Sabo. I think she kind of had a boyfriend, too. Kurt, I think, but maybe that's wrong. I know she talked about him a lot.

"I rode my bike around a lot, especially after everything happened. I built model cars in the basement to take my mind off things. The youth group at Bay Presbyterian became a big part of my life. If it hadn't been for Amy, I wouldn't have been so involved in church. Sometimes, tragedy does tend to work good things.

"I spent a year of high school in Australia, to get away from things. My mom sent me. I needed to be away from it all. It was good for me."

"And what was Bay like?" I asked. "What was it like to grow up there?"

"You mean the town that time forgot? By and large it was fairly safe. But it was snobby, homogenized."

"Do you remember your address?" I asked. I hoped the question sounded trivial, but it was probably the most important information I needed. If I was given a chance to jump into this story, I needed a place to start.

He thought for a moment. "Six twenty-eight Lindford Drive," he said. "I'll draw you directions." Jason took my pen and, on a brown

Borders napkin, drew a small map. Coming into Bay on Bassett, it's a right on Lincoln, and a direct right onto Lindford. The Mihaljevics once lived at the end of the cul-de-sac.

I thanked Jason for meeting me. I felt the ice cream story alone would be enough to sell the piece. It was the sort of personal detail *Scene* tried to fit into every article. I started gathering my things to leave, but Jason had one more story for me. It seemed the talking was doing him some good, and he wasn't through. Maybe he had been waiting for a reporter to come knocking so he could unload some of his burden.

"My mother didn't have a good night's sleep until the night before Amy's body was found down there in Ashland," he said. "She slept by the phone for three months. She'd get up in the middle of the night. But the night before Amy was found, she slept in bed. It was like somehow she knew it was over, finally."

That detail didn't sit well with me. I thought about the bonds between mothers and children, about stories of people burning their hands or dying unexpectedly and their mothers somehow feeling it from thousands of miles away. I thought of my relationship with my own mother. She was in the hospital again. I was definitely cognizant of that.

The question became, Who broke that bond? Was it Margaret, exhausted from the search, exhausted from holding out hope that Amy could be found? Or was it Amy, somewhere beyond, finally moving on? How did Margaret know that it was time to let go just before her daughter's death was confirmed?

I told Jason to call me whenever he wanted, for whatever reason. I didn't expect he would. But, as with many things I assumed about the Mihaljevics, I was wrong.

A few days later he called to invite me to a pitch meeting for a business opportunity called Team of Destiny. "We're allowed to refer friends," he said. I was touched. So I agreed to meet him at a satellite university in Independence one Tuesday evening to learn how I could make money by purchasing goods and services through a website. But it turned out Team of Destiny was just one of those multilevel marketing deals, like Amway, reworked for the Internet. I ended up using the experience for an article. Jason and his wife are still waiting to make their millions.

CHAPTER FOUR

Pitching the Story

I KEEP ON MY DESK a picture of Clint Eastwood from *The Outlaw Josey Wales*, his six-shooters raised into the air, his blue jean eyes ready to kill. I found it at a sci-fi/horror convention, tucked into a bin next to a picture of Natalie Portman, and bought it on the spot. It reminds me of something my grandfather, a veteran of World War II's Pacific theater, once told me.

"If you pull your gun, you better mean to kill," he said.

On the rare occasions when something I'm writing may mean the end of someone's career—or, at the very least, his or her good name—that picture is there to remind me of my grandpa's words. If you're going after someone, do him a favor and put him down for good.

I knew my editors at *Scene* liked stories with a visible antagonist, someone the reader wants to see picked apart in print. Mostly, they're not too hard to find. Bad guys are everywhere. There are enough crooked businessmen running warranty scams to keep a paper like *Scene* stocked with stories for years. And there's always room to skewer dirty politicians taking kickbacks from contractors or local corporations giving Cleveland jobs to Germany or India.

With the Amy story, though, the antagonist was unknown. My idea was to present the piece as an internal struggle instead, focusing on the plight of the Bay Village cop still working the case. Walking into the pitch meeting on Valentine's Day, I knew it was going to be a fight. But I thought I was prepared. After all, everyone loves a mystery.

The conference room where editorial meetings took place overlooked West 9th Street, the back end of the Rockefeller Building, and the city of Cleveland beyond. As staff writers and editors took their seats, wet snow could be heard hitting the glass and the metal ceiling overhead. For the next forty minutes, I waited while other writers bared their souls. Some ideas were laughed away. Others were written down by the editor-in-chief, Pete, who sat at the head of the table. "Jimmy Renn, whad'ya got?" Pete finally said, using the nickname he had chosen for me. It's a Minnesota thing, adding a *y* to the end of someone's Christian name. Don't ask me why he sawed my last name in half, though.

"This is Cleveland's most famous missing person's case," I began, "and it's never been solved. Once, dozens of FBI agents and every cop in Bay Village worked this case. Now, sixteen years later, it's the job of one detective to keep this investigation alive. I want to tell his story. I want to show how frustrating this is for him. Kind of a *Don Quixote* tale. Amy was taken right across from the police station in broad daylight, and his office looks out over that place. There's an added personal twist to this that drives him. The day she disappeared, he spoke to her school about child safety. He's linked to her forever because of those coincidences. And he can't let himself rest until he finds her killer."

A long pause followed, which was not unusual. Writers who are very outgoing outside of the pitch meeting clam up inside this room when asked to criticize their peers. It's an intimidating place, full of spent ego and aborted articles. Maybe they sensed this one was special to me because the pause did seem a bit longer than usual.

"What d'ya guys think?" Pete said, addressing the group.

Seated next to Pete, Kevin—the editor assigned to my stories—fidgeted in his chair. Not a good sign. I sensed he didn't like my idea but was hoping someone else would speak up first. Kevin and I had recently battled over an article about a local mechanic constructing a rocket truck in his garage. I had told him I would quit if he didn't let me tell it the way I wanted. It wasn't an idle threat. I didn't like Kevin, but I didn't envy his position either.

"So, what's timely about it?" Becky asked. She was a chick-lit writer in a steel-mill city, Cleveland's answer to Carrie Bradshaw. "I mean, has anything new happened in sixteen years? I just don't think there would be much interest in this."

"Well, a couple years ago, I think, the FBI released information about some items that have never been recovered," I said. "Items the killer might have kept as souvenirs."

"Yeah, I'm going to have to go with Becky on this one," Kevin said, leaning back in his chair and letting the words fall out of his mouth in one long sigh as he rubbed the back of his head. "I don't see it. It's sixteen years old."

"Are you saying you want to solve this?" asked Denise, sitting on the other side of Becky. Denise was an expat from the *Akron Beacon Journal*. Having worked at a daily, she knew instinctively how to construct a tight piece of journalism and the limitations of time involved in writing a piece like this.

"No," I answered quickly, lying through my teeth. "No, I don't want to solve it. I just think it could be a cool piece about this one guy's attempt to find her killer. Not that he can. But there's something to be said for the quest, I think. And the fact that he can't let himself stop."

"If there was something *new* maybe," Kevin said. "Are there suspects?"

"Yes," I said. "I have one suspect's name already."

"Still, this is old news," Kevin added.

"But should it matter if it's old?" I said. "Maybe it's worth bringing this girl's story up every few years just to generate more clues, you know? So people don't forget."

That's when I lost the rest of the writers. I had pulled out the soapbox, I was standing on it, and I couldn't put it away again. Writers should write news stories, their eyes said, not hit the reader over the head with some sixteen-year-old unsolved murder.

The room fell silent again, and in that pause I felt the story slipping away. I had wasted my chance by not finding a sharp enough angle. In that moment, I could feel all my delusions of grandeur dissolving like Alka-Seltzer in a bottle of Wild Turkey.

"There is something here, I think," Pete said.

I looked up at him, not sure I'd heard him correctly. He just sat there in his ratty T-shirt and baseball cap and stared back at me, his eyes unreadable. Pete was an editor driven by whim. If he had a feeling about something, he'd push for it, even to the detriment of his job. On the flipside, if he didn't "get" an idea, due to his distrust of or lack of familiarity with it he'd spike it, even if a roomful of writers believed he was making a mistake. He ran on instinct. Most times, he was right.

"But it's not there, yet," he continued. "Your heart's in the right place. I think you're right about wanting to help find this cute little white girl's killer. And you might be right about telling it from the perspective of this cop. But it's not there yet. Something's missing. Give us something no one else has. Go fishing and bring it back to the table."

"Go fishing" was the strange purgatory for stories that weren't spiked and weren't accepted. Rarely was a story lifted from that limbo. But he hadn't killed it. And that was enough to lift my spirits again. I still had a chance to tell Amy's story.

I decided to up the ante by getting the one interview no other reporter had yet managed to get. I decided to track down the man who interrupted a church service in 2002 with a startling confession. Shouting at the morning congregation, he proclaimed, "I killed Amy Mihaljevic."

CHAPTER FIVE

The Curious Case of Richard Alan Folbert

ON THE MORNING OF October 13, 2002, the first half of the Sunday service at St. Angela Merici Roman Catholic church in Fairview Park passed according to routine. Police Sergeant Thomas Zinsmayer sat patiently waiting as Reverend Richard Colgan gathered parishioners for communion. He certainly never expected he would need to tackle someone in church.

Then, as the rites were beginning—*I take this bread, which is the symbol of thy broken body*—a shaggy-haired man stood up in a pew, toward the front of the church, and in a loud, booming voice addressed the congregation.

"May I have your attention, please!" he shouted. "My name is Richard Alan Folbert. People know me as Satan. I killed Amy Mihaljevic."

Everyone froze. Zinsmayer saw fear in the eyes of the people around him. He was afraid, too. Still, he barely hesitated before launching himself at Folbert. Two other off-duty auxiliary officers helped subdue the large man.

Soon, Folbert was behind bars inside the Fairview Park police station. He ranted about Amy and his role in her murder but made little sense. The officer on duty called the Bay Village Police Department. B.V.P.D. called Mark Spaetzel.

I read about Folbert's outburst in the paper the day after it happened and, like many at that time, took it at face value. Of course, the person who killed Amy would be overcome with guilt and confess to a church full of parishioners. It was amazing he held out so long.

Would that it were so easy.

Subsequent articles in October 2002 contained quotes from police downplaying the event. They said Folbert was a troubled individual seeking attention—in need of psychiatric help maybe, but not a lynching. The police made one thing clear: He didn't do it. No reporter interviewed Folbert, however. And questions remained. For instance, why had he confessed to this particular crime on October 13, a few days before the thirteenth anniversary of Amy's abduction? It was well-thought-out for a crazy man.

Near the end of May 2005, I finally ran Folbert's name through whitepages.com. Two other Folberts came up in the Cleveland area, but no Richards or Richard Alans. I tried Google next.

I didn't expect to find a complete autobiography on the guy. But that's what I got.

Richard Alan Folbert, the screen said, was the author of a novel titled *Buy the Truth: Do Not Sell It!* It was listed for sale on a self-publishing website for $12.50. The introduction promised "firsthand accounts of the inner-workings of the disturbed psyche." Yeah, that sounded like my guy. I withdrew my credit card and downloaded a PDF version. As soon as it finished, I did a file search for "Amy." This took me to page 86, and a passage that read as follows:

> The story of myself in connection to Amy began in 1989. It was at that time a composite drawing of her suspected murderer was circulated. A neighbor of mine alerted me to it with the statement, "You know, Rich, the picture looks like you." My neighbor was correct, the depiction of the suspected killer bore a striking resemblance to me. At this point the possibility arose that perhaps she had been murdered to frame me on the charge to silence me.

I kept searching. There were more passages, each stranger than the one before.

> My deepest sorrow is that an innocent child, Amy, could have been used as a pawn in attempts to silence my voice on the earth.

I needed to find this man. I needed to find out why he was so focused on her.

I tried the other Folberts. On the first call, an older woman answered. "He's my son," she said. "Why do you want to talk to Richard?"

The lie was through my lips before I could stop it: "I found a copy of his book. I'd like to review it."

The woman on the other end of the line laughed oddly at that. "Yeah, he told me he was writing some book. I never thought anyone would read it, though. Never thought he'd finish it either. Richard doesn't like to see things through. We used to take bets on how long he'd hold down a job."

With support like that, lady, who'd blame him?

"Do you have his phone number?"

"No," she said. "He just moved. And I didn't write it down, but he calls me a couple times a week. I'll have him call you next time he checks in."

I doubted her sincerity, but there wasn't much I could do other than give her my office number and hope she kept her word. My stomach felt heavy and full of acid. Folbert's mother's voice seethed with condescension. I couldn't wrap my head around such contempt for one's own children.

"*To each his own,*" *said the farmer as he kissed the cow*, my grandmother likes to say.

The woman did as she promised, though. A day later, my phone rang. Folbert was on the other line.

"You read my book?" he asked, his voice deep and friendly. He *sounded* sane.

"I did. It was an interesting read," I said.

Folbert laughed. "Yeah. I guess it is. I wrote it for myself, mostly. It was cathartic."

"The reason I'm looking for you is I want to talk to you about Amy Mihaljevic."

"Oh?"

I cleared my throat. "I want to talk to you about what led you to tell a church full of people that you killed her in 2002."

"Nothing *led* me to it. I was telling the truth," he said. "I killed her."

I couldn't figure out what to say to that. Finally: "Do you have time to meet up with me?"

"Sure. When?"

"How about right now?"

* * *

It was Folbert's day off. Most days, he worked as a busboy for a deli in Lakewood, a twenty-four-hour greasy spoon popular with postgrads and chain-smoking goths. I asked him to meet me there in half an hour.

Twenty minutes later, I sat at a table overlooking the street with a Coke in hand and an order of onion rings on the way. I tried not to get my hopes up. This couldn't be the guy. The FBI and Bay Village cops had let him walk. The killer couldn't really be wandering around Cuyahoga County, confessing to anyone who listened, could he?

A husky man stepped into the restaurant as the onion rings arrived. He looked at my satchel, pegged me as the reporter, and walked over. My very first thought was that Folbert looked a lot like my father. There was the stout build, the well-toned forearms, the dark goatee streaked with gray, the short-cropped salt-and-pepper hair over blue eyes, and a wide Norse-like face. He wore a white button-down shirt over a black tee tucked into a pair of well-traveled jeans.

"Do you want something to eat?" I asked.

Folbert shook his head. "Nah. But if you have three bucks I could go across the street and get some tobacco. I roll my own cigarettes. Calms my nerves."

I gave him the last two dollars in my pocket and watched through the window as he disappeared into the drugstore across the way, emerging a minute later with a small white pouch. As soon as he returned, the papers were out and the Top Tobacco pouch opened. While we talked, I watched his stubby workman's fingers roll a fat doobie of a cigarette with an ease that spoke to the hundreds that came before it.

"Moved to Cleveland in 1980," Folbert said. "I managed restaurants. I was an efficiency expert for Little Caesar's. I would go from store to store, firing employees who weren't pulling their weight. I made a pretty good living. Got married in '81. Then on March 28, 1982, four guys came into the Little Caesar's in Brook Park, where I was working at the time. They wanted to rob the place. There was a confrontation, and I was almost beaten to death. I was in the hospital forever. I went into a deep depression after that. I could no longer relate to people. Eventually, my wife's mother convinced her to divorce me. I don't blame her." Then, he added, "I still love her."

He didn't waste any time getting to the personal stuff. With some people, you have to come at the personal details sideways, from some chit-chatter tangent. Build trust, talk about fluffy stuff, then move in for the big reveal. This man was smart enough to understand that game and honest enough to speed up the process.

Folbert shrugged as if reading my mind. He lit the cigarette with a match, inhaled, and turned his attention to the window.

"They diagnosed me schizophrenic in the hospital. Gave me some meds."

"Were you still on the medication when you walked into the church?"

He shook his head again. "Not for about three months. By that time, I was in such a state of heightened awareness . . ." His bottom lip twitched as he lost the end of that sentence. Instead of completing his thought, he took another drag.

"Did you know Amy Mihaljevic?" I asked. "Did you know her when she was still alive? Did you know the family?"

"No," he said. "Look, can I say something without sounding crazy?"

"Sure."

Staring directly into my eyes, Folbert leaned forward and spoke in a soft voice, as if sharing a secret, some dangerous secret that should never be uttered in public places. "I think I can see where humanity is heading," he said. "There are the forces of good and the forces of evil. I believe there is a head of evil working behind the scenes, working against the forces of good. And the forces of evil will do anything they can to silence the truth. I do feel I'm responsible for the death of Amy Mihaljevic. Someone killed her to frame me because I was being too vocal. Satanists did this."

"What do you mean?" I asked. "How were you being vocal?"

"I threatened George Bush Sr. In 1990, when he was president, I walked into the Lakewood police department and said I wanted to kill his spirit. Not his body, but his spirit. A Secret Service agent visited my home. He asked me if I could cast spells. I told him, 'I don't cast spells. I *dispel* myths.' Anytime I get vocal, I'm shut down. Like the time I lit a joint in the federal building.'

Odd that you can't see someone's imbalance. I mean, he looked like my dad. He looked so normal. The darker truth is that I seem like the crazy one to Folbert. Crazy because I can't really see this Satanist conspiracy.

Usually, I love conspiracies—the Magic Bullet, Roswell, the Philadelphia Experiment—but this story is about a dead girl. I made a promise to myself at that moment. No matter how many more people like Folbert I ran into during my investigation, I would not chase wild theories. I would not jump down the rabbit hole in search of Wonderland. Not with this one. Because in the end, this remained a dead girl's story. The alternative to respecting that grim reality smoked a hand-rolled cigarette in front of me. That was not where I wanted to find myself in twenty years.

I will not jump down the rabbit hole, I told myself. *No matter what.*

I thanked Folbert for his time and started to square away my things.

"Wait," he said. "One more thing."

I sat back down.

"I have a feeling she was killed with a knife. There are certain Satanic rituals that require a knife. I feel it was extremely violent." He reached over and wrapped one hand around my right arm. His bottom lip quivered with emotion. "Remember. Satanists thrive on terror. They *eat* it."

CHAPTER SIX

The Second-Worst Way to Die

I RETURNED TO THE OFFICE feeling both disappointed and exhilarated. The police distanced themselves from Folbert for good reason. Sure, he vaguely resembled the composite sketch of Amy's abductor, but beyond that . . . Still, Folbert was a fully formed, unique character even if he fell off the detectives' radar fairly quickly. It occurred to me that I might be able to build an article around the suspects in the case. Now, if I could identify a few more, if I could identify the top five suspects and show how the investigation affected their lives as well as the Mihaljevics', that might be something worth reading. My hope was that, in the process, I might drum up some new clues. My *secret* hope was to stumble upon the killer himself.

A paperback copy of Robert Ressler's book, *Whoever Fights Monsters*, sat on my desk at *Scene*, dog-eared at a short chapter near the back. I had found it in the true-crime section at Borders. Ressler's involvement with Amy's case is detailed in about four pages, centering, as Spaetzel had said, on the man who committed suicide shortly after the recovery of Amy's body from Ashland County. Ressler and his friend, Special Agent John Dunn of the Cleveland branch of the FBI, interviewed this man at his Fairview Park apartment and although they searched the room while their suspect was in the can, they found no evidence directly linking him to Amy's murder. But in closing, Ressler said he felt very strongly this was "their man." However, this short chapter contains several inaccuracies. For instance, he says Amy was twelve, not ten, and he mentions the field where she was found as being "right off the highway" when, in fact, it's a good half-hour drive. Also, the suspect's name was never mentioned, at least not in the paperback edition, although from what I gathered from Spaetzel, the last name was Strunak.

I harbored strong admiration for the Bay Village detective. He had devoted his career to solving the mystery that most fascinated me. But that didn't keep me from employing a small dirty trick to draw out a little more information from him.

He had used the name Strunak. He had never mentioned a first name.

I dialed Spaetzel's office and the detective answered.

"Just going through my notes here," I said. "I can't make out some of this chicken scratch, though. I guess I was writing too fast. We were talking about the guy that killed himself, the one you said didn't do it. I have his last name—Strunak—but I can't tell if the first name is John or Richard or . . ."

"You mean Billy?"

"Right, Billy. That's it. Man, I have to take better notes. Sorry about that."

"I've been reviewing the leads we got that first week after her disappearance," Spaetzel said. "I thought maybe we missed something early on, focused on the wrong person."

"Find anything interesting?"

"No," he said. "I was really hoping something would jump out. In a way it was disappointing. Ninety-five percent of the calls we received were related to look-alikes or strange behavior. People were using it as a way to get back at their spouses in some cases. Stuff like 'My ex-husband is a little strange and looks a little like the guy. I wouldn't put it past him.' I remember taking some of those calls."

"What about the other five percent?" I asked.

"Those were all over the map. Some were calls about some guy in the neighborhood who was a little weird."

"The friends that knew about the phone calls Amy was getting— did Amy ever give them the guy's name?" I asked.

"No," he said. "Never mentioned a name. Just that he was going to take her to the mall to buy a present for her mother. She spent at least an hour in that plaza waiting for this person. She was hanging out with different friends. A couple people remember a questioning voice saying, 'Amy?'"

"Do you remember the names of the other kids that were with her that day?"

A short pause, then: "No." I wasn't the only one being a trifle deceitful that day.

"Well, thanks for looking into those tips," I said. "I'll be taking this back to my editor soon. If he goes for the article, can we meet sometime next week?"

"Sure," Spaetzel said. "Call me anytime."

Billy Strunak. I had the name of my second suspect. The fact that he had committed suicide so close to the discovery of the body made him inherently interesting. The real question was: What had put him on the short list to begin with? Ressler and Dunn had questioned him shortly after Amy's disappearance. I called Ressler, whose contact information appeared on his website.

The voice that greeted me on the other end of the phone sounded gruff and distrustful. He claimed his memory was foggy from sixteen years of writing about other cases.

"He was working at some Wal-Mart, I think, or maybe it was BJ's Wholesale Club," Ressler said. "He was a viable suspect. He was stealing stuff from his job and sending it to the Mihaljevics. He'd sent Margaret a letter with two necklaces saying, 'Here's a trinket for you and one for your daughter when she's found.' He was working in the volunteer center at city hall. And he was stealing the supplies, reams of paper the volunteers used to print out Amy's missing poster.

"When I interviewed Strunak with Dunn, he was detached and evasive. It wasn't a hundred-percenter, but he was a good suspect. When he died, the FBI went up to search his apartment and the family had cleaned everything out. If there was anything at all that could link him to Amy, it was thrown out."

My next call was to retired FBI agent Dick Wrenn, the man who organized the FBI's presence in Bay during 1989 and 1990. The Cleveland Bureau put me in touch with him.

Wrenn either had no answering machine or had it turned off that day because the phone rang about a dozen times before he finally picked up. He was out of breath. I told him quickly who I was and why I was interested in writing about the case—opting this time for the "I was eleven in 1989 and it was the first time I realized there were adults out there that could harm children" summation. I relayed to him the conversation with Ressler.

"Ressler made some judgments on incomplete information," he said. Wrenn's voice rang with authority. His timbre was distinguished and more than a little intimidating. He also sounded peeved at Ressler's bold statements, but perhaps it was simple frustration. "John Dunn was not really involved as a case agent," he continued. "He did do some of the investigations, though. Dunn and Ressler knew one another. Ressler was doing something else at the time in Ohio, writing his book on serial killers, and he agreed to come up and take a look at the case. One of the assignments Dunn had was to accompany Ressler to Strunak's interview.

"Because of that book, people might not have come forward with important information. They thought it was solved. Those of us who were closely associated with the case were not in agreement with Bob."

"Why's that?" I asked.

"A number of different reasons. That suicide . . . there were a lot of things going on in Billy Strunak's life, some of which had nothing to do with the investigation." Wrenn sighed loudly. "I do not believe that Strunak was the individual involved in that abduction/homicide."

"Do you have any reason to believe it was anyone else?" I said. "Any hunches?"

"If I did, I really couldn't share them," he said. "I'll tell you this: This was clearly a case of abduction. This was not a runaway. The motive in these instances, the reason for it, is sexual. And it's an active case. There is a continued investigation being done. We're all hopeful that at some point in time the individual responsible will be arrested and convicted."

Armed with the full name, I pulled up Cuyahoga County's website and accessed the "criminal info" page, where county court cases are archived. I entered "William Strunak" into the system and discovered another reason why this man would have been interesting to investigators.

Strunak had a prior conviction for "disseminating material harmful to children" from 1983. It was a charge that could have included everything from showing minors porno to flashing. Tracking down the police reports to provide details on that arrest proved especially difficult because a confluence of departments was involved. The unnamed victim of the crime lived in Brook Park. In 1983, Billy lived in Parma Heights.

According to incident reports from the Parma Heights Police Department, at 10:56 a.m. on June 2, 1983, Patrolman Vincent Rackel assisted Brook Park police by executing a warrant to search Strunak's apartment. He was looking for pornographic material. What he found was ten thousand dollars' worth of stolen tickets for Cleveland Indians games and boxes of Ford Motorcraft auto parts. A call to the Cleveland Indians Baseball Company revealed the tickets were part of a shipment stolen from the Trailways bus system. Billy Strunak just happened to be a recent employee of Trailways.

Strunak was arrested. Rackel read him his Miranda rights and asked Strunak to sign a letter stating that his rights had been read. Strunak declined, opting to write "Refused—wishes to confir [*sic*] with attorney."

Later that same day, Patrolman Rackel returned with a Parma Heights detective and executed a second search warrant for the tickets and engine parts. A man answered the door of Strunak's apartment and identified himself as Billy's brother. Once he learned the details of the warrant, the brother left, saying, "I don't want anything to do with this."

Pictures taken by the detective at Strunak's home give a sense of what he was like in private. Strunak was a pack rat. Boxes littered his living room—an unopened hibachi grill, an Adidas shoe box. A small closet stood open, filled with junk. Papers lay on every surface. Knickknacks cluttered the room. A small statue of a dog. A Cleveland Browns bobblehead. Cocktail glasses. Sticking out of the eight-track player was a Neil Diamond tape.

Lying on the bed and dresser were women's underwear, condoms, and a bottle of lubricant called Act of Love.

Strunak was charged with two counts of receiving stolen property, a fourth-degree felony. But there seemed to be no further record of the "disseminating material harmful to children" charge. I found no indication as to how much time, if any, Strunak spent in jail. A check with Brook Park, Parma, Parma Heights, and Fairview Park police stations revealed no further clues. Some of the departments actually incinerate their records after seven years. I figured those details, and the identity of Strunak's alleged accuser, were reduced to ashes.

Although he was arrested, none of the departments could find his mug shot. Strunak's file at Parma Heights showed that they once had a copy of the mug shot in the folder, but it had been removed sometime in the past.

Finally, I called the county coroner's office for his autopsy report. From its pages, and further interviews, a picture of Strunak's last hours began to emerge.

The morning of February 19, 1990, William James Strunak prepared to end his life. The thirty-five-year-old wandered around his house, gathering the things he needed. Strunak was five feet, six inches tall, weighed 155 pounds, and had hazel eyes under thinning brown bangs. From a distance, he was attractive. A closer look, however, revealed patchy skin, red and flaky.

In the kitchen inside his Fairview Park efficiency, Strunak scrawled out a note to his family. The exact wording is not known to anyone but the FBI now, but those close to the man say it made no mention of Amy Mihaljevic, whose body had recently been recovered. It spoke of Strunak's depression, caused by a severe case of the psoriasis that had plagued him from birth.

After completing the letter, Strunak grabbed a can of cola from the fridge. Then, he took a bottle of dry gas, the additive that goes into a car's gas tank to improve mileage, and mixed some of the toxic liquid into the soda. He chugged it down.

Perhaps Strunak felt the chemicals burning his esophagus and got scared. In any event, he stopped drinking and set the can down. He balled up the suicide note and threw it in the trash. Instead of finishing the job, Strunak went to work. He spent the morning stocking shelves at BJ's Wholesale Club. He complained to coworkers that he felt ill.

At 6:15 p.m., Strunak was taken to St. Vincent Charity Hospital, in Fairview Park, by his brother, Gary. He didn't inform doctors of the poison he drank for breakfast. He said he was just depressed, on edge. Soon, Strunak was taken to the psych ward. Doctors there treated him for hypertension until he started to convulse. He slipped out of consciousness and lost the ability to breathe on his own. Ventilator support was given. Further testing showed a lethal amount of methanol in his system, eating away his insides.

For two days, Strunak remained unconscious, kept alive by machines. On February 21, his body shut down.

Richard Alan Folbert never viewed Strunak's autopsy report, but he would certainly find it interesting that Strunak's death came exactly thirteen days after Amy's body was found.

I made a few calls then. There were eleven different Strunaks still listed in the Cleveland white pages. I called them all. Many were not home. Gary's wife answered, though, and when I asked about Billy, she lied and said, "Never heard of him" before hanging up. I got lucky with the tenth number, though. A young man answered the phone, and when I introduced myself he laughed.

"James Renner? From *Last Call Cleveland*?"

"That's me," I said. While at Kent State in the late 1990s, I was part of a late-night TV talk show that was briefly popular with the drunken fraternity crowd.

The young man told me his name, which I promised to withhold for publication, and I realized I had met him at a friend's party in the Old Townhomes complex during the yearly May Day bash. He was the stepson of one of Billy's cousins.

I asked if he knew Billy was a suspect in the abduction of Amy Mihaljevic. His answer was as brief as it was unexpected.

"Everyone in the family thinks he did it," he said.

As I got ready to leave *Scene* for the night, I drafted a letter to Pete. I told him about my conversation with Folbert and about the information I had dug up on Strunak. I also promised him that I would soon track down a few more suspects. The angle for the story became this: "What happens to the uncharged suspects of a high-profile crime that has never been solved?"

A few minutes later, he replied: *On the Amy thing: you may have just convinced me.*

I sent an e-mail to Kevin, explaining the story again and letting him know that this would be our next feature. *Let's hit a home run,* Kevin said.

I left for that day, smiling, my body charged with adrenaline. Finally, after sixteen years, I had a chance to write about an event that transformed my life and the lives of an entire community. This was a story I was close to, one I could really get lost in. And at the end, if I closed my eyes real hard and wished it into being, maybe there would come a moment where I would knock on a door and the person who answered would be Amy's killer. Because even after uncovering these strange details about Strunak, my faith was still with Spaetzel, who had digested thousands of reports and interviews with potential suspects. I believed the killer still lived. I believed I would find him.

On a whim, I decided to drop by the apartment where Strunak had lived in 1983, when he was charged with disseminating material harmful to minors. It was on the way home and I wanted to see what sort of neighborhood it was, what condition it might be in. I thought that if I was lucky I could talk my way into the apartment and have a look around so that I could describe the arrest better in a written scene.

Strunak's apartment was on a street that bisects Brookpark Road, in a depressed section of Parma Heights that looks downright post-apocalyptic. It sat above a used-appliance store that had no hours of operation on the glass window. At 4:30 p.m. on this weekday, it was closed. I parked my car in front and walked around the brick building, down a roughly paved driveway littered with beer cans and broken bottles.

There was a bay of garages in the back, some with doors wide open like mouths of slumbering giants. A wooden staircase led me to a second floor and four apartment doors. Strunak had occupied 9-C. I rapped my fist upon the door.

No one answered.

I tried 9-B, and a skinny man with scraggly hair answered, peering out from a door half opened. "What's up?"

"I'm a reporter. I'm writing a story about a man who lived here about twenty years ago," I stammered.

"No one's been here longer than two years," he said.

"Do you mind if I take a look at the apartment? I just want to see what they look like on the inside."

The man looked me up and down in a way that made me grateful to hear him say, "No. I don't think so, sport."

"All right. Thanks anyways."

He shut the door and I started to make my way back down the stairs. The sound of 9-A's door opening, though, made me hesitate. A man in a red flannel shirt and blue jeans came out, shutting the door tight behind him.

"Hello," I said.

"Hi there," was his response.

"Do you know who lives in 9-C now?" I asked him.

"No one. Not since Michelle left. You looking for her?"

I shook my head. I introduced myself and gave him the same line: Just a reporter looking for details about a man who lived here in 1983.

The flannel-shirt guy said his name was Chris McLeish. He didn't actually live there. McLeish was staying with a friend in 9-A and didn't have a key to let himself back in. And his friend wasn't due to return from work for another six hours.

I pressed him for a little more information on 9-C. I had said nothing about Strunak or Amy at this point. All he knew was that I was looking for information about an old resident. But what he said next kept me up until the early morning hours and chilled my bones until they hurt. What he said about 9-C's "extra" occupant showed me how very unstable reality can sometimes be.

"Michelle don't live there no more, but I knew her pretty well when she was still around," he said. "She left in a real hurry. She . . . never mind." McLeish shook his head and smiled awkwardly. "It's crazy and I'm a drunk. Not drunk now, though. But it's a crazy story. She thought so too, but she still left."

"What's a crazy story?" I asked.

"Well, a couple days before Michelle packed up she come to me and says, 'Chris, I seen something in my room last night. I seen someone in my apartment.'"

"Someone broke in?"

McLeish shook his head again. "No," he said. "She said she seen a ghost in her bedroom. Said she woke up from a sound sleep and saw a little girl standing at the foot of her bed, trying to say something. The little girl's mouth was moving but no sound come out."

The hairs on my arms prickled, goose bumps breaking out. "She saw the ghost of a little girl?"

"Uh-huh," he said. "Scared her so bad she moved out. Nobody's been in there since."

"Did she know what the girl was trying to say?"

"No, no she couldn't tell."

"What did she look like?"

McLeish, seemingly frightened himself, looked around as if to make sure no one could hear. He said three words: "Little blond girl."

West Allis Sweethearts

THE VILLAGE OF WEST ALLIS, Wisconsin, got its name from its position in relation to an Allis-Chalmers manufacturing plant that once employed many of its residents. Today, this suburb of Milwaukee lacks the soft color palette of a fine place to live. It is saturated and gray, its roads filled with concrete shops and ranch-style homes.

Four generations ago, Mark Mihaljevic's grandfather settled in Milwaukee after emigrating from Serbia. Presently, in terms of progeny, the Mihaljevics are outnumbered only by the few local families as large as the McNulty clan. Margaret McNulty was the oldest of five siblings and had enough cousins and aunts and uncles to lose track of. The fair-skinned girl was easy to look at, but timid and reserved. High cheekbones accented her large brown eyes in a friendly way. It is hard to imagine a single raincloud thought ever passing behind them. Her thick light-brown hair hung in long natural curls she often wore in a ponytail.

Growing up, Margaret took to what little West Allis had to offer in the way of the fine arts. She collected old and rare books, mostly dictionaries. She deconstructed classic literature in small groups at the local library. She sang in an a cappella chorus at Nathan Hale High School. Dancing became such a part of her life that she developed ballerina feet. Her toes pointed slightly toward each other when she walked.

During the summers, the McNultys took trips to a campground in northern Wisconsin. Margaret spent days in the lake, swimming with her sister, Janice, and her younger brothers, Dale, Bill, and George. At night, there were marshmallows toasted on the fire.

An odd trait made making friends difficult for the precocious girl. Margaret had a slight lisp that, while cute in childhood, caused her to become self-conscious later in life. Socially, she found it difficult to fit in. Her grace and beauty, though, did not go unnoticed by Mark Mihaljevic. By the time they graduated, Mark was a regular fixture at the McNulty house, always at Margaret's side.

A varsity footballer and accomplished wrestler, Mark had a strong, sturdy build and short, cropped hair. He was stoic. To some, it seemed an odd pairing. But it was obvious he cherished the girl, doting on her in front of friends and family.

Margaret's mother, Henrietta, was like a good many mothers-in-law: she never thought Mark was good enough for her daughter. He was more interested in cars than Margaret's book clubs. They seemed to have little in common other than their affection for each other. Henrietta hoped Margaret might find a more suitable suitor at college.

The first of the McNultys to attend university, Margaret set her sights on a nursing degree at the University of Wisconsin–Milwaukee. In her second year, though, she came home to her mother in tears. A professor had told her she could not possibly relate to patients with a lisp as pronounced as hers. So she switched her focus to fine arts, graduating in 1970.

In 1972, Margaret and Mark married.

For three years, Mark taught an auto mechanics class at a local high school before applying for a job with Buick Motors. They offered him a position in Little Rock, Arkansas. It paid better than anything in West Allis. But Margaret didn't want to move away from family. She had just learned she was pregnant.

"Mom, I don't want to leave," she told Henrietta during one late-night phone call consisting mostly of short sentences between sobs.

Mark made his wife a promise. They would give Little Rock a try, but if either didn't like it after a few months, they would move back home. Tentatively, Margaret agreed.

Neither Mark nor Margaret enjoyed their stay in Arkansas. Shortly after they arrived, Margaret was on the phone to her mother again, crying. She wanted to come home, but Mark wouldn't have it. It hadn't been long enough, for one thing. For another, he had a steady job. Eventually both their children were born there. First, Jason in 1976. Then, a girl, on December 11, 1978. They named her Amy Renee.

In 1979, Buick transferred Mark to a new position in Jackson, Mississippi. They bought a house there and fell into a little bit of money when Mark's grandfather passed away, leaving him an inheritance. Better cash flow relieved at least a small amount of Margaret's stress. By all accounts, their sojourn in Mississippi appears to have been the best of times for the Mihaljevics.

The majority of family pictures were taken here. Margaret's mother keeps them at her apartment now. They are faded and tinged with that sickly yellow pallor of low-quality seventies-era film. But they clearly show a happy family. In one, Amy rests in a papoose slung around Margaret's shoulders. Amy is less than a year old in the photo, but as she peeks around her mother's shoulder, she looks out at the world with an eerily mature expression of curiosity.

In the summer of 1984, Buick Motors transferred Mark one last time, to Cleveland. Following a recommendation from a Buick employee, he surveyed Bay Village as a possible place to live. It seemed quiet, safe. And on Lindford Drive, at the end of a cul-de-sac, a four-bedroom colonial was for sale. It was the perfect size for a growing family. They moved in during the extended July Fourth weekend.

In her bedroom at night, Amy could hear the rumble of the trains on the nearby Norfolk & Western railroad tracks, which serve as the southern edge of Bay Village. Perhaps she listened to the gentle thunder of the trains sweeping past as she slowly rocked herself to sleep.

CHAPTER SEVEN

Best Friends

SOMETIMES STORIES ARE WRITTEN entirely from a desk, from interviews conducted over the phone. But the good ones require fieldwork and lots of driving. Nothing puts a subject at ease with sharing information more than sitting next to the person who puts it into print. With Amy, I knew I should meet as many people face to face as I possibly could. I needed to work off their memories and their lost tangents of thought, and the only way I could do that was to read their eyes to see when they veered off course or to see if they were holding onto some last tidbit they hadn't shared before. Amy was taken from Bay Village and ended up fifty-four miles away in the Ruggles Township area of Ashland County. That's a lot of ground to cover. In telling her story, I would spend plenty of time in my hand-me-down car. With the FM radio busted, I needed some new tunes.

As sad as Amy's story is, I felt from the beginning an odd sense of hope. I felt if I looked hard enough and met enough people, maybe I could solve this thing. In every photograph I have seen of her, she is smiling. There's that, too. I had a sense she really enjoyed life. I wanted to know the music she would have loved at the time.

Deep in the display case archives of the Cuyahoga Falls Record Exchange, I found a compilation CD of the eighties' greatest hits. It opens, appropriately for the MTV generation, with the Buggles' "Video Killed the Radio Star." The track I kept replaying as I drove west from Cleveland on Thursday, June 2, was number four, the Fixx's "One Thing Leads to Another."

Enveloped in my eighties experience, I headed toward a Caribou coffeehouse in Westlake. Kristen Balas, one of Amy's best friends, had agreed to meet me there.

*   *   *

I arrived early and took a seat outside, facing the door. Ten minutes later, a young woman walked in and surveyed the customers. Her eyes landed on my satchel sticking into the walkway, and she came over. She wore a business suit that still held creases from whatever display rack she'd taken it from the day before. Dark hair, fair complexion, thick eyebrows, turned-up nose. No trace of a smile. Pretty, but plain. Bay aristocracy, that look said. She eyed me like a wounded badger.

"James?"

I stood and shook her hand. And then we both sat down.

"I'm coming from an interview," she explained. "I already have the job, but they still make you go through the interview process. Just got done."

"What's the job?" I asked.

"I'm going to teach for Bay in the fall," she said. A trace of a smile played at the corner of her mouth. "The day before you showed up at my house, I was talking with my sister about Amy. I'm reading this book right now. It's called *The Lovely Bones*. It was written by Alice Sebold. It's about a young girl who is murdered and she watches from heaven as they search for her killer. It's eerie how similar it all is to Amy's abduction."

I jotted down the name of the book and the author.

"I can't imagine what sort of impact her abduction had on your life," I said as a way of drawing out a discussion.

Kristen threw my well-rehearsed response right back at me. "For the first time, I realized there were bad people out there," she said. "That there were adults who could take kids."

"Were you close friends?"

"Best friends. We were the best of friends," she said. "Near the end, it was really just her and I. We rode our bikes to school together every morning. In the winter, we would walk. Her mom was like a second mom to me. She had this little koala backpack."

"What was Amy like? What kind of things was she into at the time?"

"She loved watching *The Monkees* on Nickelodeon after school," Kristen said, wistfully. "We had a big crush on Davy Jones. She was into old things. Antiques. She had this old-fashioned bike with the big handlebars. It could have been from the 1950s. Blue and white. It stuck out from all the others. She didn't care if anyone made fun of her on that bike. She was into that. She was really artsy. Sometimes, we would flatten pennies on the tracks behind her house. I was a year ahead of her in school. She was in fifth I and was in sixth. Fifth-graders got out at 2:10. Sixth grade got out at 3:10. Some of the older kids, high-schoolers and eighth-graders, would hang out at Baskin-Robbins after school, but we were a little too young still. Believe it or not, our parents were both very protective. We had to be back inside by the time the streetlights came on."

As Kristen continued, I scribbled in my notebook. Occasionally I asked her to wait for me to catch up. Now that the gates were open, she wanted to talk. The story rushed out as she played with her cup of coffee.

"That Friday, the day it happened, was just like every day. Amy rode her bike to my house," she said. "It was still dark in the morning. She was talking about her school picture, the one with the ponytail. She didn't like it and she was looking forward to picture retake day. After school, the first thing I noticed was her bike was still in the bike rack. I figured she had a doctor's appointment. When I got home, Amy's mother called, asking if I'd seen her. She called again at 8 p.m.

"The first thing the next morning, my mother and I went to the Mihaljevics'. Margaret was hysterical. I remember walking to that house and Amy's mother hugging me. I had this feeling of déjà vu. It was a memory, but it was coming back to me so clearly. Amy was telling me about someone who had called her. This had happened a couple days before she disappeared. Amy said, 'My mom got a promotion at work and this guy is going to pick up a present for her.' He said, 'I'll pick you up after school and we'll go get a gift.' So, obviously, it wasn't some random girl they wanted. Or him or her, I don't know why I say 'they.' Anyway, I remembered it then, and that's when I told the FBI."

For a while, the FBI used Kristen as a quick reference, asking her to recall more specifics or fact-check their own. During the next two years, she was pulled out of class or interviewed by the FBI in the guidance office several times. Once, the feds showed up at a middle school dance held at St. Raphael's Catholic Church. "Do your parents have any strange male friends?" "How do you feel about Jason?" "Did you think Amy's father was weird?"

Kristen's stay-at-home stepfather, Riley Bonham, was questioned at one time. "But that didn't last long," she said. "They wanted to see if anybody knew anything. They were just very intrusive. It was weird to hear them ask about my relationship with Jason and with Amy's dad. I think they wanted to know if anyone was molested. None of that was going on. Except for Sam Sheppard, this was the biggest thing that ever happened to Bay."

I asked her what she thought about the local police.

"I think they're worthless," she said. Her eyebrows crinkled with intimidating anger. Eventually, she let them rest and returned to her drink.

"Can you tell me a little more about what Amy was doing that fall?" I asked.

"Riding horses," said Kristen. "Holly Hill Farms was her second home at the time. She had a whole wall of ribbons from shows. They told her she had a promising future in riding. She was already doing small jumps and things. She would go there when she didn't have lessons just to brush the horses. It was her favorite place for sure.

"A few weeks before she disappeared, Amy found out her parents were getting a divorce. When she told me that, I told her my mom was pregnant. We kept each other's secrets. That's why I'm the one she told about the phone calls, I think. She was very sweet and very caring." Kristen's eyes wandered somewhere over my right shoulder. "I'm not surprised Amy fell for it," she said.

"Amy's birthday was December 11," Kristen continued. "We went out and bought her a present, even though she was still missing. A board game. I gave it to her mom. Later, we bought her Christmas presents, too. But after a month, we knew she was dead. I never saw my mom cry until she told me Amy's body was found. I didn't see her cry again until her dad died.

"I thought the man who abducted her was going to come back for me. If he knew where Amy lived, he knew where I lived. If he watched her, he watched me. My brother walked me to school after that. This was someone who knew her, someone who watched her. For some reason he picked her out of all the other little girls at Bay. He wanted her specifically. It was a planned thing.

"I have two sisters who made it past the age of ten. I was always afraid for them. That word 'abduct' wasn't even in our vocabulary until Amy disappeared—not on that street."

I asked her then about the other Kristen, Kristen Sabo. No Sabos were listed in the Bay directory anymore.

"That was her other closest friend," she said. "Kristy Sabo's mother was the school secretary. Her father was weird. Used to take us all down to the lake to feed the ducks. Her father was just creepy. He committed suicide two months after they divorced."

I imagined—correctly, it turned out—that the police and FBI would have also looked closely at Kristy Sabo's father following his suicide so close to the time Amy's body turned up. I asked Kristen what she thought of the timing.

She shrugged. "There was a reason for killing himself in his mind."

(According to a report filed by a Cleveland Metroparks ranger, Martin Sabo shot himself inside the family's van with a .357 magnum in a parking lot off Valley Parkway on June 11, 1991. He left a suicide note that referred to financial difficulties. It seemed pretty straight-forward, except for one detail: the lenses had been removed from his eyeglasses. One lens was found on the driver's side floor, the other on the floor below the passenger's seat. Yet the frames were neatly folded on the dashboard. The reporting ranger ventured no explanation.)

A few minutes later, I walked Kristen back to her car. But she wasn't quite done talking. "It is strange that I came back," she said. "All I wanted was to escape my adolescence and here I am coming back to it. I feel like I have a connection to this town."

I thanked her again and moved toward my car.

"I still talk to her all the time," Kristen said. I turned back to her. Her eyes glistened in the afternoon sun. "I do. Last October, I was driving down to the BP on Crocker-Bassett Road to get my coffee before work. Amy had been on my mind for days. When I got out to walk inside, this woman came out of nowhere, put her hand on me and said, 'Excuse me, do you know where Holly Hill Farms is?' "

Kristen smiled. "I just feel that was Amy saying 'Hi' back to me, you know? She touched me. She came to me."

*   *   *

Something had been replaying over and over in my mind during that whole conversation outside Caribou. It was the beginning of the interview. I could see Kristen sitting down and telling me about the book she was reading. Something about that book was really tugging at me. I had seen the blue paperback edition of the novel *The Lovely Bones* at Borders a couple times and thought about picking it up but, after scanning the first few pages, had set it back down every time. Too close to reality for me, I guess.

The author—Alice Sebold. I could see the name. I had come across that name somewhere else, hadn't I? But where?

Just the day before, I had found a couple articles about Amy's murder online. One piece mentioned the jogger who discovered her body on a morning run. The jogger's name: Janet Seabold.

Sebold, Seabold. My mind wanted to make something more out of that connection. But I knew better than to confuse coincidence with fate. Looking for meaning in coincidence leads down that rabbit hole I'd promised myself I'd avoid—that point at which a person creates the illusion of patterns, of order, in what is really just more chaos. It can lead a person into a church on the thirteenth of October, a few days before the thirteenth anniversary of Amy's abduction.

There is some kind of answer in that name.

I pushed the thought away. There were other things to do. Since I was so close to Bay Village, I figured I might as well stop in at Holly Hill Farms. It was such a big part of Amy's life—so important that at least one close friend of hers considered its mere mention a communiqué from beyond the grave.

CHAPTER EIGHT

Holly Hill Farms

HOLLY HILL FARMS sits at the epicenter of three townships—Bay Village, Avon Lake, and Westlake—just off Nagle Road, which runs parallel to the railroad tracks that sit behind the Mihaljevics' old house. In 1989, much of Nagle was farmland, but several cookie-cutter housing developments have sprouted up in the years since. The farm is really a collection of long, narrow stables and a few fenced-in riding areas. A turn-of-the-century house sits near the road, beside a large gravel parking lot. It was abandoned when the farm's matriarch lost her senses and was committed to a home shortly before the millennium. When I visited the house, an aviation student occupied the apartment above the garage.

I pulled into the gravel lot next to a dirty pickup truck and killed the engine. I left the satchel in the car, opting for just a notebook and pen.

As I got closer to the nearest barn, I noticed a steady stream of adolescent girls walking in and out. None of them wore the black uniforms and rounded hats I associated with girls on horseback at county fairs. One carried a saddle almost half her size. Walking slowly, looking casual, I followed.

Inside the stable, the pungent smell of manure hung thick in the air, mixed with the aroma of fresh hay and grain.

"Can I help you?" a young woman asked, brushing the mane of a towering black mare. Its nostrils flared and vibrated loudly as the animal exhaled.

"I'm looking for the owner of Holly Hill Farms. Is she around?"

"She's teaching right now, out back. She'll be done in a couple minutes, though. You can wait by the fence."

I thanked the young woman and walked through the stables and out the other side. To my left was a riding circle where another girl, this one about ten years old, rode a tan horse. The girl trotted along, responding to the commands of a squat woman in dirty overalls. I leaned against the fence and watched, doing my best to not look like some leering stranger.

After about five minutes, the woman shouted, "That's enough!" The girl slipped off the horse and onto the ground before pulling at the bit and leading her animal back toward the stable. The girl did this gracefully, and I pictured Amy doing the same thing the same way. No doubt Margaret Mihaljevic had stood against this very fence, smiling with pride at the sight of her daughter managing such an adult task.

"Hello," said the riding coach. She reminded me of the sort of woman who frequents church bake sales.

"I'm writing a story about Amy."

I left the first name hanging out there in order to judge her response. How well did she remember Amy Mihaljevic? Pretty well, it seemed. She didn't even hesitate to respond.

"Oh," she said. "Well, she was out here a lot the summer before her abduction. I'm Hollie Anzenberger. I'm the owner of Holly Hill Farms."

"Can we sit down somewhere and talk for a few minutes?" I asked.

"Sure," Anzenberger said. She motioned for me to follow her to a large barn behind the stables.

Stepping through a gigantic barn door, I found myself in an enclosed riding arena, behind a wooden wall that contained the exhibition ring. The air smelled of cedar and pipe tobacco. I had been to an Amish auction once that smelled exactly like this. It reminded me of bearded farmers selling suburban ranchers a stock of inbred runt pigs. Not a good smell. It set me on edge.

"This way," Anzenberger said.

At the front of the building, accessible from inside, was a cramped office and meeting room. Brochures for leasing and boarding horses at Holly Hill Farms sat in a display case against one wall. *A Proud Equestrian Tradition in Avon Lake, Ohio—Since 1970*, one read. On the front was a picture of a girl in full uniform leaning forward on a brown horse as it jumped a short obstacle. *Indoor Riding Arena! Fun and More!*

Anzenberger sat in a chair in the center of this room, and I opened a folding chair next to her.

"So what do you remember about Amy?" I began.

"Well, it was a long time ago."

Something about Anzenberger's tone seemed strange—some indistinguishable quality under the surface. I brushed it off as a touch of annoyance at the inconvenience of my impromptu interview. After all, a riding stable is a busy enterprise, and I hadn't called ahead.

"I guess I was about thirty-six years old then," Anzenberger added. That made her fifty-two, though she looked more like someone in her early forties. But then, her face was much too round for premature wrinkles.

"My mother started this facility when I was seventeen," she said. "My dad built all the barns. I got my training certificate in England. Riding is in my blood. This is all I ever wanted to do. I wanted to teach young girls how to ride."

"Do you remember anything about Amy and her family?"

Anzenberger squinted, as if trying hard to jog her memory. Her expression struck me as unusual, since people typically look off to their left when trying to recollect a past event—a natural behavior some scientists link with visual memories being stored inside the right hemisphere of the human brain (and the fact that each brain hemisphere controls eye and hand movement on the opposite side). Anzenberger's expression didn't seem natural. It seemed showy.

"Amy came once a week for riding lessons," she said. "I taught her when her instructor was not here."

"Who was her instructor?"

"Oh, I can't remember," she said.

Why are you being difficult? I thought. *What are you holding back?*

"Amy was a very sweet girl," she continued. "She was a pretty good rider, too. Her horse was named Razzle. He was in the second stall to the left back there."

You can remember the name of her horse and not her instructor?

"I remember coming back to the farm that Saturday morning after she disappeared. The road was closed. I had to tell the police where I was going. They were heavily searching this area because of a lead. I remember buses of FBI agents. They walked a human chain down Nagle Road."

"Why were they searching over here so soon after she disappeared?" I asked.

Anzenberger shrugged. "Because she rode here. But we never saw any threatening source here."

That's a weird way to put it, I thought. This woman was not being candid.

"Who did they question here? Did they have a suspect that worked here?"

It was a leap, but a good one. Anzenberger's eyes flashed with emotion for a second, but then it was gone. She smiled thinly. "They questioned everybody," she answered. "Everybody was a suspect, of course. A couple times, I had to chase the media away. I would be teaching lessons and suddenly there would be a camera in my face."

The way she said that word, *media*, I knew she distrusted me.

"It disrupted my business," she said. "Everyone knew she rode here."

Yeah, it's a real shame the abduction of a ten-year-old girl put a damper on your riding lessons.

"Later, to find her all the way over to Ashland, it was like 'oh my gosh!' " she said, putting some *oomph* into her performance. "It will play an important part in my life. It's a tragic thing."

I nodded and stared her directly in the eyes, reading what I saw there.

Anzenberger grew uncomfortable and began to stammer. When she finally got her words straightened out, she said something so strange that I recoiled a little.

"There must not have been a struggle of any sort because someone would have seen it," she said.

I stood. "You don't remember if the FBI had a specific interest in anyone who worked here?"

Anzenberger shook her head. "No. It was so long ago," she said and smiled that thin smile once more.

"Okay then," I said. "Thanks for your time."

I had a feeling I would return to Holly Hill Farms—after I found out what this woman hadn't told me.

CHAPTER NINE

County Road Eleven Eighty-One

TWO WEEKS LATER, I was no closer to solving the mystery of Holly Hill Farms than I was to solving Amy's abduction. I spent the majority of that time in suburban libraries, poring over old editions of the *Lorain Morning Journal*, the *Cleveland Plain Dealer*, the *Akron Beacon Journal*, the *Ashland Times Gazette*, the *Mansfield Press*, and the *Sun Post*, all of which had dispatched reporters to cover the case in 1989 and 1990. I listed the names of everyone interviewed and made notations explaining their relationship to the Mihaljevic family. I made several trips to Lindford Drive to speak with neighbors and to get a sense for the community. Slowly, a kind of road map emerged, which I used to direct the remainder of my reporting. I knew who the main players were, for the most part, and where they fit into the story. My intention was to conduct an investigation in direct reverse of how the police and FBI conducted their own. As with any missing child case, the authorities started with the family and worked their way out to relatives, friends, associates, then strangers. I wanted to keep to the periphery for a while, build a strong base, learn everything I could. My last interview would be with Amy's father. My hope was that after I shared the information I had gathered with Mark Mihaljevic, some small detail would trigger a new revelation that made sense only to someone so close to Amy. Maybe an odd answer given to me by some distant subject would make a connection in his mind, pointing to a definitive conclusion overlooked until now.

I had to deal with the issue of Strunak soon, I knew, but not until I understood the case a little better. After all, both the FBI and police were certain he had nothing to do with Amy's abduction. Organizing my reporting this way might uncover new suspects. Perhaps the reason Strunak was dismissed was simply because he was a less likely suspect than some other person.

In the end, this method simply seemed the right way to go, even if it created more work. As far as my editors were concerned, what they didn't know couldn't hurt them so long as I turned the draft in on time.

The one place I hadn't yet visited was the recovery site in Ruggles Township. That was the last piece of the map that needed shading in. A call to the Ashland County sheriff's office put me in contact with a detective named Roger Martin, who was mentioned in early news reports. He was no rookie in 1989 and, by simple addition, should have been retired. He wasn't. He worked as the captain in charge of the detective bureau, and when I told him I wanted to see the site where Amy was found, he offered to drive me out there himself.

I made the drive to Ashland County on June 16, snaking over to I-71 South from Akron, first thing in the morning. An hour later, I was in the Ashland County Justice Center, a sleek, six-year-old building that housed the sheriff's department, the coroner's office, offices of county prosecutors, and a jail. Captain Martin stepped out and led me to his cruiser in the parking lot.

Captain Martin had the countenance of a lawman from some forgotten Sergio Leone Technicolor western, as well as the slow drawl. His face was stretched and pale, but ruggedly handsome. He seemed to possess the innate confidence of a good man at the end of a long career.

"Should I sit in the front?" I asked.

Martin laughed. It sounded like wind pushed through a sandpaper tunnel. " 'Less you want to go to jail, yes, I'd sit in front," he said.

The cruiser's interior smelled of leather inside and faint cologne, Brut maybe, and a law enforcement career's worth of cigarettes.

"How far away is County Road one-one-eight-one?" I asked as he climbed behind the wheel with a slight groan.

"It's not close," he said. "And we call it 'eleven eighty-one.' "

Martin wheeled the cruiser out of the parking lot and crossed the main road, then headed down a narrow lane. He pulled a cigarette from his pocket and lit it. Then he rolled down a window before looking at me again. It wasn't the stub of some black cigarillo like Clint Eastwood gnaws on in those movies, but the resemblance was enough to make me want to laugh. I didn't though. I thought he might shoot me if I did.

"Ask your questions," he said.

"Have you ever taken a reporter out to the site before?"

"No. I don't like reporters too much."

I swallowed. "Why are you taking me out there?"

"You sounded nice enough on the phone," he said. Then he looked at me from the corner of his right eye. "Don't prove me wrong."

I brought out my notebook with a shaky hand. "When did your office get the call that a body had been found in Ashland County?"

"We got a call that morning, from the jogger who found the body," he said, turning onto an even dirtier road. "We called the whole detective bureau out. We had Amy's flyers hanging up in our office for months. I figured it was her. After seeing the body, I was almost certain. Because of her size. Dispatch made the call to Bay Village police to identify the clothes. We didn't have cell phones back then, only radio, so it took a little while to get that confirmed. We couldn't ID her from appearance alone. She was already decomposing."

My face flushed with anger. Not at Martin. I welcomed his bluntness actually. It was simple anger for the man who let the girl decompose on the side of an isolated road. I felt the old eleven-year-old vigilante yearning for a meeting with that man. *One day*, I thought. *If I'm lucky enough. For now, just pay attention.*

Neither one of us had talked in a few minutes, and I slowly became aware of a new expression etched onto the man's grizzled face. It was a look that didn't belong there, so it took me a moment to recognize. It was the look of a man who wanted to tell some crazy story he only half believed himself. For a moment, he looked like Folbert.

"What's going through your mind right now?" I asked.

Martin smiled and eyed me sideways. Then he reached down and took a swig of coffee from a thermos, balancing the cigarette in the same hand. This small gesture spoke to the dexterity he had developed in the line of duty. I didn't think he'd answer the question, but after a moment he shook his head, uttered a little laugh, and began.

"After we knew it was her, the FBI sent forty-one agents down here. A helicopter flew a whole forensics crew in."

"Seems like a lot of agents," I said. "And I've heard it was more like sixty."

"They don't do that on regular cases. I've had some serious wonderings about that case. I asked, 'Why's the FBI involved if Amy didn't cross state lines, if there was no ransom, no money involved?' They said they were assisting local law enforcement. Bullshit. I've been doing this for too long to buy that.

"I worked the Buell case. This guy was killing kids in Ohio and Pennsylvania. We tracked him back to Akron. There was no FBI involved in that case, and he was killing people in two states. Yeah, there was always something about Amy's case. Voluntarily going with her kidnapper . . . usually cases like that, it's someone she knows. I'm no profiler. I'm a street cop. I just look at the evidence and go from there.

"I was on the first live *Unsolved Mysteries* show, you know? I worked the Interstate Homicide case. This serial killer murdered prostitutes and dumped them off Ohio interstates. Eventually he got caught outside Bellefonte, Pennsylvania. But this one, this one's different.

"We assumed it was somebody who knew the area," he continued. "Either someone who had lived in this area or gone camping here."

That made sense to me. If he stopped the car and let me out—taking revenge on a reporter, maybe—I wouldn't know how to get back to my car. These county roads were indistinguishable from each other. Mostly, it was the same field of wheat or corn whipping past the window. Occasional farms, wind-beaten into gray ghosts, passed by, but mostly this area was remote, desolate, and confusing. There were campgrounds out here, too. County Stage Camp and Rohr's Lake, to name a couple.

Suddenly, the road on which we traveled shot us onto State Route 224, a double-lane thoroughfare full of trucks loaded with goods bound for Sullivan and points west. Less than a mile down 224, heading east, we pulled left onto County Road 1181. It was thinly paved, cratered with potholes. There was no berm, only the edge of fields on either side. Past a set of railroad tracks and a bisecting gravel road, a gradual hill stretched to the horizon.

"It's on the other side," Martin said.

We passed an old red farmhouse on the left. The houses outside my window were ugly prefab ranches that couldn't have been older than five years. I realized how empty, how devoid of life, this road would have been in 1989. Over the hill my suspicions were confirmed. There was not a single house in sight.

Martin pulled the car a short way into the grassy field to his right and pointed across the road. "There," he said.

I stepped out of the cruiser and looked around. In the direction he pointed, the field was obstructed by a short rise. I noticed the field grew corn now, not wheat. And on our side of the road a small vehicular access led to a pond.

I walked across the road and climbed the steep rise so I could stand in the field. Martin didn't follow but walked a ways farther down the road so that he could see me clearly. The jogger, I realized, must have been coming in the opposite direction of State Route 224. It's the only direction from which the body would have been seen.

Sebold, Seabold.

"Her teeth had fallen out and were found in the earth, there," Martin said.

I looked at the ground, a part of me hoping to see a horse-head earring or some scrap of clothing. Nothing but pebbles and dirt, soft with recent rain.

"When do they harvest this field?" I asked. If it was later than October 27, Amy's body could not have been here the whole time. It would have been eaten by the combine.

"End of September," he said.

I took a couple pictures, then jumped back to the road.

"All set?" he asked.

I nodded and got back into the car. That part of each of us that listens for the voices of the departed reached out for Amy and found nothing. This was just a country road, just some cornfield. Any trace of Amy, ethereal or corporeal, had departed long ago.

We started back toward Ashland. Along the way I learned a little more about Captain Martin, but little concerning Amy. The detective served in the marine corps in southwest Asia from 1967 to 1969. He spent his spare time restoring old cars in his garage and was most proud of a '77 Trans Am, which he took out in fair weather only, but he also had a 1966 Chevelle, two Camaros, and a Corvette. Recently, he had had some time to tinker with them. Six months before our meeting he had a heart attack that nearly killed him. He had only been back at work for a couple weeks.

"I was supposed to quit smoking, quit drinking coffee, and quit my job," he said, then he took another long drag on the cigarette hanging from his mouth.

"So do you have any hunches?" I asked. "What do you think happened to Amy?"

Martin seemed to ponder this a moment, then said, "A vendetta killing would fit the profile, too. Someone killing her to get back at Dad. But I'm sure there are a lot smarter guys who looked at this than me."

The sarcasm in that last sentence was thick enough to drown in.

I was almost back to my car when I remembered the coroner's report. I had called ahead to the coroner's office, asking for a copy of Amy's file. These reports are public record under Ohio's sunshine laws, even when the victim is part of an ongoing investigation, and I had never had a problem requesting files from Cuyahoga County. Even the photographs are available for journalists and family. I doubled back and stepped into the offices next to the sheriff's department.

A man named William Emery has been the Ashland County coroner since 1987. His wife, Karen, runs the office and handles the phone calls and appointments. Karen Emery is a pudgy lady with a permanent scowl, quick to remind anyone who calls that she's the one in charge. It's also obvious she's a little touchy about Ashland County's nepotism laws. "I'd be paid, too, if I wasn't married to the coroner," she has told me on several occasions.

Already, I had met people unwilling to talk to me about Amy and the Mihaljevics. Some of the folks who have stayed on Lindford Drive since her abduction kindly shut the door in my face after cordial introductions. At first, I chalked this treatment up to normal fear of the media. Most people just don't trust journalists, and usually for good reason. But that wasn't always the case. There are people, thankfully very few, who hold onto Amy's story with a sense of dark lust. It's the same with the older generation that lived in Bay Village when Doctor

Sheppard was arrested for killing his wife. These events have become legend to those indirectly involved, a kind of communal secret not to be shared with outsiders. *You weren't here with us,* their eyes say. *You don't deserve this information.* Usually, the people touched by Amy's case explained that they just didn't want any of what they knew going public (a statement that is, at the very least, dangerous and self-important). In reality, they just didn't want to part with their secret treasure.

I had taken to calling these people "Gollums," after the character from *The Lord of the Rings.* Each of them possessed some important kernel of information regarding Amy's disappearance, which they guarded with jealous suspicion. Their *precious.* Like Bilbo Baggins, I had to acknowledge that nothing made me feel quite so good as prying that gift from their grubby little hands. Until I met Karen Emery, though, the Gollums had never held a position of power over me.

"You will not be getting the full coroner's report," Emery said the day I arrived after my drive in the country with Martin. "I spoke with the county prosecutor, and she has allowed you to view the summary of the report which was released to the newspapers back in 1990. I have also included a number of newspaper clippings for you to view. But you cannot take them with you and you cannot copy them. We close in fifteen minutes."

I thought of simply demanding the full report, telling her to comply with the open-records mandate or face a lawsuit. But I held back, barely. I thought it likely she wanted me to say something like that. Then, she could easily take away the offer to read the summary. If I argued, I got nothing.

"Great," I said. I took the file from her, trying my hardest to look grateful, and sat at a table on the other side of the room. Emery returned to her cluttered desk and eyed me over a stack of paperwork.

So that's how you want it, I thought. *All right then.*

Surprisingly, Amy's birth certificate was included in the file. I noted that she was born in Little Rock, Arkansas, on December 11, 1978. As expected, Mark Mihaljevic was listed as the father, Margaret McNulty as her mother.

Other bits of missing info I garnered from the sparse details included in the summary: Amy was cremated by West Shore Cremation.

Jenkins Funeral Chapel in Westlake handled transfer of the remains, at no charge.

Amy was pronounced dead on February 8, 1990, by Cuyahoga County coroner Elizabeth Balraj, who had conducted the autopsy at the request of William Emery. Death resulted from stab wounds to the neck.

A note from Dr. Emery claimed Amy's body had rested in the wheat field "a considerable period of time." Probably the entire three months. She was identified through dental records and fingerprints.

From the clippings, an assortment from the *Ashland Times Gazette* and the *Cleveland Plain Dealer,* I learned that police were interested in an employee of a Westlake manufacturing plant who left at noon the day Amy was kidnapped and did not return. Also, Amy was lying facedown when found by Janet Seabold, twelve feet from the side of the road. A man named Dick Stose, an air-traffic controller living in the Ashland area, claimed his daughter had almost been abducted during a walk, near the same field in which Amy was found. Most bizarre was one writer's claim that WKYC reporter Tom Beres received a phone call from a man in January 1990 who said Amy could be found in Ashland County, and for twenty thousand dollars, he'd provide the exact location. When I later spoke to Tom Beres, he assured me he never took such a call.

"I have to close up," Emery said, her gaze going to the clock mounted on the wall. I shut the half file and left it sitting on the desk.

"Thanks a bunch," I said. I had to be going anyway. I had another meeting with Spaetzel in Bay Village later that afternoon. This time, the FBI would be there, too.

CHAPTER TEN

The Feds

SPECIAL AGENT LAURA HENRY of the Cleveland branch of the FBI stands only as high as my shoulders. She has short and spiky white hair and a gentle handshake. She joined the Bureau in 1990 after serving a number of years in the military. Henry spent her first two years as a federal agent in Washington, D.C. Then she was reassigned to Mississippi, where she investigated white-collar crime and longed for a return north of the Mason-Dixon. "Nobody wants Mississippi," she'll say with a wry smile when pushed on this subject. In 1999, Henry was transferred to Cleveland, where she was reassigned to the Violent Crimes division, a reactive squad for bank robberies, kidnappings, and murder-for-hire schemes.

Inside the cramped confines of the 29th floor of the old federal building on Superior, personal space ran at a premium. Offices were unheard of. Special agents toiled at desks crammed together, and hers sat next to one occupied by a distinguished older agent named Gary Belluomini. He retired two weeks after Henry's arrival, but she got to know him fairly well before his departure. The first thing she noticed was the photo on his desk, a photograph of a young girl with a side-saddle ponytail.

Belluomini, as it happened, was a key player in the search for Amy Mihaljevic, and he told Henry what he knew of the case as his retirement party approached. It was obvious he was passionate about finding Amy's killer and believed such a thing was possible even after many years. "When I retire, I want that Amy poster always hanging in this office as a reminder that her case is not closed," he said to Henry one day.

That poster, a twin of the one that hangs in Spaetzel's office, is supposedly hanging on a wall in the sleek new FBI building on Lakeside Road today. Henry inherited the case in 2001.

"No one has forgotten this case," Special Agent Henry said to me as I sat in what had become my usual chair beside Spaetzel's desk. She wore a sharp business suit, and I thought at first she looked as unintimidating as a grade school teacher. As her eyes studied me during the interview, as she took notes and appeared to listen closely to everything Spaetzel and I said, I realized that was probably the impression she wanted to project. Behind those eyes, I could see her mind collecting cold data and comparing it with what she already knew, like some cybernetic calculator, making deductions about the human condition.

As a gesture of good faith or to keep her from writing for a while, I handed her a copy of Folbert's self-published autobiography.

Spaetzel, I think, could read my nervousness. I imagine he felt the same way. Henry was a hard read. "It would be very easy for the FBI to just let this go," he said, smiling at the woman. "But they're always helping. They're still investigating the Amanda Berry and Gina DeJesus cases. They just don't let them go."

Special Agent Henry nodded. "Earlier this week, we got a walk-in," she said. "Someone had information on Amy's case and just walked in with it."

"We had two this week," Spaetzel said. It did not seem like an attempt to one-up her, more like an example of how often the Bay Village police get their own leads.

"Can we talk about Billy Strunak a little?" I asked.

Agent Henry didn't say anything. She looked to Spaetzel and he responded with a shrug, as if to say *What can it hurt?* "Still hung up on him?" Spaetzel asked me.

"I don't know," I said. "The timing of his death, coming so soon after Amy was found. What do you make of that?"

"Well, we ran across a lot of people who acted strangely," Spaetzel said. "Some other people we talked to committed suicide."

Kristen Sabo's father, for one, I thought. *Were there others?*

"Why was Ressler so sure that Billy did it when he wrote his book?" I asked.

Spaetzel sighed and rolled his eyes. "At some point, Ressler inserts himself into the timeline of the investigation," he says. "And then Billy commits suicide. What Ressler didn't know was that Billy was having problems with his ex-girlfriend. He was personally involved with the volunteer center upstairs, searching for Amy. A lot of people were personally involved like that. And when they heard her body was discovered, that affected some people. A guy like this who's mentally unstable anyway, that could push him over the edge. The unfortunate thing was Ressler decided to write about it. Our fear is people will read his book and think Billy did it. It's difficult when someone takes facts out of context and exploits them."

Tread lightly was how I read Spaetzel's warning.

"Where were the phone calls coming from? Did you trace them?" I asked.

Henry's pen was scribbling again. Was she writing down Spaetzel's answers or my questions?

Shaking his head, Spaetzel said, "The technology at the time wasn't what it is today. The Mihaljevics had two lines coming into that house. A family phone and a work phone."

"Which one did it come through?"

"We don't know," he said. "But it was a local call. The phone company logged all long-distance calls at that time, but not local ones. There were no records of any long-distance phone calls during the times Amy would have been home alone that were not accounted for."

"You mentioned there were a number of suspects early on," I went on, "and that all but one of them took a polygraph. The ones that took the polygraphs, did they all pass?"

"Failing a polygraph doesn't mean you're guilty. It's just another tool," Spaetzel said, deftly side-stepping a direct answer.

I chose to detail my interview with Hollie Anzenberger and the way she avoided some specific questions. Henry gave Spaetzel another look. His response this time came across as an odd mixture of surprise and humor. It felt like another confirmation that I was on the right track, that I was beginning to mirror at least part of their investigation.

"Holly Hill was looked at pretty closely," Spaetzel said, sounding like he was weighing his words. He might share information with me once I had it, but he didn't feel comfortable handing it to me. "Obviously, this person had to have seen Amy before. So, you look at where she is most often. You look at the stables, the school, the neighborhood. Riding horses at Holly Hill—that was one thing she and her mother did together. So there was a connection there."

"What about Margaret's job? The guy on the phone told Amy that he worked with her mom. I'm assuming her coworkers were looked at pretty closely."

"Yes," he said. "Each person at *Tradin' Times* was definitely looked at."

"How many suspects are there currently?"

"There are a lot of people who are still suspects," he said. "You can't always rule someone out 100 percent."

"Have you seen this MO anywhere else?" I asked.

"The phone call, that was a very unique way of getting to someone," Spaetzel said. "Today, that would probably happen over the Internet. We sent the specifics to VICAP. [The Violent Criminal Apprehension Program is a nationwide database that collects details on crimes of violence.] I've never been contacted. At least to law enforcement's knowledge, another crime like this one has never occurred."

I set my own pen down and started putting things away. Henry stopped writing. "Can I say something real quick?" she asked. "There's a child killer walking among us. There is someone out there who is responsible for this who is not accounted for on October 27, 1989. This happened in the middle of the afternoon when most people would be at work. It's someone with a connection to Ashland County."

I thought of the long back roads that lead to County Road 1181. She had to be right. Nobody just ended up there.

Her statement prompted Spaetzel to speak up once more, too. "We feel that this is not the only person who has direct knowledge of the crime," he said. "That's the phone call I'm waiting for. From the sheer guilt of this, they would have talked to somebody."

Gary Belluomini, the man who worked Amy's case before it was assigned to Special Agent Henry, grew up in a rough section of Chicago still controlled by the mob. It was so Old World, the man still has a clippy *Goodfellas* accent forty years later. As a teenager, he saw the Mafia's rampant extortion games as a problem, not a future occupation. He discovered an urge within himself to make this world a safer place in which to live. In 1968, he joined the army and after two years signed up as an investigative aide with the FBI. The Bureau didn't require college degrees then, and new recruits were often drafted from a stock of young apprentices. These were the days of Patty Hearst, of Wounded Knee, of Kent State. In 1975, he was accepted into a new agent training class. By the end of that year, he was a full-fledged G-man working in Cleveland.

His first day on the job was not a quiet one. A local antihero named "Fast Eddie" Watkins held up a bank at the corner of West 136th and Lorain. Though Watkins was adept at stick-'em-ups, so much so that he enjoyed a kind of Clyde Barker celebrity status, things did not go well for him that day. He was cornered. He took hostages.

Belluomini watched from a safe distance throughout the night as agents debated a course of action. He was still there the next day when Watkins surrendered. But that wasn't the last time they would see each other.

In 1980, Watkins escaped from a prison in Atlanta and fled back to Cleveland, where he proceeded to the Central National Bank building on West 177th. He wanted to withdraw some money they were holding for him—though not in an account per se.

"I'm Eddie Watkins and I'm here to rob you," he announced as he entered the bank. This was a man who loved his job. And this time he got away . . . for a while.

Belluomini loved his job, too, especially when it involved taking Watkins down. An FBI agent driving near Lodi spotted Watkins rocketing down 71 South and contacted Belluomini. Soon the agent was racing toward Ashland County after his old nemesis. Watkins, not in the mood to return to a Georgia prison, turned off the highway and pulled over next to a cornfield. There he proceeded to hold himself hostage, pointing a firearm at his own temple. By the time Belluomini got to the scene, Watkins was throwing money out the window.

The retired agent laughed as he recalled these desperate actions of a once-notorious criminal. He seemed to admire Watkins's brazen style; he was the last of a dying breed of celebrity bank robbers.

"I knew he didn't like dogs," Belluomini said, a sparkle in his eye. "So we brought out the dog. There was a short shootout. A bullet hit Watkins' pinky finger. Then it was over. We arrested him."

I sat next to Belluomini inside a busy café on Superior Avenue downtown, next to the regional headquarters of Fifth Third Bank, while I listened to the circumstances that delivered him to Cleveland. Belluomini works as a criminal investigator for Fifth Third these days but still dresses classic FBI: sharp suit, well pressed, with a smart tie.

"I had worked on some other kidnapping cases before this one," Belluomini said, moving on to Amy with a non sequitur worthy of a dime-store novel's first sentence. "When you're an agent for the FBI, and there's a kidnapping, especially of a child, everybody wants to be involved."

Belluomini coordinated the federal investigation from a command bunker set up in the basement of the Bay Village Police Department, alongside Special Agent Dick Wrenn. They were supplied at regular intervals with paper, coffee, and food by the civilian volunteers on the second floor. If not for the dedication of those volunteers, not to mention the police department itself, the investigation would never have been able to cover so much ground so quickly.

"We hit the ground running," Belluomini said. "It was a wonderful marriage between the FBI and a local police department. Usually, you have to cut through some jealousy with some local departments. But that was not the case here. Jim Tompkins was the detective lieutenant at that time. We were both doing our best to find Amy. We retired the same day in 1998, too. Jim and I, we talked to *thousands* of people."

"People like Billy Strunak?"

Belluomini didn't flinch. Whatever I knew, he *knew* I knew. "He was one of a number of people we looked at who did not fit the bill. But some people you just can't rule out completely. There were a lot of 'persons of interest.' To this day, we don't forget about them. I don't want to say more than that."

The morning of February 8, 1990, Belluomini was in the command center talking on the phone with an agent in Sandusky who was investigating a lead there. During the conversation, the Sandusky agent's police-band radio squawked to life in the background.

"He said, 'Gary, I've been hearing some chatter over the radio between Huron County and Ashland County. I think they may have found the body,' " Belluomini recalled. "As soon as he said that, I got a chill down my back. I just knew they had found her. I called our agent working out of Mansfield and said, 'I need you to do me a favor.' He said, 'I can't. I gotta go check this body out.' I said, 'I know. I want you to see if it's Amy.' And it was.

"I went down with a bunch of agents and conducted a crime scene investigation. We set up another command post at the Ashland County Sheriff's Department. For the next three weeks, I led the case down there. The main goal had always been to find Amy when she was alive. The second goal was to find the person who took her. When her body was found, we focused on that second goal."

By the end of 1990, Belluomini returned to Bay Village and Dick Wrenn. Over the course of the next year, the other agents working the case were reassigned. Belluomini and Wrenn continued to follow leads and interview suspects. Finally, in February of 1991, the duo packed up crates of information and returned to their offices in Cleveland.

"We weren't giving up on the case," Belluomini obviously wanted to make clear. "But there wasn't enough work anymore to keep us out there." He paused then and shook his head. "It was difficult for everyone not to have that case solved. We live with this case today. It will never leave us."

"Is there anything you can tell me that I don't already know?" I said, making sure not to sound disrespectful.

He laughed and shook his head again. "There may come a time when we have to confront a person," he said. "We don't want to reveal certain facts that might disrupt that."

"So you think this guy is still around? That there's a serial killer living in Bay?"

Belluomini waited a second before he answered, his eyes traveling to that familiar space behind my right shoulder. "It's possible this was the first murder for this person," he said. "It's possible this was the only one. I think that's what happened here."

CHAPTER ELEVEN

Back to Holly Hill

IN AN ARTICLE in the *Plain Dealer* in 1989, I found a picture taken at Holly Hill Farms that showed a young man leaning against a fence, his eyes cast sadly downward. His name was Jeff Taylor, and the article said he worked for the farm and knew Amy. Naively, I immediately figured he was a suspect in the case, probably because he was white and in his twenties. Determined to surprise the man with a visit, I tracked his personal information on the Internet and found he still worked in the area, training riders.

On Wednesday, June 22, I drove out to a set of stables in western Cuyahoga County. A number of high-school girls were leaving as I parked. I asked one where I could find Mr. Taylor, and she pointed to a man sitting on a golf cart watching a teen galloping along a small track. A woman, college age by my estimate, sat in the passenger seat next to him.

Taylor watched me cross the distance to him, a curious expression on his face. Sixteen years had been kind to him. The young man's face from the *Plain Dealer* had only grown distinguished and handsome over time, a thinner, less ruddy visage of Robert Redford—a *GQ* magazine cowboy. "Can I help you?" he said.

"I hope so," I said. "I was hoping you could tell me what you know about Amy Mihaljevic."

Taylor's face went blank. He scrunched his eyes as if trying to remember the name.

"The young girl from Holly Hill who was abducted in 1989," I prompted, feeling a little disappointed. I determined by his initial reaction he'd never been a "person of interest." People don't forget an interrogation by the feds. In fact, Taylor was nowhere near Bay Village on October 27, 1989. As it turned out, he was halfway across the state, selling a horse.

"Oh! Right. Amy. Yeah, I remember that," he said. "I was leasing the farm from the Fettingers. Wow. How long's it been?"

"About sixteen years."

Taylor nodded. "That sounds about right. I heard Mrs. Fettinger's in a nursing home now and her daughter, Hollie, runs the farm."

"The FBI was interested in the farm in the first few days after Amy disappeared," I said.

"Yeah, they had Nagle Road blocked. There were planes flying everywhere. They had heat sensors pointed at the ground."

"Do you know if anyone at Holly Hill Farms was a suspect in the case?"

"H.B.," he said. "H.B. Fettinger. The owner's son. Hollie's brother. He was living above the garage at the farm. He was about thirty years old at that time. He had had nervous breakdowns in the past. He wasn't allowed down at the stables because he had some issues before, some altercations with the old owners of the farm. He had so many weird problems. This guy was off the wall. He was big into hunting. And he had this van. I know the FBI had seen stuff in his van that made them want to talk to him. They sat H.B. in the house and grilled him for hours. H.B. told them he needed a lawyer. I almost felt bad for him. They were pressing so hard. They questioned another employee of mine, Sean Hillock, but he was working on the farm when Amy was taken."

My intuition had been correct. Hollie Fettinger (married name Anzenberger) had been holding back about her brother. "Do you know H.B.'s full name?" I asked.

"Nah. Sorry."

"Do you know where I could find him?"

"No, I don't," he said. "I haven't seen him since then. But maybe one of the girls that worked for me would remember more. Sue Tomsu was Amy's instructor. And you could try Shannon Conway. She rode with Amy."

I discovered that Sue Tomsu had changed her name since 1989, after marrying. She had moved to Florida, and her number was unlisted. However, family members still living in the Bay Village area passed along an interview request for me. Her husband called soon after and said he would speak to Sue when she returned home. She never called me, and later family members would only say, "She just doesn't want to relive it."

Thankfully, Shannon Conway was a little more helpful.

"Of course I knew Amy," Conway said when I reached her by phone. "She was a cute kid who rode at the barn. She was about five years younger than me, and we both rode with Sue Tomsu. Once or twice a year, Holly Hill Farms had their own little horse show, the kind of thing where every kid gets a ribbon. Amy was proud of her awards."

"Did you hear anyone talk about H.B. in relation to her abduction?" I asked. "What were people saying at the barn after she disappeared?"

"There was a lot of speculation," Conway said. "All of us girls at the barn thought he was really creepy. There already had been a creepy vibe about him. He would wander around at the barn sometimes. I think I saw his dark shadow disappear into his apartment one time. He was sort of like the Boogeyman. But the person you should talk with is Jennifer O'Brien. She rode at Holly Hill. And she happened to work at the Baskin-Robbins where Amy was taken."

O'Brien was as eager to talk to me as her friend. It was as if both had been waiting for someone to track the events back to them so they could share what they knew.

"I was in a couple of lessons with Amy and her mother," O'Brien said. "They really seemed to enjoy riding together. Ah yes, H.B. It was more folklore than knowledge. He had a lot of guns in his apartment. Sue Tomsu had been in his apartment and told us that. He was a Vietnam vet. We thought he suffered from posttraumatic stress disorder. I was in the field behind Holly Hill once, and I remember seeing him back there in camouflage. He had a high-tech bow. And he just never acknowledged you. We were definitely intimidated by him. The FBI came to my house and asked me about Holly Hill and about Baskin-Robbins. They asked me about the woods to the left of the barn."

Unfortunately, O'Brien cannot recall if she worked at Baskin-Robbins on October 27. As with most minimum-wage jobs, her shifts blended together. She does remember Amy coming in for ice cream once, but she cannot link that memory to a specific date, let alone identify Amy's favorite flavor.

After speaking to Conway and O'Brien, I practically shook with the anticipation of being able to unveil the man whose identity the FBI and Bay Village police had kept secret all these years. A quick search of whitepages.com found no H.B. Fettinger, nor any similar name. It seemed useless to conduct a wider search without at least a first name. Logging onto the Cuyahoga County website, I scanned its pages, looking for a possible solution. I tried the marriage registry archives. Nothing. Same with a civil and criminal case search. I tried Lorain County, too, as the farm straddles the border of the two counties. Nothing. I stared blankly at the computer screen for a few minutes, slowly realizing there was only one way to get the information I needed.

I grabbed my satchel and peeked into Kevin's office.

"I'm going back to Holly Hill Farms to check on something," I said. "I might head home after that."

"How's it coming?" he asked.

"Good. I might have something to talk to you about tomorrow morning."

Hollie Anzenberger spread soil around a newly constructed fence near the back of Holly Hill Farms as I arrived twenty minutes later. The summer sun beat down, and I saw beads of perspiration hanging from under her thin blond hair. She's not a young woman, but she was quite up to the task. She had the type of solid, hardworking farmer's physique seldom seen north of Canton, and strength enough to rival the young men who shovel shit out of the horse stalls. If she got her hands on me, I was sure she would be able to work me over.

As I approached, she looked up but did not immediately recognize me. I came unarmed—no notebook, no satchel to encumber a quick escape. And I was dressed down in jeans and a T-shirt, not having expected to do an interview that day. She stood as I neared the fence separating us.

"Hello," she said.

"Hi, Mrs. Anzenberger, I'm the reporter from *Scene* magazine," I said. "I spoke to you a little while ago."

"Right, about Amy," she said.

"That's right. And you said you didn't remember who the FBI was interested in out here."

"Well, it was a long time ago. I really can't remember."

I nodded and regarded her for a moment. "I've talked to some people who used to work for you. They say the FBI interviewed your brother."

Anzenberger's face pinched into a glare. "Harold had nothing to do with it," she said. "The FBI told me he didn't do it. This whole thing has hurt my business enough. Just leave my family alone."

"Harold Fettinger?"

"Bound," she said. "Harold and Greg Bound are my half brothers. But Harold had nothing to do with it."

Harold Bound. *H.B.*

"Well, I'm writing about the suspects in this case," I said. "And I think Harold was one of them. I think I should talk with him."

"I don't know where he is," she said. "I haven't seen him in about ten years."

I didn't believe that.

"That's all right," I said. "I'll find him. I was just hoping you'd save me some time." No longer afraid of this woman, I felt a red rage growing inside me. *Just tell me to my face you aren't going to help me.*

"You won't find him," she said as I turned and walked away.

If only to prove you wrong, I will, I thought. *I won't do anything else until I do.*

Less than ten minutes later, I parked in front of an old house on the border of Cleveland and Tremont, an older neighborhood very close to downtown. I had called the office and asked our editorial assitant to do a quick records search on the Web. It didn't take long. Greg Bound lived in the "up" apartment. I stepped to the door farthest to the right and pressed a button. I couldn't be sure, but I didn't think it worked. I didn't hear a bell. I knocked. Peering through the dirty glass of the door's wide window, I could make out the stairs leading to the second-floor apartment. Junk cluttered steps blackened with crud. I knocked again and listened. I couldn't hear a thing. I knocked on the other door for a while, hoping to find neighbors that could tell me something about Greg Bound. No answer. I looked in their window only to find the apartment empty, a cable cord sticking out of the wall, attached to nothing.

I stepped back onto the sidewalk and looked up to the second-floor windows. A blue light flickered in the dreariness there. Someone was watching TV.

Reaching into my car, I honked the horn. When no one came to the windows, I returned to the door and really hammered. I kicked the bottom for added reverb. Now, I heard the sound of heavy footsteps from above. I discerned through the glass the dark outline of a man negotiating the junk on the steps. My heart throbbed against my shirt again. I wondered if twenty-seven was too young for a heart attack.

A slender man with thinning hair hanging limply over his ears opened the door and looked out at me. "Hello?" he said.

"Are you Greg Bound?"

"I am."

"Can I talk to you about Amy Mihaljevic?"

Greg's eyes shot open and his face stretched into comical surprise. He stepped outside and shut the door behind him. "You a reporter?"

"I am," I said. "I'm with *Scene.*"

"I knew one day a reporter would come along and ask me that question," he said. "It's been a long time."

"Do you think your brother was a suspect?"

Greg laughed at that. "Yes," he said. "My brother *is* the main suspect in the abduction of Amy Mihaljevic."

"What can you tell me about that?" I asked, my voice suddenly a notch higher than normal. I kept my distance from this man, though it probably wasn't necessary. He almost seemed relieved that I had stopped by.

"All I know is that the FBI said it was a blue truck that Amy was driven off in," said Greg. "The farm had a blue truck. The day she disappeared, Harold came home really late at night, driving that truck."

"Where is your brother?"

"When the FBI started questioning him, he checked himself into a

VA hospital. He had himself committed," he said. "I haven't seen him for a long time."

"Do you think he did it?"

Greg looked off across the street and shrugged. "I don't know," he said.

The main Veterans Affairs hospital in northeastern Ohio is a sprawling brick campus in Brecksville, a suburb halfway between Cleveland and Akron. I arrived early the next morning, hoping to talk myself into a casual meeting with Bound.

Elderly men mixed in the grassy spaces outside the psychiatric wing, some of them smoking and watching the woods beyond the parking lot, some just sitting next to each other, eyes unfocused as they relived some long-ago insurgency.

Inside it smelled of urine and bleach, and the linoleum floor sparkled in the fluorescent lights above. A platoon of men in wheelchairs guarded the door, monitoring the slight actions of the troops in drab scrubs outside. One of them smiled up at me as I passed, greeting me with toothless gums.

In the hallway, men slid about on slippers as if the will to lift their feet had abandoned them. Gravity was too strong. Many didn't look old enough for Vietnam. I realized that some had to be vets from the first Gulf War. And a few were young enough to have seen action in Iraq.

At the reception desk, I found a large woman leaning over an old computer, the screen grimy with dust and lord knows what. She smiled at me.

"I'm looking for a gentleman named Harold Bound," I said.

"Are you family?"

"He served with my father," I said—a lie. My dad had been too young for the draft. "My father lives out of state now, and he wanted me to pass along a personal message to Harold."

"All right," she said. "Let me see what I can find." I watched as she typed on the keypad. "You just missed him. He was here for group yesterday."

"So, he's not a patient here anymore?"

"No, he lives in a group home," she said. "But I don't have the name of the place. He'll be back for group therapy next Monday at 9 a.m., though."

"I thought it was this Billy Strunak guy," Kevin said when I gave him an update the next day. "You can't keep switching suspects."

"I know," I said. "But this guy's own brother believes he's the FBI's main suspect."

"Well, we can try looking him up online. We have a subscription to a website that can find anybody," he said with a smile. "We don't tell everyone about it because it would be too expensive to use all the time."

Kevin entered Bound's name into the search engine. A name and number flashed onscreen. There he was, and he lived only a few streets from his brother, Greg. Five minutes from the office.

"Go get him," said Kevin.

CHAPTER TWELVE

Bound

THERE ARE A NUMBER of group homes in the Cleveland area for veterans who are too healthy to remain at the Brecksville VA hospital. Most are ramshackle two-story structures with a decent view of the Mittal steel factory. Harold Bound lived on the second floor of just such a place; his caregiver, Mrs. Reed, was on the ground floor. A wrought-iron gate protecting a patch of green grass separated the property from the sun-battered dirt lawns of its neighbors.

Mrs. Reed said Bound was at church, a daily routine of his. She didn't know when he would return, so I staked out the house from up the street. Inside my car, the day dragged on. Except for a quick trip to a nearby fast-food joint I waited for Bound's truck to return to the gravel lot next to the house. The smell of stale fries soon filled up the car as I slipped into a blood-sugar daze. I drifted toward sleep as I watched a family of raccoons wander out of their home inside an abandoned building across the street. Twilight approached over the smokestacks of Mittal in the valley below.

Some time later, a truck drove past and pulled into the lot. It was so new it still shined. A man got out. I couldn't see his features too well from the distance in the low light, but, then, I had no idea what Bound looked like anyway. When he started toward the group home, I got out of the car and jogged up to him just as he entered the front gate.

"Excuse me, I'm looking for Harold Bound," I said.

"That's me," he answered. Standing close to him, I could see him quite well. He was a pear-shaped man, wide around the hips. He wore a polo shirt and slacks and thick round glasses. He was mostly bald on top, but the hair was still thick enough on the sides. Jowls hung like pasty-white sacks at the sides of his face, making his neck appear wider than it was. I caught a whiff of something. Cologne maybe. Old Spice?

Here was the question by which I might learn his secret: "Can I talk to you about Amy Mihaljevic?"

Strangely, Bound did not react at all, except for the smallest trace of a smile. "Are you James Renner?" he asked.

It was my turn to act surprised. So surprised, actually, that I couldn't respond immediately.

Bound uttered a rough laugh. "My sister told me about you," he said. "Why don't you come in and sit down?"

"Can we sit on the steps here?"

"Yeah, that's fine." Actually, Bound sat on the steps and I hunkered down Indian-style on the sidewalk in front of him.

I opened the notebook in my hands and tried not to appear too nervous. Names are powerful things, as many voodoo doctors would testify. In the age of the Internet, where a person's address can be located by pushing "Enter," that's never been so true. I didn't much like that Bound already knew mine. "Do you want to talk to me?" I said.

Bound shrugged. I couldn't see his eyes through the thick tinted glasses, but I felt like he was staring away from me, maybe watching the raccoons filing out of the house across the way. "Sure," he said. "I don't care."

"Do you remember Amy from when you lived above the garage at Holly Hill Farms?"

"No," he said. "I wouldn't be able to pick her out of a lineup of ten kids."

"Then what do you remember?"

Now I felt his eyes on me. "I remember Dick Wrenn," he said.

For the next hour, I listened to Bound's tale, documenting in my notepad while keeping one eye on him as the light slowly drained away from the earth, enfolding us in a warm summer void.

According to Bound, this is how things went down:

On Saturday, October 28, 1989, there was a loud knock on the door to his apartment. He opened it and there was Special Agent Dick Wrenn. He was with another agent he only remembers as "Mr. Hendricks."

"We want to talk to you," Wrenn said, stepping inside.

Normally, other people in the house attached to the garage might have intervened. Bound's mother lived there with his stepfather, but they had gone to Florida on vacation. And so much the better, as far as Bound was concerned. They didn't get along. To his mother, he was just someone who picked up the shavings in the horse stalls. When he was younger, he had asked his mother for a pair of riding boots but was told he wasn't worth the money.

However, Bound was frightened by the feds and so he called his mother, hoping she might help. Over the phone, Wrenn told Bound's mother that he wanted his agents to look over the entire house. When he returned the phone to Bound, his mother said simply, "Let them."

Wrenn escorted Bound to the garage below as other men rooted through Bound's possessions.

Bound gave Wrenn his history. He had served nine years in military intelligence in the air force. He had a bronze star and two presidential unit citations. He was diagnosed as paranoid schizophrenic, a condition that had been aggravated by combat.

Wrenn questioned him about Amy. "Where were you yesterday?" he asked.

"I was here," Bound said. He had no alibi. "Give me a lie-detector test. Give me a Sodium Pentothal test," he pleaded. He was familiar with Sodium Pentothal, a "truth serum," from his years in air force intelligence.

"You need a lawyer first," Wrenn said.

Eventually, Wrenn and his agents left, and Bound returned to his apartment. Wrenn had said he would be back, and Bound knew he meant it. He had no intention of helping a man who seemed focused on pinning this crime on him, so he sat down and wrote a detailed list of items he would need to pack for an extended stay inside the VA hospital. He figured Wrenn wouldn't dare set foot inside the military facility. People needed special clearance to interrogate people under the watchful eye of Uncle Sam.

Bound's brother, Greg, drove him to Brecksville. But Brecksville psychiatrists refused to admit him. He was too lucid, they said. The detailed list of his belongings proved he was highly functional, too precise. He was quickly transferred to Wade Park, a facility with less strict military oversight.

The next day, Wrenn came to his room and escorted him to a car, then to a Holiday Inn on Crocker-Bassett where another agent named Singleton waited. A lie-detector machine sat on a table inside their room. They interrogated him every day that first week Amy was missing. Sometimes they met at the Radisson Inn instead.

"Tell us what you did," Wrenn demanded one day, Bound's arm attached to the lie detector. "Tell us what you did!"

Wrenn asked Bound a series of questions and Bound knew enough about manual lie detectors to understand that he was consistently failing one specific answer. This only seemed to fuel the rage of the FBI agents.

Finally, they gave Bound what he had asked for, the Sodium Pentothal test. Someone injected the drug into Bound's arm and the next thing he remembered was Wrenn staring into his eyes as the interrogation ended. "Harold, I'm very disappointed in you," he said.

There were no more interrogations after that. Bound returned to a regular routine at Wade Park. He never left the VA system.

As Bound finished his story, I looked up at him but could judge no emotion in his expression. Without pause, he had provided me with far more detail than I had hoped for. I wondered how much of it I could believe.

"What happened when Amy was found in February of 1990?" I asked.

"Well, her being found in Ashland County jogged my memory of something. I remember seeing a guy who worked for Jeff Taylor at the stables right before Amy went missing. He talked to me about the Ashland County Gun Club. I called Bay Village police to give them that information and they hung the phone up on me. That guy that worked for Jeff looked just like the composite sketch."

"And you're sure you don't remember Amy specifically?" I asked.

For a full five seconds, Bound didn't say anything. Then, he nodded, almost reluctantly. "I remember this one time, Amy's mother dropped her off for riding lessons. I was on my porch and I saw their van pull in. Amy got out and her mother just threw her boots out the window and drove off. I watched Amy sit down in the parking lot to put her boots on. That's when I met her. She was putting on her boots. I walked down to her and asked, 'Do you need any help with that?' But she wouldn't talk to me. So I walked back to my apartment."

I didn't like that story one bit. Especially since Bound had denied remembering Amy only an hour earlier.

"You seem pretty self-sufficient," I said. "How are you doing in general?"

"I work a booth at gun shows," he said. "I arrange hunting trips for small groups for extra money. They have me on clozapine now. I still have problems with voices. I still hear them. But I haven't had a problem in ten years. I'll tell you one thing, though. I'm glad I wouldn't be able to recognize Wrenn or his agents anymore."

I got up to leave then but turned to him again when I was on the other side of the gate. Putting as much edge in my voice as I could muster, I said, "Mr. Bound, I have to ask you straight up. Did you kill Amy Mihaljevic?"

"No," he said. "I didn't."

On the way home, I tried to process our conversation. Was it possible to control your answers under the influence of Sodium Pentothal? I didn't think so. Who knows what someone like Bound, an ex–intelligence officer for the air force, might say under such conditions?

What interested me more was Bound's story about the man he met at Holly Hill Farms, the one who had mentioned the Ashland County Gun Club. There were two options concerning that tale. One: Bound made it up to take the heat off him. Two: Someone who worked at Holly Hill Farms, where Amy spent most of her free time, was familiar with the isolated area where her body was found.

In 1989, the Ashland County Gun Club sat a block and a half away from County Road 1181.

The next morning I called Dick Wrenn. I asked him to meet with me, but again he declined. I relayed the conversation with Bound.

"Harold Bound is a name that is known to me, certainly," he said. "I wouldn't classify him as our main suspect. I wouldn't classify anybody as the main suspect. Obviously we would have conducted an investigation at the barns. Holly Hill Farms was a logical extension of the investigation. That's where Amy spent a lot of time. Amy had some contact with her abductor at some point in time prior to her kidnapping, based on what the investigation determined.

"There has to be a reason to ask somebody to take a polygraph in the first place. He wasn't the only person to take them. Maybe it was for ruling some people out. Maybe we didn't like the answers to the questions we asked them. If you want to go with what Bound tells you, that's up to you. Harold's memory and my memory are slightly different. There were a number of people we spent a good deal of time with. There were many others we talked to at the stables as well."

"What did you find at the stables that was so interesting?" I asked.

There was a brief pause, then a stern answer. "I'm not able to discuss the results of the investigation at the barn," he said.

"Do you think Harold Bound was involved?"

"If Harold was someone we felt was responsible for the abduction and murder of Amy Mihaljevic, we would have spent a lot more time with him than what we did," Wrenn said.

A further call to Jeff Taylor only blurred the already confusing picture painted by Bound and his interrogator. "I don't remember this guy working for me," Taylor said about the man from the Ashland County Gun Club. "H.B. was the main person the FBI looked at over at Holly Hill."

Somebody was holding something back. Maybe everybody was. I didn't know who to believe. A plan formed slowly in my mind as I went over their stories again and again. I thought of two things I discovered during my first trip to Holly Hill Farms. First, an aviation student lived in Bound's old apartment above the garage. Secondly, Hollie Anzenberger usually left the farm around 6 p.m.

It was already a quarter till. I grabbed my car keys.

The aviator sat at the picnic table beside the farmhouse, sharing a bottle of wine with a young woman when I arrived. Besides his car and mine, there was only the horse trailer in the parking lot. I thought

I knew what I was doing, but I also considered that the young woman's presence might complicate the situation.

They looked up as I came over empty-handed. She was a thin, debutante-ball blonde, he a well-groomed respectable type. They both smiled. That was good.

"Is Hollie Anzenberger here?" I asked.

"No," the aviator said. "You just missed her."

"Shoot," I said. "I wanted to talk to her about something. It can't really wait until morning, either. I'm a reporter with *Scene* magazine. I'm writing this story on the man that used to live in the apartment above the garage."

"Oh, that's where I live," he said.

"Really? Huh."

"What did he do?" the young woman asked. "The man you're writing about that used to live there?"

"He may have been a suspect in a crime that happened a long time ago," I said. "I have to describe his apartment in the article. I was hoping to catch Hollie before she left, so she would show me the place. Ah, well. Thanks anyway." I started to return to the car, hoping I had made the proper impression.

"Well, I can show you the place if all you want to do is look inside," the aviator said.

"No, you guys are in the middle of that bottle," I said.

The young woman tipped the last few drops into her glass. I could see her flushed cheeks in the softening light. "Not anymore," she said.

"C'mon, I'll take you inside," he said. His girlfriend stayed behind as I followed him up a set of weather-beaten wooden steps that led to a claustrophobic apartment above the garage.

The aviator's efficiency resembled a thousand other college sublets: a kitchenette in one corner; a bed set up next to a television so that it doubled as a couch; clothes strewn about like flotsam; a cramped half bath in the back. The ceiling slanted to a sharp eave in the middle, making it impossible to stand at the sides of the room without hunching over. It smelled of American boy with a trace of American girl. Something like Polo mixed with Herbal Essence.

"Sorry about the mess," he said.

"That's all right," I replied, walking into his bathroom without an invitation to do so and opening up the medicine cabinet. I wasn't sure exactly what I was looking for. "Did you find anything strange in this apartment when you moved in?" I asked.

"No, nothing."

I came back into the main room and looked around again. In the corner opposite the door, I noticed a tiny hatch set into the wall. "What's that?" I asked.

"Storage," said the aviator. "It's an access space over the house. I haven't really been in there."

"Let's check it out," I said.

He looked apprehensive for the first time. "Yeah?"

"I just want to take a quick look."

"All right," he said. He opened the door. A high-tech crossbow sat inside, next to an outboard motor. "Those are my things."

I pulled the crossbow into the room. It took both of us to pull the outboard out of the way, however. A blaring hotness drifted out of the dark hole, as if a dragon lay pent up there, breathing sulfur fumes in its sleep. "Got a flashlight?" I asked.

The aviator fished one out of a drawer in the kitchenette. After shaking the energy back into it, he handed it to me. I shined the light inside.

The space was long, squat, and narrow. The shingled roof of the house sloped up to the beams on my right; insulation covered the floor to my left. Across the middle someone had set plywood, creating a walkway. It looked empty, except for a few pieces of paper scattered about.

"I'm going to go inside for a second," I said.

Now the aviator looked very nervous. "Is it safe?" he asked.

"Yeah," I said. "I'll be back in a minute."

Bent at the knees, I waddled inside the access space, testing the plywood with an outstretched foot. It seemed dry and sturdy enough. It held my weight as I stepped onto it. Inside, it was easily a hundred degrees, and stale, the air thick in my lungs. I picked up a letter-size piece of yellow paper and read the fine print. It was a tax statement for Harold Bound. The smaller scraps were receipts. Bound had stored his financial records here, and they had remained undisturbed since he had himself committed to avoid the FBI.

I aimed the light along the old roof. Near the back I noticed some shingles were covered with some kind of fabric. I saw it was a small carpet fragment, crimson in color, draped along one section of the slanted roof. I stared at it for a moment, trying to riddle out its purpose. Why would someone put a piece of carpet there?

The simple answer came to me: to sit on, of course.

Turning around, and backing up to it, I leaned back against the carpeting. The angle was such that I was more comfortable lying on my back. When I had situated myself, the flashlight illuminated the wooden beams that enclosed this little nook. Jackpot.

There was writing on every exposed surface in black and red ink: *666 ... Hail, Satan ... Metallica rules ... marijuana ... FUCK YOU!* In the joint of two beams, a candle dribbled petrified pink wax. A couple beer cans rested on overhangs. Once upon a time, had this had been Bound's secret place?

"Is everything okay?" the aviator asked from the doorway.

"Yeah," I said. "I'm coming out."

Quickly, I scanned every word. I was searching for her name, Amy's. But it wasn't there. Only more references to heavy metal and drugs. Sensing I was overstaying whatever welcome I had exacted, I climbed back out of the access space, brushing cobwebs out of my hair as I handed the flashlight back to the young man.

"Did you find what you were looking for?" he asked.

I thought for a moment and said, "Maybe I did."

In the car, heading quickly away from Holly Hill Farms, I dialed Spaetzel's office number. I knew he wasn't in, but I wanted him to have the message first thing in the morning.

"I just got out of Holly Hill Farms," I said. "There's a small access space in Harold Bound's old apartment. There's lots of stuff written on the walls there. And a long piece of red carpeting. I just wanted to know if that meant anything to you. Red fibers. I think it's possible the FBI missed the place. The door was small enough that it could be hidden behind a dresser or something. Anyway, hopefully this is helpful to you. Let me know if the red carpeting means anything to you."

As it happened, Spaetzel was on vacation that week. But when he returned, he called me. No *red* fibers were found on Amy's body. This case wasn't going to come together like a Richard North Patterson novel or an episode of *CSI*. It had a hundred variables, any of which could be interpreted in a dozen ways, like some quatrain by Nostradamus.

CHAPTER THIRTEEN

Ragamuffin

I HAD COME TO KNOW Kristen Balas. She had lived nine houses down from Amy on Lindford Drive. They had pressed pennies on the railroad tracks behind their houses and ridden their bikes to school and back when the weather was good, and sometimes when it wasn't. Kristen Sabo, however, was still a mystery to me. All I knew was that her father had committed suicide about a year after Amy was found in Ashland County. In a very short span of time, this girl lost a close friend and a father. I doubted she would want to talk even if I managed to track her down. But I had to try.

A check of the listed Cuyahoga County phone numbers turned up nothing. I finally found her name listed as a codefendant in a civil suit against the Crazy Horse Saloon on St. Clair. An address was provided—a Bay Village address, to be specific—but the case was a few years old and a reverse-address search found the property belonged to a Jeanne Silver. Most likely, she had already moved, and this Jeanne Silver was the new occupant.

I called the number, hoping that the woman would know where Kristy had moved. When I discovered that Mrs. Silver was actually Kristen Sabo's mother, I scolded myself for not making the obvious deduction. Of course her mother would have remarried by now.

"I'm so glad I found you," I said. "I've been looking for Kristen."

"Oh, yes," she said, her voice pleasant and inviting. "Kristy was a good friend of Amy's. It's so strange you called. We were just talking about Amy the other day. She was my other daughter, you know? My adopted daughter. She spent so much time at my house."

"Well, I'd love to talk with you and Kristy sometime," I said.

"That would be fine. Have you found anything new? There's some things I know about the case, but I probably shouldn't say too much."

"Too much about what?" I asked.

"Oh, you know, suspects," she said.

"I think I have that information already," I said.

"You know about Brad Harvey[*], the handyman from hell?" she said.

I wrote down his name quickly, before I could forget. "Actually, that's a new name to me," I said.

"Oops," she said, sarcastically.

The development in which the Silvers live is the nicer part of Bay Village, the richer side of a rich town. Mansions stretch out behind tall shrubbery there, blanketed in a cool shade. Lake Erie can be felt, if not seen, nearby.

I pulled into the driveway of a tall brick and stone home. Tall trees obscured the home from the street. I wondered, vaguely, what Mr. Silver must have done for a living. Evidently, whatever it was, he was good at it.

Another car pulled behind mine as I walked up to the door. A young woman stepped out of the sleek, black vehicle. She was stunning. Her hair was dark and tied up in a bow; a few loose strands framed her eyes. Fair skin. A cute, upturned nose. She wore a short green skirt that fluttered in the breeze, revealing her long legs. As she skipped up to meet me I felt my cheeks flush brightly.

"Hello," I said, more faintly than I'd intended, my voice halting in her presence.

She smiled a smile with enough dimples and laugh wrinkles to make even someone on as grim an errand as mine feel at ease, welcome even. "Hi. I'm Kristy," she said.

"I'm James. I've been looking for you," I said. "You're a hard person to find."

She laughed at that. "I wish it was harder for the police to find me," she said.

Then the door was open and Kristy was leading me inside.

"Mom! The reporter's here!" she shouted in no particular direction.

A woman who appeared to be in her early forties (though simple

---

[*] Not his real name. I've changed that, and his occupation and some incidental details, because he did not consent to an interview.

addition made it unlikely she was quite *that* young) came in from the back porch. She had a smile as warm as her daughter's. "I'm Jeanne," she said. "Kristy, let's have some wine."

Already in the kitchen, Kristy said, "What do you like, James?"

I tried to say something about not drinking on the job, but it got lost somewhere in my throat. When a beautiful girl speaks your name, it's like a certain kind of magic that endears her to you. At least it's always been that way for me.

"Do you like white or red?" Kristy asked.

"Let's have red," Jeanne answered.

Kristy fished in the cabinet and pulled out a bottle. "Cabernet?"

We adjourned to the porch then, and I took a seat in a wrought-iron chair overlooking a backyard full of shrubs and flowers. Jeanne's mother was seated at the table as well, a regal older woman with an air of gentle wisdom. She regarded me for a moment, made up her mind about something, and smiled.

"I was laying out on the boat when my mother called me," Kristy said, taking a seat beside Jeanne. The skirt, I realized, was little more than scant covering for the bikini underneath. "It's so weird. We were just talking about Amy yesterday."

I noticed Kristy had a peculiar way of speaking, an accent all her own. It was some mixture of Valley Girl and Rust Belt, but the pacing, the rocking up of her vowels, could only be California Beach. For instance, "weird" became two syllables: "wee-erd," with a stress on both. I'm not implying she was somehow dim—far from it, actually. It just sounded different from Ohio, a little more playful.

"Let's have a toast," Jeanne said, raising her glass.

"To what?" Kristy asked.

There was a brief pause as they considered it. "To Amy," I said, raising my own.

Kristy nodded. "To Amy."

"So," I said at last to Jeanne. "What do you remember about Amy after all these years?"

"There's not one thing I don't remember. I remember every second. I remember Margaret calling my house and asking, 'Is Amy there?' "

"That whole week, Amy was acting weird," Kristy said. "She said she was going to meet somebody after school on Friday."

I held up one hand, a gesture for them to slow down. People who survive tragedies almost always start in the middle of things, inside the effects, working their way back toward the causes, which are usually less dramatic. "What can you tell me about *Amy*?" I asked. "Tell me what she was like."

Jeanne smiled. "She always tilted her head when she talked. She wore her hair over one eye. She was very smart. Probably would have been valedictorian had she lived."

"I used to get annoyed with her because she was better at everything than me," Kristy said.

"They didn't have a lot of money," Jeanne said, "so she always wore sweats."

Money can be quite subjective in a place like Bay Village. The house standing behind me was testament to that. The Mihaljevics may not have been rich, but they had certainly been comfortable.

"We watched *Dirty Dancing* over and over again," Kristy said. "We always sat in the same chair. It was big enough for both of us to just fit. We memorized every line. *Dirty Dancing* and *Sixteen Candles*."

Kristy recalled that Amy had one peculiar habit: Every night, she would lie on her back and rock herself to sleep.

"Do you mind if I rock?" Amy would ask.

"Rock on, Amy," Kristy would answer. "Rock on."

There were trips to Huntington Beach with Amy's father. Margaret brought Kristy along to see a concert with them at the Richfield Coliseum on Amy's tenth birthday. There was a blizzard that night, and Jeanne remembered sitting up late, worrying.

Jeanne remembered, too, the times Margaret showed up late at night, unannounced, asking her to watch Amy until morning. "She drank," Jeanne said.

In the summer of 1989, Kristy and Amy formed a "babysitter's club" and passed out flyers around the neighborhood with their home phone numbers printed on the front. But by fall, they saw less of each other outside of school. Kristy didn't share Amy's love of horses. She preferred soccer.

The last time Kristy saw Amy was when she walked by her classroom on October 27. Amy was at her desk, writing.

Jeanne was in charge of the PTA for Bay schools. When Margaret called, looking for Amy, Jeanne asked the school moms to call every fifth-grader's parents to find out if anyone knew where Amy might be. Around 10 p.m., she took Amy's class photo to the Channel 3 News office in Cleveland.

"It hasn't been long enough," a reporter told her.

But Jeanne didn't leave. She pleaded with managers to listen to the details of Amy's disappearance. *Amy told friends she was meeting some man.* Obviously, this was not simply a misplaced kid. Finally, they agreed to air the photo.

As Jeanne pulled into the Mihaljevics' driveway, she heard a primal scream let loose from inside the house. Amy's picture had just come up on the news.

For the next three months, Kristy remained hopeful. She heard rumors that someone had seen Amy at Heinen's, a grocery store located behind the shopping plaza, after she left Baskin-Robbins. Jeanne stayed in touch with the volunteers working at the police department, who provided regular updates. During that time, Kristy was aware of FBI agents following her to school in the morning and home at night.

Even though Margaret was hounded by reporters, she wouldn't change her phone number because Amy knew it, and one day she might call. The phone company agreed to set up a call-forwarding system for the Mihaljevics that transferred incoming calls to Jeanne's house whenever Margaret was not home. Because of this arrangement, it was Jeanne who first heard from police on February 8, 1990.

Kristy was home sick that day with strep throat. That morning, the television news reported that a body had been found in Ashland County. People were predicting it was Amy. But Kristy knew it couldn't be.

In the late afternoon, the phone rang. Jeanne picked up. The police were on the other line. The message was for Margaret. The body had been identified as that of her lost daughter.

Kristy pulled away from her mother and ran to her room upstairs. She ripped posters off the wall, broke toys, tore the room apart. "Amy, how could you be so stupid?" she screamed.

*   *   *

"Amy has been a ghost in our lives since that day," Jeanne said. "You know, when they found her, they also found a single earring. A small horse-head earring."

This was news to me. The FBI has always maintained that Amy's abductor took *both* her earrings.

"What do you think Amy would have done once she realized she was in danger?" I said.

Kristy's eyes grew cold. "She would have fought and fought and fought until the death of her."

"She was a survivor," Jeanne said. "She was brilliant. She wanted to be a pediatrician when she grew up."

Jeanne shook her head, as though fighting back a bit of unexpected emotion. "She was my ragamuffin. That's what I called her because her hair was always messy and hanging over her eyes, but I meant it lovingly. She was my little ragamuffin. And whoever did this, they've been living a life for sixteen years, and she hasn't."

"Who do you think it was?" I said. "Who's this handyman from hell?"

"Some people think Brad Harvey was a suspect," she said. "He worked on the house next door to the Mihaljevics shortly before Amy's disappearance."

Harvey had an alibi, she said. "But he started going to church every day of the week for a while after Amy disappeared. That I know for a fact. Why did he suddenly become religious?"

Jeanne paused, seeming to follow her train of thought into deep reflection, then emerged on a different track: "Look, if you wanted to get to Amy," she said, "all you would have to do would be to tell her how to please her mother. Her mother was always mad at her. She would have done anything to please Margaret."

CHAPTER FOURTEEN

The Naked Neighbor

A FEW WEEKS BEFORE Amy's abduction, the Mihaljevics' next-door neighbors hired local handyman Brad Harvey to work on the exterior of their two-story colonial. He had the reputation around town of being a lady's man. Women throughout Bay Village were drawn to his tan, well-toned physique earned from hard work under the Ohio sun, and his chiseled face framed by sun-bleached surfer's hair lent him an exotic look. He was a Don Juan in a town full of white-collar dweebs with trophy wives—an interloper, a snake, a threat.

While working on the house next door to the Mihaljevics, he might have met both Amy and Margaret. Amy was the social butterfly of Lindford Drive and never missed an opportunity to chat up a newcomer. Often, she would shadow her mother on such well-wishing visits. Sometimes Amy would go it alone.

Harvey lived on a road lined with overpriced cottages graced with prim lawns and leased cars parked in the driveways. Harvey's place, however, was the exception.

His house was little more than a two-story shanty. It had been painted once—white, maybe—but had taken on the color of rain clouds. Ancient curtains drooped behind windows like cataracts. Yet it was not an entirely unpleasant place; it evoked the character of a cool bachelor pad, the last respite of a lifelong partier.

When I visited Harvey's residence at around 4 p.m. the day after my conversation with Jeanne Silver and her daughter, he was not home. A neighbor told me he usually returned after five, so I made a trip to the Bay Village shopping plaza for a cappuccino to kill some time. Between sips, I watched families come and go. A new generation of middle-school students ran up and down the sidewalks, oblivious to the location's morbid history. People, for the most part, had forgotten about the Mihaljevics. The parental paranoia so pervasive in my youth had been replaced by a stubborn naiveté, as though parents believe lightning never strikes the same shopping plaza twice.

A truck was parked behind Harvey's house when I returned. I left my car on the street with the doors unlocked in case I needed to make a quick retreat and walked up to the front door. A screenless window was propped open to my right, letting in the evening air. From somewhere inside, I heard running water, what sounded like someone washing dishes. I knocked loudly. No answer. I tried again. Nothing. I peered in through the window as best as I could without looking like a creep. "Hello?" I said. Again, nothing. I listened some more. Yes, it sounded like someone doing the dishes near the back of the house.

As I walked around back, the sound of running water grew louder. Stepping around the corner, I saw that the back door was wide open. "Hello?" I tried again. I was nearly ten feet from the door when the water suddenly shut off. It was then I realized Brad Harvey was not doing dishes. I saw a tall curtain hanging just inside the doorway and smelled shampoo. *Oh no*, I thought.

The curtain was pulled back, revealing Harvey's dripping nude body. He looked up at the stranger with more curiosity than surprise.

"Whoa. Hey there, partner," he said, stepping behind the door, half-closing it.

"I'm . . . I'm sorry," I stammered. "I tried knocking on the front door, and then I heard the water. I thought you were doing dishes. I tried knocking first."

"Maybe I didn't want to answer the door. I don't want what you're selling." He started to shut the door completely.

"Mr. Harvey," I said. "Mr. Harvey, I want to talk to you about Amy Mihaljevic."

He froze, his mouth gaping.

"I don't have anything to say to you," Harvey said.

"Were you a suspect in that case?"

"Get off my property, boss," he replied.

I weighed my options, which did not take but a moment. I turned around and walked back to my car. I had made a mistake—poor timing. If I hadn't caught him stepping out of the shower, I might have pressed my luck a little further. I knew I wouldn't overcome that intrusive introduction, no matter how hard I tried. No, this man was not going to talk with me.

Still, I did not feel completely finished with Brad Harvey, so later I called and left a message at his place, a kind of apology for the way we met, but he never returned my call.

I contacted Dick Wrenn, the retired FBI agent who had been in charge of Amy's case, for a final comment on Harvey. I knew Harvey had an alibi, provided by a man with a solid reputation in the community, a man with no reason to lie. I'd been told that, and I confirmed it with the man himself. He said Harvey sat next to him at a public sporting event on the evening of October 27, 1989. So I asked Wrenn if Harvey could still be considered a suspect.

"I will tell you this," Wrenn said. "During the course of these investigations, you do as much as you can to confirm alibis. We took the time necessary to check out Brad Harvey's alibi. We only took that effort with people who were particularly interesting for one reason or another."

Every statement I managed to get from Wrenn was a riddle. I took this one to mean: Nobody should be ruled out completely.

CHAPTER FIFTEEN

Fearful Symmetry

ANY CLOSURE FOR THIS CASE will be bittersweet. Margaret McNulty is dead. She died alone in a Las Vegas apartment on September 29, 2001. She was fifty-four. The official cause of death, as listed by the Clark County coroner, was chronic alcoholism. Friends and family, however, claim she really died of a broken heart in 1989. It simply took her body twelve years to catch up.

Already preparing to leave Mark Mihaljevic at the time of their daughter's abduction, Margaret officially divorced him in 1991. In April of that year, Ohio attorney general Lee Fisher hired Margaret as a victims' rights advocate in his Cleveland office.

During this time, her body began to weaken. She was diagnosed with lupus, for which she prescribed herself voluminous amounts of alcohol. Coworkers smelled it on her breath but blamed the escalating problem on the loss of Amy. Alcoholism, however, did not keep her from seeking out her daughter's killer.

Margaret appeared on *The Oprah Winfrey Show* on November 23, 1992, for a special "unsolved child murders" episode. There she met several other women in her tragic situation.

Winfrey appeared to sympathize with their plight. "I know all of you have been in the green room together and you all were here this morning," she said to her guests. "Is there some sense of, I don't know, some tiny bit of relief—knowing that you're not the only one?"

Margaret answered for her peers. "I wouldn't call it a sense of relief," she said. "Obviously, you know, we have a common thread. Other people hear about it and go, you know . . . [Margaret's face contorted into a look of shock] . . . in astonishment. They think, 'What would it be like?' We know. We've been through it. We live it."

Then the composite sketch of Amy's abductor was flashed on the screen. "That may or may not have been the person, and he may or may not look like that now," Margaret said. "It's more important to really take a look at a person's behavior—changes in attitude, becoming religious, abusing alcohol or drugs, a change in job, a change in residence, a loss of time from work around that time—erratic behavior is really important. I believe in my gut that there is someone, either one or more persons that know who killed Amy, but they have not come forward. So I would personally like to plead with this person or persons, to have a little human . . . humanity, a little bit of conscience and call the police with information."

Once a shy girl, uncertain of how to be sociable, Margaret had become a national spokesperson for the lost children of strangers.

In 1993, she sold the house in Bay and moved across town to Shaker Heights. (Jason stayed in Bay with his father.) When Betty Jane Montgomery was elected attorney general in 1995, Margaret was let go. She took a job delivering papers for the *Cleveland Plain Dealer*, working out of a South Euclid bagging depot.

Slowly, the lupus destroyed her immune system and riddled her body with pain. It was so bad at times, all she could manage was to bag the papers for other carriers to deliver. In 2000, she suffered a stroke.

Upon leaving the hospital, Margaret moved to Las Vegas to be with her elderly mother, Henrietta. They shared an apartment until Margaret's chain smoking became too much for Henrietta. In August 2001, Margaret got a place of her own. A month later she died.

My own mother started getting sick a few years before I began writing this book—not the two-day, common-cold kind of sick, but the monthlong, full-body-scan, let's-get-some-bloodwork type of scary sick. No one could explain the symptoms. No one could tell my mother why her entire body ached with a dull throbbing most days or why sometimes it felt like a thousand tiny hands were ripping her intestines apart.

In 2004 she ended up in the hospital again, and for the first time, I thought she might not come out. My mother, by the way, was only in her forties when she fell ill. She took care of herself. People have said that she looks "just like Princess Leia," meaning she could pass for a young Carrie Fisher. None of this illness stuff made any sense to me.

I visited her in the hospital. She was thin under the covers, bone shaping the skin around her hips. Dark circles surrounded her eyes, and she spoke in labored, barking gasps.

"What are the doctors saying?" I said.

"It's lupus," she said. "They told me I have lupus. But it's the good kind of lupus."

I looked at her and wondered what the bad lupus could look like.

My mother has not died. Her immune system rebounded. The good lupus, it turns out, is the kind that lies dormant as long as you take care of yourself.

I've seen enough of this disease to picture Margaret's last years quite well. It was neither quick nor quiet. An alcoholic who tries to deaden the pain by drinking is like someone stranded on a raft in the middle of the ocean, reaching a cupped hand toward the salty sea: relief will only mask future agony. My mother is strong enough to respect this principle these days. But, then, she's never lost a kid.

To borrow an appropriate metaphor, I sometimes felt as if Margaret and my mother grew up in the same house. One day Amy's mother left through the back door and my mother went out the front. And both of them, in their own ways, remind me of my wife.

I celebrated my one-year wedding anniversary with my wife, Julie, during the peak of my research for the *Scene* article on Amy Mihaljevic in the summer of 2005. Julie is a public school teacher, with the same dark hair and easy sense of humor my father once noticed in my mother. Though, to me, Julie's more Kirsten Dunst than Carrie Fisher.

After years of living in a boxlike Cuyahoga Falls apartment, we had just moved into a quaint house in a secluded neighborhood in Akron. It's the sort of safe environment where everyone knows each other and strangers' cars are spotted as soon as they pull onto the road. It was a welcome change from the overpopulated rental communities we had known since college. At the apartment, we had problems with a peeper. But here, we were safe. Or so I thought when we bought the house. Weeks of hunting Amy's killer and conversations with suspects caused me to reconsider. I bought new locks for all the doors, adding deadbolts and chains. Then I had a home security system installed. Finally, I got the bowling pin out of storage.

The bowling pin appeared outside my house one night when I was fourteen years old. Some neighborhood pranksters had played three full frames at about 4 a.m. on the street below my bedroom window. By the time my father managed to get outside, they were gone. The next morning, I picked one pin to keep. The others were burned in summer bonfires.

Once, in 1994, I woke to a shaking at about 3:30 a.m. It was my dad again, and he looked scared in the faint light that filtered through the window next to my bed. He held in his hand an aluminum bat. It was the second time that month I'd been awakened like this. "What is it?" I said.

He answered by putting a finger up to his mouth. I listened.

Something fell downstairs. I heard footsteps on the living room floor.

"Come on," he said.

I picked up the bowling pin and followed in white briefs as he led the way downstairs. As we approached the landing, something larger crashed to floor in the dark below. This was no false alarm. I tightened my grip, and the two of us charged.

In the living room, my father flicked on the light. Nothing. Slowly, we made a circle around the house, turning on every light along the way. In the office, my father's business papers were scattered. Receipts and memos lay on the floor. He looked at them and then at me. I couldn't tell what he was thinking.

We checked behind every couch and table, in closets and behind the shower curtain. Whoever was in the house had apparently gone out the bathroom window, which did not lock.

The trespasser never came back. That was the last night we had to go downstairs with our blunt instruments. Apparently, they had found what they were looking for.

I think about that night sometimes and what would have happened if we had found some disgruntled subcontractor hidden behind the sofa. The intruder could have fought back against the aluminum bat for awhile. If I had gotten in one hit with that bowling pin, though, it would have been over. The pin is as dense as a brick and twice as heavy.

The bowling pin traveled with me when I moved into the dorms at Kent State, and it stood beside my bed at University Townhomes before ending up in a box in the basement of my house in Akron. I wielded it again from time to time—when I heard noises in the night—but I never had to use it. Sometimes, when I drifted off to sleep alone, just knowing it was there made me feel safe. As I grew older, I became complacent. I started feeling secure. It wasn't until I started introducing myself to the suspects in Amy's murder that I even thought about it again.

My last interview with Harold Bound brought the bowling pin back to mind. He told me it was a good thing he couldn't remember Dick Wrenn's face, inferring that he didn't know what he might do if he ran into the retired agent on the street. That kind of talk made me paranoid. Bound knew my face very well. And he knew I was writing about him. Add to that my surprise visit to a burly naked man and constant inquiries about Amy's old neighbors and friends, and I figured there were a number of people out there who wouldn't mind roughing me up a little. I was turning over rocks in Bay Village that had rested for sixteen years, and I was leaving my business card under every single one.

"Monsters under the bed?" Julie asked with a grin and a raised eyebrow as I returned from the basement with the bowling pin during the first week of July in 2005.

I smiled back. "No, no monsters."

"What do you need it for then?"

I paused on the steps leading up to the second floor and thought about lying. I'd been doing that a lot lately. I had lied to the young pilot living in Bound's old apartment. I had lied to the secretary at the veterans' hospital. I had told a hundred white lies to get extra information out of others I spoke to, my justification being that finding Amy's killer outweighed all venial sins. Thankfully, I couldn't justify doing the same to Jules.

"It's just in case," I said. "I've been talking to a lot of strange people lately."

"You think someone's going to break into our house?"

"No. I don't know."

"This is a safe neighborhood," she said.

"I know. But, maybe you shouldn't open the door for anybody for a while, okay? If someone comes by when I'm not here?"

"Okay."

"Look through the eyehole."

"Okay. Are you going to put it under your pillow?"

"No," I said. "I'm going to put it on the other side of the room so I don't accidentally club you with it in my sleep."

I have a habit of sleepwalking when I'm stressed. When I was a teenager and it was at its worst, I often didn't wake up until I was out of my bedroom. Once, I didn't wake up until I was outside the house. I was never a violent sleepwalker, but I didn't want to find out the hard way that I could be.

"Oh, okay then," Julie said, a note of sarcasm mixed in with her agreement.

Less than a week later, I wielded the bowling pin once more.

CHAPTER SIXTEEN

Breakfast with Amy

ONE NIGHT IN JULY 2005, I closed my eyes at the end of the evening, and when I opened them again, it was October 27, 1989.

This dream had none of the qualities associated with my typical dreams. The scene did not change suddenly halfway through. No one became a monster or an elephant or anything like that. Like simple reality, my surroundings remained static, and I simply took them in with all five senses, like some well-played memory.

I was seated at a white Formica table in the kitchen of a large house. The walls were covered in a blue-and-white patterned wallpaper. The room smelled of coffee and cereal and toast. Outside, it was still dark. The living room beyond the kitchen was pitch black.

Other people were seated at the table, their eyes puffy with inter-rupted sleep. To my right sat Margaret, her hair short and curly and brown. She ate a piece of toast and picked at a half-shelled grapefruit. To my left was Jason, age twelve. He was going to town on a bowl of Peanut Butter Cap'n Crunch.

"Amy!" Margaret yelled. "You're going to be late!"

The sound of padded footsteps on the stairs. Suddenly, there she was. Amy in 3-D. She wore a light-green sweatshirt with laven-der pants. Her hair was not done up like the yearbook picture, but hung slightly brushed to her shoulders, parted to favor her right eye. I felt my breath stolen away as she looked up and acknowledged my presence.

"Hi," she said, tilting her head to the left and smiling. "Can you pass the cereal, James?"

I looked down at a large blue box in front of me. Wheat Chex. I passed them across the table to her.

Amy poured herself a small bowl, then added a little milk.

What the hell is going on? I wondered.

Finished with his breakfast, Jason got up from the table and took his bowl to the sink. He trundled gracefully over to Margaret and kissed her quickly before bounding out the front door. "See ya," he said over his shoulder.

"And what's your day look like, little miss?" Margaret said.

"Choir tryouts," Amy said.

"Oh, right," her mother said. "That's right. Well, good luck."

I opened my mouth to say something—something like "She doesn't have choir tryouts, Margaret. She's lying." But nothing would come out. I could feel the air collecting in my lungs, but I couldn't push it through my vocal cords. I thought if I tried real hard, I might be able to force out just a few words. I concentrated on being heard.

Margaret walked over to the trash can beside the refrigerator and pitched in the last of her grapefruit. "Come on," she said. "Kristen's waiting for you." Then she stepped into the blackness of the living room.

Amy tilted the bowl and drank the sugary milk at the bottom.

Mustering all the strength available to me, I pushed out two words: "Don't go," I said.

Amy set the bowl down and wiped her chin. She looked at me for a moment but didn't smile this time. It wasn't sadness on her face, but a kind of wistfulness. "I have to," she said. "You know that."

I watched her drop the dish in the sink. I watched her take a light jacket from the closet by the stairs. I watched her grab her backpack and wrap it around her shoulders.

Then she was gone.

"Don't go!" I screamed, so loudly and distinctly that Julie sat up in bed beside me.

"What? What's going on?" she said.

The room around me came into focus. It was our bedroom. In our house. In 2005. It was 3:30 a.m.

"Are you okay?" Julie said.

"Yeah," I said. Then I heard it: a sound like someone walking down the creaky old wooden steps outside our bedroom door. The sound of small, padded feet. I looked at Julie. "Did you hear that?"

Julie shook her head. "I didn't hear anything," she said. "You're having a nightmare."

I put a finger to my lips. There it was again. Something was almost to the bottom of the stairs now, walking away from our bedroom. As quietly as I could, I slipped out from under the covers. In my boxer briefs, I walked over to the bowling pin next to the door and picked it up. It felt good in my hands again. Like some slugger's favorite bat. Or Excalibur, maybe. I opened the door and stepped into the upstairs hallway.

I listened hard. *CREAK!* Downstairs now, in the kitchen. I flicked on the stairway light and rushed down the steps, raising the bowling pin above my head in preparation to deliver a death blow.

As I hit the first-floor landing, I spun around the corner and slid into the kitchen, turning on the light with a deft flick of one hand.

Empty. The door was locked, the deadbolt in place. Same with the front door. An exhaustive search of the house turned up absolutely no intruders.

Confused and headachy, I returned to my bedroom, where Julie still sat in bed.

"No Boogeyman?" she said.

"No," I said. "No Boogeyman."

I set the bowling pin down by the door and climbed back into bed. My wife put a hand on my back and rubbed.

"Are you all right?" she said.

"I don't think so."

"What's wrong?"

"No matter what I do, she's still going to be dead," I said. "I don't think I really thought about that. Not really. I think I thought I could find her. She's always going to be dead."

And your mother's always going to have lupus, said a voice somewhere deep inside. It sounded like the voice of my father. *And you can't save either one.*

Bullshit.

Eventually, I found sleep again. And dreams found me. Random images amidst the flotsam of consciousness we're used to, life seen through a faulty shutter. Horse-head earrings and bowling pins. Margaret and my own mother. Seabold and Sebold. And somewhere, beneath it all, the smell of toast and cereal and coffee.

CHAPTER SEVENTEEN

Mark and Henrietta

MARK MIHALJEVIC, Amy's father, remained in northeastern Ohio, though most everyone I met in Bay Village believed he had left the state years ago. I caught up with him at his modern two-story in Avon, very near the terminus of Interstate 480 West, where he lives with his new wife and stepdaughter. At fifty-eight, he had been working as a bus driver for the physically and mentally handicapped. His number was unlisted, so I reached him through Jason, corresponding through e-mail before he finally agreed to let me drop by on a Wednesday morning.

Inside, the home was sterile, the walls primer white, clean. The place had only a moderately lived-in feel. When I arrived, his new family was not there. I imagined they were dispatched on errands that would take most of the day. It seemed to me that Mark did his best to separate his old life from his new one.

He and his dog, a large golden lab, greeted me at the door and led me to a table in the kitchen that served as a breakfast nook. A large man, sturdy and stout like his son, with the round face I saw in Jason, Mark came across as welcoming but, unlike his progeny, also a little reluctant. He seemed put out, angry, and only outwardly kind. Given the circumstances of my visit, though, I couldn't blame him. I felt like an intruder. Margaret was the one who talked to the reporters. Mark had been quoted rarely and photographed even less so.

"Take a seat," he said, motioning to a wooden chair. I sat and let him regard me for a moment while I dug into the satchel for pen and paper. "What can I do for you?"

"I was hoping we could talk about Amy," I said. "What was your daughter like, growing up?"

Mark sighed, leaned back in his chair, and stroked the thick neck of the dog at his heel. "Amy always had the 'can do' attitude," he began.

"She thought she could do everything. If she knew how to do it, she didn't want any help doing it, you know? And she was very quiet. Amy wouldn't talk when a stranger came into the house.

"She wasn't afraid of much, though. Amy was jumping off the high-dive at five years old over at the Blue Marlin Club. She acquired the nickname Moose sometime around then. We used to call her Moose. Don't remember how that came about. Amy was smart. Amy was smart, smart. She really liked her science classes."

"You had a dog then, too," I said. "Do you remember its name?"

"Jake," said Mark. "He's buried under a rosebush here in Avon. We got him for the kids back then, but as usual, he became a parents' dog."

"Where did the name come from?" I asked. "Jake?"

"It came from the pound named Jake. We didn't want to confuse him anymore."

"What do you remember about the day she went missing?" I said, not looking up from the notepad.

Mark cleared his throat and paused for just a second. "I came home from work—from Buick, where I handled warranties and complaints—and Margaret was in a tizzy. Amy hadn't been home. She had told Margaret she had choir tryouts that day." Mark looked into the empty living room. "I taught school for three years. Nobody holds tryouts on Friday nights. That should have been a signal, should have been a red flag.

"Margaret was on the phone calling everyone we knew. I patrolled Bay Village in my car. I checked back at the middle school for her friends. I checked the park by the lake. When I came back home, one of my friends was there. By the middle school there's a creek that runs all the way to Lake Erie. He and I walked that whole ravine. We thought maybe she had been playing there and something had happened. Jason stayed at home with Margaret. Margaret slept right by the phone that night. She lied down on the kitchen floor next to the phone, there.

"The next day, the police were in the house. Chief William Gareau. They always look closely at the parents when children are missing. In a day, day and a half, they got past that. Margaret and I took polygraphs at the FBI headquarters in Cleveland.

"After a day or two, Margaret's mother, Henrietta, came down from Wisconsin. She would cook for us. Then *my* mother came down. We had a lot of people bring food to the house."

"Did you participate in any of the searches going on out at Holly Hill Farms or around Bay Village?"

"No," Mark said. "I was mostly at home, answering the phone. The police would call and ask, 'Do you know this person?' And either we did or we didn't. It was tough going back to work. The Buick dealers all banded together and put up reward money."

"Was there a point when you began to think Amy wasn't going to come home again?"

"Her eleventh birthday. They had kind of a birthday party for Amy at our house in December, when she would have turned eleven. I don't know why, but that was the day I knew she wasn't coming back. That's when I mentally threw in the towel."

"And when did you discover your daughter had been found in Ashland County?"

Mark was in some kind of zone now. I could tell that this was not a conversation he had ever had outside of family, if anywhere. These events resided in an area of his psyche he kept to himself, behind a mental door triple locked and marked RESTRICTED ACCESS. That door was open now, and he was walking around inside this room, dusting off the shelves and reacquainting himself with its contents.

"I was out making a dealer contact in Cleveland for Buick when Margaret called," he said. " 'You need to be home,' she told me. 'They found Amy's remains.' It was a relief. I thought if they found her remains, they would find some DNA. That wasn't the case, though."

"Did you have to ID your daughter?" I said.

"No, we never did. We never ID'd the remains. There was no sense in it. I've never really cared to know. Amy was cremated, buried in a Wisconsin cemetery. There was a church service, but I did not go. Margaret and I were not seeing eye to eye. I would have spread Amy's ashes over at the horse barn or over Lake Erie or something like that."

I let him have a moment to rest, as he was breathing harder and looked ten years older than the person who had greeted me at the door. Looking around the room, I noticed a collection of Father's Day cards arranged on the counter behind the living room couch.

"When did you remarry?" I asked.

"Nineteen ninety-five," he said. "My present wife, Georgette, went to high school with Kristen Balas's mother. Small world, huh?"

"Do you still hear from the Bay Village police?"

"They call. They called again a few months ago. Wanted to know if a name was familiar to me. It wasn't. That's typically how the calls go. I'm amazed they're still working on this case. My theory is when they know who did this, before anything else, they'll come knocking at my door."

"Did you read Robert Ressler's book?" I said. "The one that named Billy Strunak as the likely suspect in the chapter on Amy?"

"The FBI told me that book was a piece of shit," he said. "No, I didn't read it."

"Had you ever taken your family to Ashland County before Amy was abducted?"

"We went to Mohican Park out there," he said. "But we didn't stay in the campgrounds. We stayed at a hotel. Amy was in Brownies and the Girl Scouts, though, so I don't know if they ever camped out in that area."

I tried to think of more questions to ask Mark while he was still in that zone of recall. There were so many open-ended questions whenever I thought about the case, but at the moment I couldn't remember them all. So I fell back on something more or less factual:

"Did your phone records from the day Amy went missing show anything odd?" I said.

Mark seemed to think hard for a minute before nodding. "If I remember right, somebody called our house from the Euclid mall. From a pay phone."

"Was Margaret always with Amy when she went to Holly Hill?"

"No," he said. "Right at the end, Amy would just take her bike out there. She was totally unsupervised. You think of stable hands as strange people . . ." He trailed off.

"Do you remember what the last thing Amy said to you would have been?" I said. "Or what she was doing?"

"I don't remember the last time I saw my daughter," he said. "I don't remember."

I tucked my notebook into the satchel and started closing it up.

Mark offered me a glass of water, and I sat for a moment in silence with him and his dog as I drank it down, thinking of more questions to ask, feeling like I might be wasting an opportunity. It was then that I realized something odd. I looked around the room again, at the walls, and at the shelf of pictures and cards behind the sofa. As further proof of Mark's self-imposed isolation from tragedy, I found no evidence of his lost daughter or even of Jason, his son.

"Do you have any pictures of Amy?" I said.

"Oh, I think we have one somewhere," he said. "I gave most of them to Margaret's mother, I think, a long time ago."

I followed Mark to a small room off the foyer. It was an office, the only cluttered room on the first floor. An old roll-top desk hulked at an awkward angle near the center. He pointed to a picture on the wall, a framed portrait of Jason and Amy, circa 1984. Amy's hair was done up in what had to be a permanent, her blond locks curling like Little Orphan Annie's. Both kids looked radiant and happy.

Behind me, Mark rummaged through the contents of his desk. Eventually he pulled out something pink and handed it gently over to me. It was a ceramic pig, shiny from the kiln's fire. On its underside, Amy had carved her name.

"I've always at least kept that," he said. "She made it for me in art class. It's really rather well done, isn't it?"

"Yeah, it is," I said. It was, too. Especially for a fifth-grader. I handed it back. "I should be getting back to the office. Is there anything else you think might help?"

"Knowing Amy, you'd have to assume she knew this person," he said. "She must have known this person. She would never had gotten into a car with a stranger."

I wondered if that were really true.

Returning to my desk, I phoned Henrietta McNulty. She answered on the second ring. I quickly explained what I wanted.

Her voice was loud and clear. This woman may have been old, but her mental functions were sharp. She was a feisty matriarch of one of West Allis's biggest clans, and it sounded like she had plenty of fight left in her.

"What's the point?" she said. "My Margaret's dead. The person who did this is probably dead or in prison somewhere."

"Wouldn't your family like some closure?" I said.

"Won't change anything now. Amy's long gone. She's in a cemetery with her mother. I think we would just like to not think about it anymore."

A long pause fell between us. I really didn't know what to say.

"You talk to the police?" she said.

"Yeah."

"Then do me a favor. Ask them if I can have Margaret's things back now."

"What do you mean?" I asked.

"When Margaret died, someone showed up at her apartment and took all her address books," she said. "All her phone numbers and addresses and a bunch of other things. Some man. Said he was from the Bay Village Police Department. He said he'd send me the stuff in the mail after he took a look at it, but he never did."

Las Vegas is slightly out of Bay's jurisdiction, I thought. It's possible that someone with the FBI had taken Margaret's things, and she only assumed they were with Bay P.D. Still, it was certainly an interesting detail. Was it possible Margaret didn't share everything she knew with the authorities? This seemed to suggest someone thought so.

"Did Margaret think she knew who took Amy?" I said.

"No. At least she never told me she did."

Henrietta wasn't up for talking about Amy anymore. She did promise to send some pictures of her granddaughter—an empty promise to get me off the phone, I thought at the time.

A few days later, though, an enveloped showed up on my chair. Inside were color pictures someone had copied onto nice paper for me. Attached was a handwritten sheet, in Henrietta's scrawl, describing the images. "*1986: Amy made a apple pie!! 1987: Amy Walleye catch from fishing with Dad (Mark) (27¼"-9 lbs). Amy with ribbons won from horseback riding.*"

I tacked the sheet onto the wall in front of me, next to Amy's "missing" poster. As I began to assemble the story, I looked to them often for inspiration, knowing I could never do that girl justice. Not even close.

CHAPTER EIGHTEEN

The Tragic Life of Billy Strunak

"I NEED TO SEE SOMETHING by the end of the week," Kevin said. Pete could be distracted no longer. Our boss wanted to see what his biggest liability had been working on for so long.

But what did I have, really? Some suspects' names, sure. Though every paper in Northeast Ohio had covered Amy's abduction, mostly in front-page, above-the-fold stories, the local news had never named suspects. I had several. I knew Bound had been of particular interest to Dick Wrenn and the FBI. And his proximity to Amy, his fondness for her, and his character certainly made him interesting to me. Still, I had originally pitched the story believing Billy Strunak was the most likely suspect. As far as Pete knew, I still believed this. Interviews with the police and FBI, however, made me think Strunak couldn't be the one. If sixty agents and the entire Bay police force thought he didn't do it, why should I? I figured they knew things about Strunak I didn't. Those details—still hidden among thousands of lead sheets and field reports in Amy's investigatory file—must show that Strunak had other reasons to commit suicide thirteen days after Amy's body was found in Ashland. Besides, everyone said the murderer had to have known the Mihaljevics. Bound knew them well. So far as I knew, Strunak didn't meet the family until *after* the abduction, when he worked inside the volunteer center.

To assuage any doubt, and in preparation for my inevitable defense of this change of focus with my editor, I again attempted to contact the Strunak family for an interview. When my calls went unreturned, I drove out to the houses where Billy Strunak's brothers lived and left my cards in mailboxes or doors. I thought Gary Strunak's wife might actually spit on me during one visit. "He doesn't want to talk to you!" she yelled. "None of the family does. Leave us alone." Finally, I sent messages on *Scene* letterhead, informing them that I would be mentioning Billy in my article and they should call me if they wanted any response from the family to run with the story.

Two days after the letters were mailed, I received a call from Billy's older brother, Jeff. He sounded displeased.

"Why are you harassing my family?" he said.

"I'm trying to help you," I replied. "A book came out a couple years ago that said it was Billy that the writer believed murdered Amy Mihaljevic. I've done some research, and I believe it was somebody else. The cops do, too. That's what I'm going to say in my article, but I'm still going to mention his name. There are people in Bay Village who think the case is solved, that your brother did this. I need to talk about that so they realize it was somebody else."

Jeff paused, perhaps weighing my explanation. "I'll talk to you," he said. "But leave the rest of my family alone, all right?"

"Can you please tell me a little about your brother?" I asked. "I don't know much about him. What was he like?"

"Billy was always trying to be the nice guy and he usually got crapped on for his efforts," Jeff said. "And this was kind of the final straw for him, being implicated in Amy's death, when all he wanted to do was help find her. People think he did this just because he decided to commit suicide shortly after Amy was found. But that would be like saying that when my grandfather died three days after Kennedy died, that he had something to do with Kennedy's assassination."

I typed Jeff's responses into my computer as he described growing up with his brother. One detail struck me as unusual: a genetic trait afflicted Billy and many of his family members with a severe and savage form of psoriasis.

In their youth, Billy and Jeff shared a bedroom in a modest house in Fairview Park. While Jeff somehow escaped the family skin disease, Billy had it the worst. The simple act of bending over to retrieve a dropped pencil caused Billy's skin to break open across his body, and he would bleed all over. His skin had a perpetually sunburned look that drew ridicule from classmates. People on the street stared at him as he passed. There were many days Billy did not even get out of bed. He lay there, in the dark, covered in Vaseline from head to toe, wrapped in oil cloth so the goo would not rub off on the walls.

"When you're the freak out there, you just feel funny about it," Jeff said. "As much as that could have tarnished him, he was always trying to help somebody. He'd pick up people on the way home that had a flat tire or something. He took in stray cats. If you knew Billy, Billy was one of those people who wore his heart on his sleeve." Jeff suggested that his brother's good-heartedness made up for his lack of smarts. "He could read and repeat anything, but when it came to horse sense, he didn't have a heck of a lot of it," Jeff said.

In 1989, Billy worked for BJ's Wholesale Club, in the auto department, sometimes driving a company van for deliveries, Jeff recalled. He lived in an efficiency apartment off Fairview Circle, with an on-again-off-again girlfriend named Lori, who had a young child. There was no real furniture in the apartment, Jeff noted, as Billy couldn't afford anything decent. He drove a beat-up Maverick.

By October that year, Billy was on the outs again with Lori. He made regular trips to University Hospital, where a doctor tested new psoriasis medication on him—none of which did much for Billy besides make him more uncomfortable. In his spare time, he ran a booth at a West Side flea market.

"That's where he met Margaret Mihaljevic," Jeff said. "He met her there, so when her kid vanished, that's why he wanted to help."

This was a revelation, for sure, but one the police had undoubtedly uncovered. I was not much impressed. Perhaps I was distracted by my interest in more compelling characters. "Do you know if Margaret ever had Amy with her at the flea market?" I asked.

"Probably," Jeff said.

As the investigation into Amy's abduction picked up speed, the FBI visited Billy several times, but Billy did not seem stressed by his status as a suspect. He told Jeff about every interrogation as if he were describing some crime show he'd seen on TV, as if it were something removed and interesting. "They called me today and were asking some questions," Jeff remembers his brother saying shortly after Amy's body was found.

"Then he mixed the dry gas with his Coca-Cola," Jeff said. "I don't think he thought he'd taken enough, and I think he was too embarrassed to tell somebody. I think he thought it would just make him sick. He wanted to be readmitted into the hospital. He'd go in sometimes, and they would give him sleeping pills. He was depressed about breaking up with Lori and about his psoriasis and other things. The only time he felt all right was when he was in the hospital and they gave him sleeping pills. But the poison just overpowered him."

Coworkers from BJ's Wholesale Club drove Billy to his parents' house after he started acting sick. Billy and Jeff's father took him to the emergency room at St. Vincent Charity Hospital. There Billy slipped into a coma at around 9 p.m.

"Let me tell you what happens when you drink dry gas," Jeff said. "Your brain dies from top to bottom, and the only thing that's working at the end is the base at the core of your brain, which is the reflex to breathe."

Eventually, that reflex died, too. At 10 p.m. on Wednesday, February 21, 1990, doctors removed Billy's respirator. He died seventeen minutes later.

Billy's suicide note was found wadded up in the kitchen trashcan, another clue that he thought this was a failed attempt at taking his life. According to Jeff, it made no mention of Amy. "The letter said he was tired of fighting the big battle, which was life," Jeff said. "He couldn't find a decent-paying job. He was just frustrated like a lot of people get."

In his book, Ressler writes that the Strunaks cleaned Billy's apartment before any police arrived. Not true, Jeff said. The Fairview Park police were the first ones inside the efficiency after the suicide, and only after they left did the family go in and clean it up. Everything went to the Salvation Army.

"The FBI took the Maverick for a couple days," Jeff said. "They took the stuff he committed suicide with. They took the note. They took hair, blood, whatever they could take. They checked the car inside and out, front and back, the whole kit and caboodle. I talked to the FBI for four to five hours one day. Our biggest crime was cooperating. With the DNA and everything they have now, if they have something, we would have heard by now. But six weeks after it was over with, they told us our brother was no longer a suspect."

But Ressler's book and the Bay Village rumor mill did not let Strunak rest. The family's name remained tarnished in public, even among relatives. "You just get beat up so long about something that nobody had anything to do with," Jeff said. "My mother, until the day she died, anytime someone said the name 'Amy,' she used to get all freaked out about it. There's just nothing left. Everybody is buried and gone. It's just a horrible feeling—every year when October comes around, you're looking in the paper for something to come up again. We're the scapegoats for this thing, and when you're a Strunak, there are not a lot of other Strunaks out there."

By the end of our conversation I felt more confident than ever that Billy was not Amy's murderer. In the months since, I have come to wonder if this was just false hope, if maybe I shared the wishful thinking of the authorities: that Amy's killer was still living and will eventually be brought to justice.

The article I wrote for *Scene* was not the end of my relationship with Billy Strunak, not by far. Billy may not have murdered Amy Mihaljevic, but he remained suspect—and for very good reason.

I only wish I had discovered the rest of Billy's story before the article went to press.

HAVE YOU SEEN THIS CHILD?

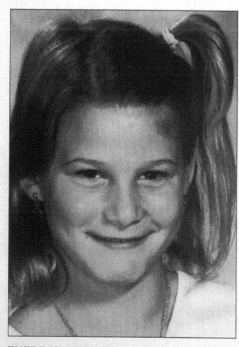

VICTIM:
AMY MIHALJEVIC

DATE OF BIRTH:
12-11-78

GRADE IN SCHOOL:
5th Grade, Middle School,
Bay Village, Ohio

DESCRIPTION:
White female, 4'10", 90 lbs.,
medium build, straight shoulder-
length blonde hair, brown eyes,
clear complexion, last seen
wearing green sweatpants,
lavender/green sweatshirt, denim
& red backpack, and black boots
with silver studs. Has a white
windbreaker with her. Wearing
horse head silhouette earrings or
turquoise earrings.

DETAILS:
At 5:58 p.m. on 10-27-89, Amy
Mihaljevic was reported to the Bay
Village Police as missing. Amy left
school and did not return home.
Amy has not been seen since.

THERE IS A REWARD OF UP TO $13,000

For information on the whereabouts of Amy Mihaljevic and the identification of her abductor.

CALL BAY VILLAGE POLICE (216) 871-1234

CALL FBI (216) 522-1400

These two artist's depictions are recollections of two different witnesses.

SUSPECT:
White Male

AGE:
30-35

DESCRIPTION:
5'8"-5'10" tall, medium
build, dark hair, possibly
curly, with bald spot top/rear,
trace of beard growth,
possibly wearing round
glasses and a tan jacket.

Volunteers distributed hundreds of thousands of copies of Amy's missing poster in
November and December 1989. It generated leads from as far away as Australia. Ironically,
Amy hated the way her hair looked in this picture.

628 Lindford Drive, Bay Village, Ohio: The killer called when Amy was home alone. *(Courtesy of the Morning Journal)*

Amy wins another ribbon for "excellent riding" at Holly Hill Farms in 1989. *(Courtesy of Mark Mihaljevic)*

Amy poses with horse-back riding awards, shortly before her murder. *(Courtesy of Mark Mihaljevic)*

Amy and her brother, Jason, in 1988.
(Courtesy of Mark Mihaljevic)

These illustrations, first published in a 1999 *Cleveland Magazine* article, were based on information released by the FBI. They show items Amy's killer may have taken from her body and kept for himself. *(Courtesy of Jim Mravec)*

Thousands of leads were phoned into Bay Village detectives in the weeks following Amy's disappearance. All were dead-ends. *(Courtesy of the Morning Journal)*

Bay Village police detectives and FBI agents scoured this desolate stretch of County Road 1181 in Ruggles Township for clues after a jogger discovered Amy's body there. *(Courtesy of the Ashland Times Gazette)*

Police Chief William Gareau, seen here n 1989, believes the man who murdered Amy still lives in Bay Village. *(Courtesy of the Morning Journal)*

Margaret and Mark Mihaljevic speak to Bill O'Reilley (offscreen) live from their home in 1989 for a segment of the television show *Inside Edition*. *(Courtesy of the Morning Journal)*

Even Bay Village mayor Ed Chapman was glued to the television as local stations updated viewers on the latest developments. *(Courtesy of the Morning Journal)*

Ashland County coroner William Emery, seen here with reporters in 1989, has kept the findings of Amy's autopsy report secret. *(Courtesy of the Ashland Times Gazette)*

Flanked by FBI Special Agent in Charge Bill Brannon and police spokesman Richard Wilson, Margaret Mihaljevic answers questions at a press conference. *(Courtesy of the Morning Journal)*

In 1983, Billy Strunak stalked a young waitress. In 1989, he became a suspect in the death of Amy Mihaljevic. He drank a lethal cocktail of dry-gas and cola thirteen days after Amy's body was found. *(Courtesy of the Cuyahoga County Sheriff's Office)*

Captain Roger Martin of the Ashland County Sheriff's Office returned to the recovery site with me in 2005 to share his theories of what really happened to Amy Mihaljevic. *(James Renner)*

Harold Bound lived at the riding stables where Amy took riding lessons. He said he checked himself into a mental hospital to avoid further interrogations by the FBI. *(Courtesy of Walter Novak)*

Doyle Matlock being sentenced for stabbing his girlfriend to death in 2005. *(Courtesy of the Wooster Daily Record)*

Bay Village detective Lieutenant Mark Spaetzel was a rookie in 1989, but now leads the investigation. "I will not retire until this case is solved," he said. *(Courtesy of Walter Novak)*

Amy's ashes are buried beneath those of her mother in West Berlin, Wisconsin.
(James Renner)

CHAPTER NINETEEN

Disillusionment

"DON'T DO THIS AGAIN," Kevin said.

On the filthy table in front of us, next to baskets of hot wings and two pints of Miller Lite, was a printed copy of my article, which included his editorial notes—more notes than my original content. He didn't want a story centered around uncharged suspects anymore. He wanted to rehash the entire abduction, search, recovery, and investigation. And he wanted me to do it in a standardized framework in less than five thousand words—which amounts to about five printed pages, four columns wide. I was fighting him.

"You're not from around here, Kevin," I said. "This story is a part of the area's history. The readers don't need another story about the search. They want to hear about the suspects. That's the new stuff, anyway."

Across from me, Kevin grimaced and lit a cigarette. "You don't know what our readership is," he reminded me. "And there are a lot of people living in Cleveland who didn't grow up here. I mean, it's not chronological, and you jag off the topic on every page. There are a lot of problems with it. I can help you if you'll listen to me."

"No," I said. "Not on this one."

"This one?" He was nearly yelling now. "You do this every time. It's always a fight with you."

"This one's different," I said. "Amy's different."

"They're all different. What's different about this one?"

"If we do this right, maybe we can catch this guy."

"Yeah, that'd be great, but that's not our job. Just write your story this way, and it will turn out good."

"No," I said. "You're wrong. We can't just squeeze Amy's story into the alternative-weekly format you're comfortable with."

"The formula works. This doesn't."

"I'm not doing that with Amy. I won't."

For a solid minute he stared at me, smoking his cigarette. Finally, he crushed it into the ashtray. "We're done, then," he said. "You and me. We're done. I'll tell Pete when we get back. I can't edit you anymore."

"That's fine," I said. What remained unsaid was the simple fact that this probably meant I would be fired and the article in any form would not see the light of day.

We ate our wings in silence, sipping beer between bites, pretending to watch some sports program on television.

I might not be able to save my job, I thought, *but maybe I can save the article.*

While the *Plain Dealer* enjoys a daily newspaper monopoly in Cleveland, two alternative weeklies duke it out every Wednesday for readers and bragging rights. *Scene* is the older paper, having celebrated its thirtieth anniversary in 2005. The *Free Times* is the underdog, a younger, more progressive rag with a staff populated by mostly *Scene* expats. If you work at one, it's practically required that you verbally trash the other. Each paper fights desperately each week to shut the other one down so that its profit margins will increase. It's a fight that has raged for more than a decade, with no end in sight. The discouraging fact of the matter is, most readers can't tell them apart.

My previous editor at *Scene* had become the new editor-in-chief at *Free Times*, I and a few other *Scene* staff members had kept in touch with him. We thought Frank was a decent guy. So, when I got back to the office I had Frank's number handy. As I gathered my notes on Amy and a copy of the first draft, I dialed his cell. "Frank, it's James," I said. "If I came by the *Free Times*, would you have a minute to meet with me?"

He did.

On the way out of *Scene*'s offices I bumped into Pete returning from a cigarette break. Kevin was with him. Pete looked pissed. "Let's talk tomorrow morning," he said.

I nodded and hurried to the elevator. Once outside, I made sure no one was watching before I crossed the street and headed toward a brick building on St. Clair. The *Free Times* was only half a block from *Scene*'s offices on West 9th. It would be quite easy to be spotted walking into the *Free Times* building by some classified sales manager on a Starbucks run. I'd rather Pete not find out about my betrayal until after he fired me.

Frank waited for me downstairs. The reunion was brief.

"So, what's up?" he said.

"I have this story that's really important to me," I said. "It's important it gets in print."

"What's it about?"

"It's a sixteen-year-old unsolved murder. I've found the names of several suspects that I want people to know about."

"I'll take a look," he said.

I handed over a rolled-up copy of Amy's article, one without any edits. "Kevin wants to chop it to pieces," I said. "I just don't want to see that happen to this one."

"I'll read it tonight, and I'll call you."

It was nearly nine o'clock when Frank called me at home. The hours that followed our meeting gave me just enough time to begin to doubt whatever skill I might have had as a writer. I could be too close to this one, I considered, too close to see it as a piece of writing.

"It's good," Frank said. "It's really good. But there's a lot of work to be done. I really think it needs to be chronological."

His comment was a stab to the heart. I obviously *was* too close to this one to see it objectively anymore. I had banked my job on that structure. If Frank wanted the structure changed, I really had lost my way.

I listened as Frank edited the piece over the phone. It would start with the discovery of the body, then move on to a short rehashing of events, finally ending with Billy Strunak, Harold Bound, and the other minor people of interest. Frank's notes were not identical to Kevin's, but it was close enough for me to realize I had made a mistake.

"Will you run it if I get fired tomorrow?" I said.

"Sure. I'd love to have it in *Free Times*."

That night, I told Julie I would most likely be fired in the morning. She was pleasantly disinterested. I made the forty-minute commute the next day, resigned to my fate.

*   *   *

"I ought to take you downstairs and throw you off the top of the parking deck," Pete said, scowling. "If I hadn't given myself a night to sleep on it, that's what I would have done."

I wasn't alone in Pete's office. Kevin was there. So was Erich, the paper's associate editor. Behind Pete, floor-to-ceiling windows permitted a view of the Cuyahoga River and the Scene Pavilion beyond. I could see Rock Bottom Brewery there, too, where I once worked as a waiter.

"You think you know how to write better than Kevin, but you don't know shit," Pete continued. "You can turn a pretty phrase every once in a while, but you don't understand the fucking *fundamentals*. You don't understand the easy stuff. And you won't let Kevin teach you. What is wrong with you? Why won't you listen to him?"

I knew Pete well enough to know he hated passive people and kiss-asses. So I defended myself the best I could instead of backing down.

"Kevin might know the fundamentals," I said. "But there's no heart in what he writes. And he doesn't want to learn that from *me*."

"You've got a pretty big set of balls," Pete said. "But you're stupid. You're one of those people who has to touch the flame to make sure it's hot every time."

I started to say something in protest, but he cut me off.

"This is where you shut up and listen to what I have to say because I'm going to save your job," Pete said. "I don't care that you write pretty. I need writers who know how to write *well*. Because I don't want to lose *my* job. If I don't have stories to put in the paper I lose *my* job. I've got a fucking family to feed. And so does this guy." He pointed at Erich. "That's your new editor. Are you going to listen to him? Do you want his family to eat next week, or do you want to dick around?"

"All right, Pete," I said. "All right."

"You're going to listen to what Erich tells you to do," he said. "And you're going to fucking get it done."

"All right."

He looked me in the eyes, coldly. "I'm not going to talk to you again. I'm just going to throw you off the parking deck."

*   *   *

"I can't read this," Erich said, when we were safe and alone in his office. He held Amy in his hands, covered with the bright yellow corrections of Kevin's edit. Erich was generally a pretty low-key family man sort of fellow, with dark hair and an intelligent face. I hadn't seen him mad, ever. This was pretty close.

"What do you mean?" I asked.

"It's all jumbled," he said. "It doesn't make any sense the way you have it. And, I *am* from around here, okay? But we'll fix it. We'll work together and make it great, okay?"

"All right," I said. "Thank you."

He looked at the draft for a long time, leaning back in his desk, before finally saying what I already knew he would. "I don't disagree with anything Kevin says here. Except I might have said it a little nicer," he admitted, with a smile.

The next afternoon, it was Kevin, not Erich, who visited my desk. I could tell by the look on his face that he had already read my second draft. I had stayed until two in the morning, fitting Amy's story into a chronological structure, adding new information to smooth the transitions.

"Hey man," he said. "I just wanted to tell you I really liked your changes. It's a really good read. How the hell did you do that in one night?"

"I followed your notes," I said.

For a second, I thought he might cry. I really did. For the first time, I felt a little guilty about how I had treated him. Kevin wasn't so bad; he just wasn't nice.

Amy's story hit the stands July 20. People called all week, feeding me new information on the case, names of suspects I had not known about. I realized that I didn't want to give up searching for Amy's killer just yet—not when there were new leads to follow, not when there were friends of hers yet to be interviewed. The biggest regret was that I had not managed to locate Janet Seabold, the jogger who had found her body. *Sebold, Seabold.* That correlation haunted me. I wanted to find out why.

On a whim, I e-mailed a copy of Amy's article and a proposal to a book publisher. In a week, I had a handshake agreement to do a more complete investigation into Amy's abduction and murder. In a month, I had an advance. On one hand, I was exhilarated. I had the chance to follow these new leads, a new chance to solve the case. On the other hand, I had no time to devote to the project. Working for *Scene* had never been more difficult.

Things might have turned out differently had I moved on to happier stories after Amy's. But the only ideas of mine that got approved at pitch meetings were gritty true-crime or hard-news stories. I was soon having lunches with Jeffrey Krotine, a man acquitted in the murder of his wife in 2005, after surviving two mistrials. I talked to family members involved in the tragedy and studied gruesome pictures from the woman's autopsy report. I formed an odd friendship with Krotine in the process, but living among the dead for so long eventually brings a person down.

The end for me was my next assignment. Steven Spade was an Eagle Scout from the Akron area who left home one night to catch a concert in Cleveland with some friends. His body was discovered the next day in West Virginia, though it was a while before it could be identified. Someone cut his head off with a hacksaw and then burned what remained. Erich asked me to talk to the dead kid's parents.

I found Steven's father sitting in a foldout chair behind his house. He wore a red flannel shirt that hung on his wiry frame in a sickly way. A dark mullet completed the picture. Next to him sat his wife and another man I could not identify.

"What do you want?" Mr. Spade asked.

"I want to help, if I can," I said. "I'm a reporter."

The man was out of the chair and rushing at me before anyone could hold him back. "Leave us alone, you sonofabitch! Leave us the fuck alone!"

I held my hands in the air and began backing toward my car. I avoided direct eye contact. It felt like I had crossed a rabid dog, insane with anger. "I obviously shouldn't have come," I said. "I only wanted to help. I'm sorry."

"Get the fuck off my property, you sick fuck!" he screamed. Neighbors were coming out of their houses now. "Leave us the fuck alone! I'll fucking kill you!"

The other man was now trying to take him by the arms. "Come on, man," he said. "It's not worth it. He's scum. He's just a reporter."

I climbed into my car, my heart pounding so fast my head felt weak and much too warm. Looking in the rearview mirror as I drove away, I could still see the boy's father trying to get me, held back by his friend and his wife, too.

"What's wrong with you?" Julie asked that night. She didn't say this because I looked terrible. She said this because I had removed all the furniture from the living room and was spraying the house with a variety of pungent chemicals.

"Something in this house is making me sick," I said. "I came home, and I couldn't breathe."

"There's nothing here. I don't smell anything except bleach."

"I couldn't *breathe*," I said. "I feel awful. I think there's dust or mites or mold or something."

"I just cleaned. That's not what it is."

And suddenly, I knew she was right. I looked at the empty room and the can of Lysol in my hand. In order to keep my job, to keep Pete thinking that I could be the writer he wanted, I had pushed myself further than my body and mind wanted me to go. This was not an allergic reaction. This was months of stress shutting me down. Months of sixteen-hour days and interviews with suspected murderers. Months of court documents and autopsy photos.

"I think I need to quit my job," I said.

Julie nodded. "I do too."

This is it, I thought. *Am I doing the right thing? Am I going to lose my house? Am I really quitting the job I worked so hard to get? Am I insane?*

"I'm giving you my two weeks' notice," I said to Pete.

He didn't throw me out the window. In fact, he didn't even seem surprised. "Okay," he said.

I told him I wanted to concentrate on writing movie scripts again. It was a half-truth. I really wanted to get away, to spend some time vegging on the couch and fixing my mind. Then, I wanted to start looking for Amy's killer again.

There wasn't much to say beyond that. He wished me well, and the following week the writers had a little party for me at Kevin's apartment. We sat out on the rooftop patio and drank beer. The Cleveland skyline rose in the distance, and the air was so clear it felt as if the Terminal Tower was close enough to touch.

"Look at all those people," Kevin said to me. "It's our job to tell them what to care about, you know?"

"I always thought it was our job to protect them."

Kevin sighed. "They don't want us to protect them."

I was cleaning out my desk when the call came. I picked up the phone.

"Hello?" I said.

"Is this James Renner?" The voice, with its deep timbre, sounded like it belonged to an older man.

"Yes."

"I have some information about the Amy Mihaljevic case," he said.

"Oh yeah? What's that?" I slipped a pen out of my pocket and pulled a notebook out of the half-filled box.

"Ever wondered why there were so many FBI agents involved in this case?" he said.

"Yeah, that's a big question mark."

"Well, that's because Amy's father was in the witness protection program."

I laughed. "Mark's not in witness protection," I said. "He works for Buick. He's from Wisconsin. He never changed his name."

"Mark is not Amy's father," the man said.

I listened as he told a story that explained the overwhelming FBI presence, the method of murder, and the motive behind the act itself. I listened as he divulged how he had come by this information. As he continued, a disturbing possibility began to emerge: that Amy Mihaljevic was not even dead.

Case # BV-8900713

A FEW YEARS AGO, the FBI released a video of Amy giving a book report in front of her fifth-grade classmates. It was filmed a few days before she was abducted. She looks older than she does in the year-book photo, as if she'd matured a full year in the span of a month. Her voice is not high pitched, but low and smooth, with the slightest trace of her mother's speech impediment. She wore her hair down that day, her bangs hanging over her left eye. As she speaks, she cannot stand still and pivots about on her feet, tilting her head to the left and smiling out at her classmates.

Who can blame Dan Pederson for falling in love with this girl? A fellow fifth-grader at Bay Middle, Dan had developed quite a crush on Amy the year before. She was the first girl he ever called on the phone, though he can no longer remember the details of their conversation. He hoped one day she would go steady with him. And she had started referring to Dan as her "boyfriend" to several close confidants. But Amy had developed a crush on a boy named Brian, the bad boy of Bay Middle School, who looked like one of the singers from New Kids on the Block. Brian would eventually break a few hearts of his own, including Kristy Sabo's. It was a typical tumultuous peewee soap opera they can look back on with hesitant nostalgia, those that survived.

Many claim Amy would have been valedictorian had she lived long enough. Possibly. She was certainly on the right track, being a part of GATE (Gifted and Talented Education), taking accelerated classes in English and math. Like her mother, Amy was gifted in academics. And, like Margaret, her passion seemed to be for the arts, specifically sculpting and drawing. She excelled in ceramics and spun out an as-sembly line of kiln-dried pigs and horses. One of those pigs went to her father. Another ended up with her Uncle Bill in California.

She showed an advanced understanding of aesthetics. Her sketches were finely detailed and demonstrated a rare subtlety for someone so young. She loved antiques, opting to ride a fifties-style bike with banana handlebars instead of something more modern.

On October 4, 1989, a photographer visited Bay Middle with a crew from Ohio School Pictures, a company out of Berea providing services to many local schools. Margaret had forgotten it was picture day, and so Amy had done her own hair. She tried a new style, a single ponytail on the left side. When the samples came back, she told her friends she was counting the days until the photographers returned for retakes on November 30. The ponytail wasn't her. She hated the picture.

Her daily ensemble of choice was sweats. She preferred oversized clothes, possibly to disguise her tiny frame. Amy was all of ninety pounds and stood four feet, ten inches.

She was a particularly busy 'tween. Her parents kept Amy active in a variety of social activities. She was a Brownie. She was an excellent swimmer, earning trophies for her efforts at the Blue Marlin Club. Later, she became consumed with horseback riding, which began with family lessons before she started going alone. Sue Tomsu trained her at Holly Hill Farms, usually on the back of a horse named Razzle. In 1988, she won a Grand Champion prize for excellent riding.

Though she was sometimes shy around new people, Amy had an army of friends. There were the two Kristys, as well as Elizabeth Jeffers, Renee Moran, Julie Meier, and Cindy Meeks. When a new girl, Katy, moved onto Lindford Drive a month before school started in 1989, Amy was quick to invite her along for bike rides.

Neighbors remember Amy darting about with her pals during the summer block parties held in the cul-de-sac. Adults set up buffet tables along the sidewalks. Every week families from odd- and even-numbered houses would alternate between bringing appetizers and desserts. When Amy was younger, she was little more than Margaret's shadow at these events but by age ten had become quite social, flitting about and making idle conversation with anyone who would lend an ear.

Sometimes, Amy and Elizabeth would put on roller skates in Amy's basement and spin around the center poles until they got dizzy. They tried their best to avoid Jason's model car collection and Jake the dog, who was rescued from a pound and forced to wear a red bandanna for the rest of his life. Later, Margaret would cook "baloney boats" in the oven, a strange treat that consisted of melted cheese on dried out bologna rolls, twisted from heat.

In her bedroom, Amy kept a large collection of My Little Pony figurines. She was not spoiled but was favored by Margaret. Their mother–daughter relationship evolved into a unique friendship as Amy grew older.

In 1989 the fifth-grade class had just become a part of the middle school in Bay Village. While the teachers moved with the students from Westerly Elementary School to the main facility on Wolf Road, they kept to their old schedule; their day ended at 2:10 p.m., an hour before the rest of the middle school.

One of Amy's favorite parts of the day was Jody Jurich's English class. Jurich was a young teacher at the time and concocted fun projects for her upper-level fifth-grade classes. In early October, Amy's class read *Dicey's Song,* a popular young-adult novel about a girl learning to manage her life after being abandoned by her mother. Part of the reading assignment was also to describe what you would do if you found yourself in a similar situation. Amy's take on the subject was humorous, and she gave a short speech in front of her class, banging into the wall for emphasis, mimicking the character of Dicey's loony mother.

During recess, Amy socialized with a clique of friends that included Olivia Masiak. Olivia remembers playing jump-rope with Amy one afternoon in October, near a fence that stood near a side road. Amy noticed that they were being watched by a man in a parked car. He was white. The car was a small four-door, maybe blue. It upset Olivia enough that she reported it to a teacher. But the man left before an adult could ask him why he was there.

At the end of each day, Amy would grab her bike and either head home to watch TV or follow friends to the Bay Village shopping plaza.

In the back corner of the plaza was Bay Lanes. Inside the bowling alley was an arcade run by Tim Haley. Amy whiled away whole afternoons there on occasion.

Also in the plaza was the Sunkist Tanning Salon, where Patricia

Draeger worked. She was a friend of the Mihaljevics and rode horses at Holly Hill Farms.

The evening of October 26, 1989, Patricia picked Amy up for a riding lesson. She gave the girl a present: a used saddle for her horse. She seemed very happy.

Patricia saw Amy once more. As Amy approached the plaza the next afternoon, they waved at each other through the wide window of the salon. Amy smiled back at Patricia. Neither understood it was a wave good-bye.

CHAPTER TWENTY

Down the Rabbit Hole

MY INFORMANT WAS A middle-aged restaurateur named David Bodnar. He owned a little sit-down sandwich shop in a small Olmsted Falls shopping plaza that is hard to see from the street. On October 5, I stepped into the deli for an afternoon meeting. Behind the counter was a cramped office where stacks of receipts, employee time cards, and old menus rested precariously on every surface. There was just enough room for two chairs amidst the clutter and not enough left over to shut the door. I sat in the chair closest to the deli while Bodnar sat facing me.

Bodnar was a man balding in a way that was almost endearing. Remnants of dark hair still shielded the majority of his head. Over the phone he had seemed eager to talk, but in person he measured his words very carefully.

"Now, I can't give you any names," he began. "That wouldn't be good for me. But I'll tell you this, I've worked in the restaurant business for years, so I've gotten to know a few FBI agents as customers. I also know some people in Bay Village. Anyway, I knew everyone in the entire game."

"What can you tell me?" I asked.

Bodnar hesitated, scratched his head, then plowed forward. "It was a mob hit," he said. "Most of the FBI agents working the case and the Bay police were never told. The Bay Village police were in the dark the whole time. The reason why they were not told was that the real investigation was handled by the U.S. marshals—the organization that handles the witness protection program. Margaret was married before. And Amy's real father was in the New Jersey mob before he turned on them in court. Her real father was in witness protection. It looks like they kidnapped her to get to him."

These things he was saying with such conviction sounded quite implausible. "How do you know Amy had some other father?" I said.

"I knew Amy's neighbors," Bodnar said. "Her next-door neighbors saw some man come to the Mihaljevics' on weekends and pick up Amy for visitation. I know about the witness protection because I know the family in Bay Village who housed the federal judge from New Jersey when they flew him in after Amy disappeared. The family had to sign some confidentiality agreement. If they told anyone about it, they could be prosecuted.

"Then I found out through another connection the way she died. I heard this directly from the doctor who performed the autopsy. He told me it looked as if someone had drained her blood slowly out of a cut in the neck. It was almost as if they were doing it in a manner that would allow someone to watch her while she died. Those aren't stab wounds on her neck. Those are small incisions."

"How can this possibly be true?" I said. "You can't cover something like that up."

"If it's not true," he said, "what *is* true? Nothing else makes sense. What is even more suspicious is how they left the body. Whoever killed her left the body for someone to find. And why did he only do it to this one girl and not continue killing?"

"I don't know," I said. "But I have some time now to look into these things and see where it takes me. It would be helpful if you could give me at least one name."

But Bodnar wasn't biting. "I can't do that. Look, ask the FBI who gave the order to bring in all these agents. That order had to come from Washington. They didn't treat this case like any other. For instance, I know the FBI broke into a Bay Village doctor's office looking for information. Broke in without a warrant. Somebody was directing that. Here's another thing: They ID'd Amy by her fingerprints. Why would a ten-year-old girl's prints be on file? Why would some strange little girl from Bay Village be that important? Everything is a lie."

I considered what he was saying for a moment. "If anything you're telling me is true, then why stop there?" I said. "If you believe Amy's father was in the witness protection program, what's stopping you from believing she was found and returned? She could never have returned to normal life after that. Maybe the government faked her death and sent her to live with her real dad? After all, her parents never saw the body." I laced this statement with heavy sarcasm. That was crazy talk, I-just-saw-Bigfoot-in-the-woods talk.

Bodnar smiled. "Why not?" he said. "A few years ago, I told an FBI agent what I just told you. I told him to ask his director about it. He went to his boss and asked him. Guess what? The guy never talked to me again."

Driving back home to the makeshift office I had set up, I compared what I knew about the Mihaljevics against these so-called substantiated rumors. Mark and Margaret met in high school. For Margaret to be remarried, she would have had to marry Mark, divorce him in Little Rock, marry this mob guy from New Jersey, divorce *him*, then remarry Mark before moving to Bay. That kind of thing may happen in daytime soaps, but I doubted if such things took place in real life.

Then there were the little odd things about this case—to start, an abnormal amount of FBI attention. And, what about the guy who showed up at Margaret's house a day or two after her body was found in her Las Vegas apartment, the guy who represented himself to Margaret's mother as a Bay Village policeman? Why did he take her address books?

I wanted to dispel these rumors quickly. I was down the rabbit hole now, desperate to see a coherent sign in a disordered jumble, and I didn't want to indulge that desire too long. Everyone knows somebody who has gone down a rabbit hole and lost his way—people who banter about alien abductions the way others talk sports. I figured the easiest way to disprove this train of thought would be to call the U.S. marshal's office in Cleveland.

Once home, I made them my first phone call. The switchboard operator transferred me to the office that handles witness protection. "Can you tell me if Amy Mihaljevic had a father who was in witness protection?" I asked.

I heard an intake of breath on the other end that I read as simple recognition. "I couldn't talk to you about that even if I wanted to," the man said.

Mark Mihaljevic is listed as the father on Amy's birth certificate. No family member on the Mihaljevic or the McNulty side has ever said anything about Amy not being Mark's biological daughter. Most important, I had looked into Mark's eyes as he spoke of Amy. He undoubtedly loved her as his daughter.

As much as I'd have liked to believe in some grand conspiracy, a government- and mob-related cover-up, Amy is dead. And now her mother is too. The best I could hope for was to solve her murder before it became an urban legend, some down-the-rabbit-hole fable to be bandied about in the backs of delis.

CHAPTER TWENTY-ONE

Game On

AS THE POLICE AND FBI had discovered before me, once a lead was investigated, two more usually popped up in its place. I didn't know where to resume work on the case. There were no editors around to tell me what to do. Should I talk to the family some more? Should I hit the streets and question additional Bay Village residents? Should I take another look at some of the suspects?

I came to the conclusion the best place to begin again would be with Dick Wrenn. He was the FBI agent most central to the case. I was sure he had read the article by now. Maybe he could tell me where to look next. I fumbled through my old notes and called his house one evening in the beginning of October.

"Yeah?" came the odd greeting. *Must have caller ID*, I thought.

"I just wanted to see what you thought of the article I wrote about Amy a few months ago," I said.

"Well, to tell the truth, James, I didn't care for it."

My skin grew cold. Realizing I'd pissed off an FBI agent, even though he was retired, I was unnerved in a way I'd never been before. "Can I ask why?"

"There was a lot you got wrong," he said. "First of all, the volunteer center was on the second floor, not the basement. You got those reversed. Secondly, I was never furious with Robert Ressler about his book. You said I was furious. I never said I was furious."

I quickly thumbed through my notes from our conversation about Ressler's book. "Well, I guess I got the floors reversed on the volunteer thing," I said. "And for that, I apologize. But, I do think you said you were furious. You were certainly upset about it because you thought people would assume the case had been solved, that they would think Billy Strunak did it and not come forward with more information."

"I never said I was furious."

I tried to think of a way to continue as the silence dragged on. "I'm calling you because I wanted you to know that I'm writing a book about the case now. I wanted to see if you'd meet with me. Maybe you could tell me where I fell short with the article and help me do better with the book."

"No," he said. "I don't think I'll do that."

"All right," I said. "Can I give you a call after I finish the first draft and fact-check with you?"

"You can call," he said. "But I'm afraid the answer is still going to be no."

I hung up. My head felt dizzy and slightly overloaded.

Underneath Wrenn's number was Jason Mihaljevic's. *Amy's brother would want to hear about the book*, I thought. I was sure her family would have appreciated the story in *Scene*. If it did nothing else, it brought attention to her case again and reminded people that it was unsolved.

"No, I didn't read it," Jason said. "But I know my father was pretty upset about it. He said there were a lot of lies in there."

"What? What lies?"

"The stuff you put in there about my mother," he said. "The stuff about her being an alcoholic."

I didn't know what to say. I wasn't about to argue with Jason the facts of his mother's addiction. Not once did I consider the family would take that revelation so personally. Surely they were aware. Even Jason, as young as he was at the time, must have had a clue. Then again, I knew better, didn't I? Alcoholics are more adept at misdirection than many magicians. They share their secrets with strangers, but the ones they love rarely see the sleight of hand.

This was an evening of lows. By the time I got off the phone with Jason, I felt depressed. These calls were supposed to motivate me to finish the investigation. I began thinking about spiking the whole thing. If the family didn't want it, what was the point?

Of course, there *was* a person close to Amy who wanted answers—one of her best friends, as a matter of fact. I gathered my things for a trip to Lakewood. If Kristy Sabo told me she hated the article and told me I was a bastard, there the book would die.

*   *   *

This was one of those times when everything falls into place just so, when the universe lines up and shows you a pattern to things. When we met at her mother's Kristy had mentioned tending bar at O'Donnell's in Lakewood. I knew she would be there. I just didn't know how she would react to seeing me again.

I was barely through the door before Kristy spotted me across the dark, smoky room. She looked older in jeans instead of a tank-top and skirt, and her hair was longer, pulled back into a tight ponytail. She smiled warmly and waved.

The place was nearly empty at nine o'clock on a weeknight. A couple of men sat on barstools toward the front. Two women on stools chatted at the far end. I stepped up to the bar nearer the women and took a seat.

"Read your article," Kristy said. Her dimples appeared again, above both corners of her mouth. "Really liked it. You really got Amy down, man. You really got close to how she was, you know? My mom liked it, too."

"Thanks. I've gotten a lot of phone calls about the story."

"Really? Like from who?"

"Different people," I said. "There's a lot more to look at, I think. A lot more to do. I left my job so I could focus on writing a book about the case."

"That would be great," she said. "I think about her every day, you know? It's just so sad. I miss her, still."

A beat passed quietly as I wondered again how my life, how both our lives, might have been different had Amy lived. Half the weight Kristy carried behind those deep eyes would not exist. Sadly, she still had the loss of her father to bear either way.

Ought not to get lost in those eyes, I reminded myself. *Or reflections on futures that might have been.*

I ordered a Labatt's, which Kristy served me on the house, and I followed her down the bar to meet her friends—the two older women at the far end.

During the next several hours, I got to know these women well. We traded sad stories and shots of Jameson. Whenever Kristy had a moment, which was often, she would sit with us, too. This was the good omen I needed to begin again. This was what I was looking for.

And suddenly it was 1:30 in the morning, and I was drunk. I needed some serious detox soon. I tried to remember where the closest Taco Bell was located.

"Why don't you come back to my apartment?" Kristy said.

I tried to read her intentions. She knew I was married. She saw my bling-bling wedding ring. No. She only wanted to make sure I wouldn't drive home like this. It was a sweet gesture, nothing more. I thought I might cry. Now that, *that* would have been really awkward.

"Thanks, though," I said. "Really. I had fun." I stood and staggered a bit on my feet.

"You can't drive like that," Kristy said.

"Not gonna," I said. "I'm gonna get a taco and some water."

With a final wave, I dragged myself out of O'Donnell's and into the warm night air of Lakewood in autumn. That night, I would throw up. And in the morning, I would start investigating again.

Game on.

CHAPTER TWENTY-TWO

The Jogger

THE FIRST THING I DID was find Janet Seabold.

It took a little more sleuthing than normal. She did not want to be found and went to great lengths to remain hidden. Amy's death, as far as Seabold was concerned, might as well have happened yesterday.

I found her in a remote part of Ohio, away from any large cities. Her house sat at the end of a one-lane road bordered by nothing but forest and more forest, up a long and winding driveway that wrapped around a mountain.

At the top, I pulled my car into a parking space below a mansion of a house with impeccably landscaped grounds. I stayed in the car for a minute and watched as a fawn nibbled at Seabold's hostas. Being from the country myself, I had seen plenty of deer but seldom this close. When I finally stepped out of the vehicle, yonder fawn merely lifted her head, sniffed at the air, then returned to consuming Seabold's shrubbery.

There was no back door. A winding wooden staircase led to a porch in the back, and as I approached, a middle-aged woman stepped out of the house. Her hair was mostly gray and there were years of anguish in her eyes, but her graceful gait suggested that she had continued those daily runs years after coming across Amy in the wheat field off County Road 1181.

I raised my hands in greeting and also to show they were empty. "Mrs. Seabold, I came by to ask you if there's anything you'd like to tell me about Amy Mihaljevic," I said.

"You're that reporter then," she replied. "From, what's it? *Scene* magazine?"

"That's right. I tried to find you for the article."

"Uh-huh. I know. I didn't really want to talk about it," she said.

"Can I ask why not?" When she didn't say anything for ten seconds or so, I followed up with "Look, I drove a long way, and I'll leave if you want me to. But I've always had this feeling like you have something important to tell me. I'm a good guy, Mrs. Seabold. All I want to do is find out who did this to Amy."

"I've had headaches ever since that morning," she said. "I've been depressed ever since. Can't keep from thinking about her. I think about her every single day. It was my morning routine, you know? I went jogging every day along that route. I lived one street over, on County Road 1281, so I would make a big circuit, running past that field. And I didn't see her there until that morning in February. I thought it was somebody playing a joke on me. I thought it was a doll or something. And then I saw that it wasn't. I ran to Pat Kidd's house on the corner there, because the people in the farmhouse next door weren't home or they weren't awake. And I told Pat what happened and I told her not to give my name to the reporters, but she did anyways. We didn't talk after that. It was only last year, when I bumped into her at a store, that I even said 'hi' again."

I could tell she was building toward something, but she kept stalling out. I just gave her time and let her come to it herself.

"Have you talked with the FBI?" she asked.

I hadn't moved from my spot on the driveway below her. I could tell she wanted me to remain somewhat distant. "I have," I said. "They've been pretty open with me."

"Do you know if they ever looked into what I told them?"

"What did you tell them?"

"There was a man that lived on my street," she said. "He ran a plumbing business. Right around the time they found that girl, he quit the business and checked himself into a mental hospital. I knew his partner's son, and he told me this guy looked like that composite sketch the police made."

"Can you tell me this guy's name?" I asked.

She shook her head.

"Can you tell me the name of his partner or the name of the company?"

"No," she said. "I don't want to say any more. I'm sorry."

I held up my hands again. "It's all right. Thanks for talking to me."

"Can you do me a favor?" she said.

"Sure thing."

"If you find out who did this, can you let me know?"

I promised.

CHAPTER TWENTY-THREE

Dead Ringer

ALL I HAD WAS a road and an idea of the sort of business this new suspect once owned. With the light fading over the countryside of middle Ohio, I decided to head to Ashland County and try my luck anyway.

Traveling down State Route 224, County Road 1281 is just a mile farther west than 1181. I pulled into the first driveway I saw. "Did somebody around here run a plumbing business sixteen years ago?" I asked a woman who spoke to me through the latched screen door of a modified trailer.

"Not that I know of."

Same response from the next few houses. Then I arrived at a dilapidated farmhouse. There an elderly couple, evidently both hard of hearing, watched a television cranked up full blast.

"Next door," the old woman yelled. "Sam Tillerman* ran a plumbing business years ago."

My pulse quickened as I approached a wide two-story painted blue, set back from the road on a rolling hill. It was eventide now, one last sliver of sunlight peeking above the horizon. The colors of the world were muted, becoming shadow, losing substance. I spied the figure of a man leaning under the hood of a pickup truck. He stood up stiffly and followed my progress toward him. *There goes the element of surprise*, I thought.

Not that I had hoped for much from this guy. If he were of any particular interest, I figured I would have heard of him by now. Still, there was a pestering urge to see this hunch through.

As I got out of the car, the man stepped toward me, wiping his

---

* Not his real name. I've changed that, and his occupation and some incidental details, because he did not consent to an interview.

hands on a rag he then slipped into his back pocket. Something crunched underfoot. I looked down and saw a Coors can that had been smashed flat for recycling. Dozens more littered the gravel drive and twinkled in the fading light.

"Can I help you?" he asked.

My eyesight fails me at night, and so I couldn't discern his features until we were almost three feet apart. By then, it was too late to hide my surprise.

I never really trusted the composite sketch of Amy's abductor. For one thing, I thought it was too vague. I thought it looked like any average Midwestern white man. Secondly, no reporter, as far as I knew, had met the person or persons who witnessed Amy's kidnapping and supplied the information for the sketch artist. I had begun to think these witnesses didn't exist.

Sam Tillerman, however, didn't just resemble the composite sketch; he was its three-dimensional twin. It was as if somebody had taken the composite sketch and made a mask and this guy was wearing it as an early Halloween joke. But Tillerman was real.

"Can I help you?" he repeated.

Thump thump thump, went my heart. "Hi," I said. "I'm a writer. I'm in Ashland writing about true crime, about Amy Mihaljevic, and someone said you might have some information for me, since it only happened one road over."

Now it was his turn to act surprised. He stopped wiping the grease from his hand. His mouth slipped open like a door with a faulty hinge. I stared at him as he struggled to say something. He began moving his mouth like a fish, forming words I could not hear.

A sound to my left startled me. A woman—presumably Tillerman's wife—leaned out the front door. He waved her back in with a flick of his wrist. She obeyed.

Tillerman turned to me again and seemed to collect himself a little. "What can I do?" he said. "What can you do?" He raised his arms, palms to the sky, and shrugged, as if that gesture said everything.

How cruel would fate be, I wondered, *to put a man resembling the sketch of a kidnapper so close to the scene of the crime if he hadn't done it? What kind of a world would that be?*

Tillerman turned from me, lightning fast, and moved toward the darkness of his garage. It was my impression at the time that he wanted to retrieve something there. But then he stopped in his tracks, turned, and walked back toward me. He just stood there, silent, until I climbed back into my Plymouth and pulled away.

CHAPTER TWENTY-FOUR

Special Agent Father Dunn

BEFORE JOHN DUNN RAN security for the Cuyahoga County Public Library, he was a special agent for the FBI. And before that, he was a priest.

A thick-bodied man with a full head of white hair, Dunn was dressed like a G-man when he and I met. There was an aura of serenity surrounding him, something people feel around good men of faith but never put into words. It could have been no more than wise confidence, but I found it very calming to be in his presence. From the start I knew this was not a man who lied to strangers.

I had tried to get Dunn to sit down with me during my research at *Scene* but never managed to catch him in the library's central office in Parma. Dunn bounces between all of the branches in Cuyahoga County, making sure everything is up to spec. As I found myself with little else to do during the month of October besides research Amy's case, I simply called several times a day until he picked up his line. Surprisingly, he sounded quite anxious to talk, and later that week I sat on a comfortable chair in front of his wide desk inside his office at the library system's administration building.

The office was well-ordered, clean, and neat—the kind of office one would expect to find inside a diocese. Pictures of Dunn's family sat in front of a wide window.

I discovered pretty quickly that Dunn was an excellent observer with an enviable recall for past events. He had the conversational skills of an excellent agent and an even better storyteller. It was a challenge to keep up with him as he relayed his involvement with the search to find Amy Mihaljevic.

*   *   *

The call came Sunday morning, October 29. "Report to Bay Village," he was told. A command post was already set up in the basement.

Once Dunn arrived at the Bay Village town hall, he was asked to drive out to the Mihaljevic residence with a female agent named Babetta Chiarito, nicknamed Bebe. Chiarito was young, in her mid-twenties, and short and petite enough that, from behind, someone could easily mistake her for a teenager. But her stature belied the skill and cunning of one of Cleveland's finest feds. Dunn and Chiarito were asked to stay with the Mihaljevics and await any ransom demands that might be phoned in and to try to obtain a better description from the mother of what Amy might be wearing, a task easier said than done.

Inside the colonial on Lindford, the mood was funereal, grim, tense. Nearly forty-eight hours had passed since Margaret had reported Amy missing. Dunn knew there was no time to waste with well-intentioned obfuscation.

"There is going to be a lot of scrutiny," Dunn said to Margaret and Mark. "We're going to look at everything. What I need you to do now is tell me if there is anything we should know about. I need to know if either of you are having an affair right now. Because if it comes out later, it will cast a different light on you." Both denied seeing anyone outside the marriage.

Margaret and Mark had been planning to separate for a while by then. Chiarito stayed with Margaret while Dunn took Mark aside. Dunn asked Mark to walk him through his activities on Friday, and together they constructed a timeline. This was partly an exercise to discern when the search for Amy had truly begun. Another reason for it, though, was to rule Mark out as a suspect in his daughter's disappearance. Dunn found Mark to be open, concerned, and straightforward. His alibis checked out.

Dunn and Chiarito also searched Amy's room. It was the very essence of Young American Girl: stuffed animals, frilly bed sheets, pink stuff. On a desk, Dunn spied a writing tablet. Taking the end of a pencil, he rubbed against the pad, watching Amy's last message materialize in hazy relief. It wasn't telling, though, just the simple scribbling of a ten-year-old. No phone number or name of her abductor. Nothing about this case, Dunn came to realize, would be that easy.

It was the first of several days Dunn spent inside the Mihaljevic home with Agent Chiarito. During their stay, the two learned a great deal about Amy's parents' already splintered relationship.

At the time of Amy's abduction, Margaret had been preparing to divorce Mark. She had taken out a post office box in her name and was beginning to separate their finances.

It also became obvious that alcohol was an active ingredient in Margaret's life. The agents became more frustrated with this the more Margaret drank in front of them. Dunn questioned everything she told them. Was the description she provided for Amy accurate, or was Margaret too inebriated to remember correctly? Other things she told them did not check out at all.

"Who did you talk to at work on Friday?" Dunn asked her.

But Margaret couldn't concentrate, couldn't remember.

"Let's pass the glass over," Dunn said. He took the tumbler she held in one hand. "Let's talk."

Dunn and Chiarito walked Margaret out to the backyard and conducted their own impromptu intervention.

"Your drinking is impairing our job," he told her.

"I know it's a problem," she said. She promised to quit.

When Dunn finally left the home a few days later, he concentrated on interviewing every bartender in town for further information on Margaret's friends and behavior. It was not a pleasant assignment. Questioning the habits of a missing girl's mother was one thing. Implying she was an alcoholic during such a tragic time was just brutal.

Dunn did not leave Bay Village for nine months.

"I remember being so bummed that Halloween," Dunn said to me. "What that must have been like for the kids in Bay Village. Nobody trick-or-treated. I have four kids of my own. I used to come home at the end of the day and just hold my kids. I'm not saying it was hard to work the job. These jobs are actually the easiest. Everyone wants to give it their all. But I needed to hold my kids at the end of the day."

"You and Robert Ressler interviewed Billy Strunak," I said. "Can you tell me about that meeting?"

"There were a number of questions we had about Strunak," he

said. "He had some trouble at the volunteer center." Dunn paused for a moment. "He never wanted to talk to us. One time I went out to Billy's apartment with an agent named Scott Brantley. We were going out there to interview him. We called him on the phone, and he said he was on his way out and couldn't talk to us. Another time, an answering machine picked up and I said, 'Billy pick up the phone.' And he picked up. 'Look, we need to talk to you,' I said. 'We're right outside the building, so let us in.'

"His involvement with the volunteer center was interesting to me," Dunn added. "He sent a trinket in the mail to Margaret, a little gift. There were unresolved issues attached to him—like there were to some other people. For instance, we found surveillance photos of Strunak visiting a bank at West 220th and Lorain Avenue (ten minutes from Bay Village) the day of Amy's abduction. And his behavior was odd. That's what you key in on. One of the maddening things about all this is, after he died someone cleaned his apartment. We went in with the Fairview Park P.D. I had the distinct impression the apartment had been gone through."

I thought of Strunak's brother, who said the police were the first ones in the house. Had he been wrong? Had someone else gotten there first?

"You've had a lot of years to think about this," I said. "What do you believe happened to Amy that day?"

Dunn rearranged himself in his chair and rubbed his chin. "Things that end up as homicides sometimes don't start out that way," he said. "Maybe Amy got in that vehicle and this person touched her the wrong way, and she started screaming. Then he hits her to make her stop, but he hits her too hard. We just don't know. And we don't know who did it for sure. The FBI vetted several dozen people who were interesting for one reason or another. There are any number of people who have verifiable alibis up to a point."

"And her body," I said. "How long was it in that field?"

Dunn shrugged. "We know that area was used by hunters during the winter," he said. "No one saw the body until the jogger found her."

CHAPTER TWENTY-FIVE

The Man in Charge

THE SAC—SPECIAL AGENT IN CHARGE—OF the Cleveland Bureau at the time of the FBI's search for Amy Mihaljevic was a guy named Bill Brannon. His tenure ran from 1989 through 1993, which were formative years for his children as well. Although the Brannons eventually left Cleveland, residing in the warmer climate of New Mexico and subsequently the city of Chicago, when Brannon finally retired from active duty the family opted to return to Ohio. "We had a family vote," Brannon said. "My son and daughter wanted to come back to Cleveland and, by God, we came back to Cleveland."

Reached by phone, Brannon agreed to meet for a cup of coffee at a Starbucks on the West Side. By that time, October 18, 2005, I had met several agents, so I found it interesting that the person who looked the least like a fed was the man who had been in charge. Unlike Belluomini and Dunn, Brannon would not have been the one I would peg as the covert op, and perhaps that had something to do with his position. He blended well with the Cleveland population. At first glance, he resembled some Irish transplant, tall and burly. A union boss maybe, but not a fed. He looked like a suburban Cub Scout leader and his voice had the pleasant timbre of an uncle who likes to tell tall tales. He greeted me with a warm clap on the shoulder and remarked that I looked far too young to be a *real* reporter. It wasn't meant as an insult, and I didn't take it that way. In fact, I smiled and couldn't stop the whole time we talked, though the subject was often morose. At first, I thought everyone must feel this way in the big guy's company. As the conversation progressed, however, I sensed an underlying awareness behind his mild-mannered exterior. We joked, we laughed, but he was privately measuring me, judging me, isolating my tells in a way that I found a little frightening, a little robotic. I thought this man could be an excellent interrogator. It was an idea I didn't want to test because I knew a little about his dual personality already. Here was a man devoted to his family. At the same time, he was also the man who helped put away Melvin Mays, a terrorist who tried to buy missiles from Muammar Khaddafi to shoot down an airplane at Dulles International.

"I was always convinced it was someone local," Brannon said between giant gulps of steaming java. "Half the FBI lived in Bay Village or Westlake at that time. So, we really wanted to find this guy. And when we started overturning rocks in Bay Village . . ." He paused, clearly censoring himself a little. "It amazed me the things we uncovered. It amazed me, the number of sexual deviants and perverts in Bay Village. There are things I could tell you that you wouldn't believe. There are some things about this case that are only known to the FBI for good reason. I spent thirty-one years in the FBI. The most disappointing thing in my career is not having this solved."

From the office, Brannon allocated the resources needed for the search. He brought in retired FBI agents to answer phones. He pushed the Bay Village City Council for an early computerized system to catalogue leads for cross-referencing. For the search over at Holly Hill Farms, he ordered heat-seeking equipment mounted on low-flying planes. It was so powerful, the airborne operator could radio to a particular agent on the ground and say, "There's something on the ground, three feet to your left." Only rabbits and the occasional deer hunter were found in the woods, though.

"Everything was done that could be," Brannon said. "Things you'll probably never hear about. But despite all those resources, we couldn't get this guy. The FBI gave their heart and soul to this case. This affects your life."

At the beginning, Brannon said, there were a lot of false starts, generated mostly from phone calls by people who began their report with "This might not mean anything, but . . ." Each lead was pursued until it dead-ended.

On weekends and before Brannon drove to work in the mornings, he would stop at the command center inside the Bay Village city hall. He does not remember ever seeing better cooperation between local law enforcement and the FBI. It was a relationship that was used as an example for many cases in the future. Though Brannon's personality was obviously a part of what made that relationship work, his counterpart at the Bay P.D., Bill Gareau, was just as affable and open.

I asked Brannon about Sam Tillerman and then Billy Strunak. He seemed rather uninterested. His response suggested that only evidence would be intriguing at this point. Symmetry and plain weirdness were only circumstantial.

"So, what do you think happened?" I said. "Where's the guy that did this?"

"I think the guy crawled under a rock and hasn't come out since," Brannon said. "I think the answer is in those FBI files somewhere."

"I'd love to take a look in those filing cabinets," I told him. "I've seen the room in Bay Village where they keep them. Four filing cabinets and a shelf full of some type of evidence. That's a lot of information."

"Yes, but those aren't the FBI's files," he said. "You can only imagine what *we* have. You know, the person you should talk to is Dick Wrenn. He took the case to heart. He's the guy you should talk to."

"He won't talk to me anymore," I said. "He didn't really care for the article."

"Well, let me see if I can mend that bridge," Brannon said. I saw the twinkle in his eye and knew Wrenn would be calling soon. Even in retirement Brannon had the ability to lead Cleveland's best detectives.

CHAPTER TWENTY-SIX

Visiting Amy

IT SEEMED WRONG, even presumptuous, to write an entire book about Amy Mihaljevic without visiting her grave. I needed to see where she ended up after all this. I needed to see the condition of her resting place, to see if it was tranquil. I wanted to leave flowers, something to serve as a promise or maybe an atonement for bringing her name into the open again. So on October 20, I swapped my Plymouth Breeze for my wife's more reliable Cavalier and drove to Wisconsin.

This was a drive Amy made with her family on a regular basis. Margaret may have given in to Mark's desire to live far from family, but the trade-off, apparently, was routine trips out of state. They drove out for holidays and a majority of the summers. Sometimes the McNultys would travel to Ohio instead, but Margaret preferred to visit West Allis.

On a good day, the total drive time from Cleveland to West Allis is just under eight hours. However, a leg of this trip winds around Chicago. I happened to be near the Windy City at rush hour. Edging forward at a foot a minute for three miles set my timing off by a good little bit. By the time I found a motel in Milwaukee, the sun had set, and all there was time to do was get something to eat.

Mark Mihaljevic once told me it's hard to tell the difference between the suburbs of Cleveland and the suburbs of Milwaukee. On the surface, that may be true. It's a hodgepodge of strip malls, gas stations, and parks in a flat, gray world. But I noticed differences in the inhabitants. People there seemed rough-edged, depressed. Perhaps this was Cleveland ten years down the road, when the last steel mill shuts down and our economy depends on the service industry alone. It's a sad thought.

West Allis has something else in common with Bay Village. A serial killer prowled those streets in the not too distant past. After Jeffrey Dahmer moved to West Allis from Bath, Ohio, he hunted down and murdered seventeen young men between 1978 and 1991. Some of them he ate. Their remains were dumped into large acid vats in his basement. He was later convicted of these crimes and was subsequently murdered in prison. In 2002, *Dahmer*, the movie, was filmed on location. An actor named Jeremy Renner portrayed the killer.

As I was heading to the hotel, my cell phone rang. A Wisconsin number flashed on the readout, and I naturally assumed it was Henrietta, Amy's grandmother. We were supposed to meet in person the following morning, a Saturday. But the woman on the other end sounded much younger.

"James, this is Kathy, Henrietta's daughter-in-law," she said. "I'm calling on Henrietta's behalf. She can't meet with you tomorrow."

"Why not? Is everything all right?"

"Henrietta's not feeling well, and I don't think it would be good for her to talk about all this again. She's had some health problems these last few years. So I have to ask that you not contact her anymore. If you have any questions, you should call me instead."

"Well, can you meet with me tomorrow?"

"No, I can't," she said. "I really don't think the family wants to talk about this anymore."

"Well, I won't call Henrietta again," I said. "But I can't really cancel the trip to West Allis at this point. I'm going to visit a couple places in town and then head home tomorrow night. This will probably be the only time I can meet the family in person, so please see if anyone will talk to me. You can reach me at this number."

"All right, thank you."

What could I do? I couldn't be mad at Henrietta or the McNultys. Here I was, intruding on their personal space a week before the sixteenth anniversary of Amy's abduction. Timing can be everything, and my timing sucked.

At the motel, a thirty-dollar-a-night deal with scratchy sheets, I flipped through the white pages to the M's. A few Mihaljevics but literally dozens of McNultys. I recognized one. Dale, Margaret's brother. I flipped through my folders and found an old newspaper article that quotes Dale at the time of his sister's death. He seemed nice enough inside quotation marks. In the morning, I drove out to his listed address.

Two miles from town, down a winding country road, I found Dale's home. It was a farm, really, where a tired old house sat in front of a pasture. The house was once painted white, I could tell, but by now had taken on the color of used gauze. Chips of white had fallen away, revealing darker wood underneath. The grass in front was overgrown. Still, it was not unkempt. I knew farms from my youth, and this one was fair.

I parked the car, walked to the front door, then rapped my knuckle upon the glass. The satchel and all my notes remained in the Cavalier. I carried no notebook. I wanted to look unthreatening, wholesome. I stuck my bottom lip out just a tad—a trick to make myself appear charming. It was something I noticed David Duchovny do once in an interview. I'm not a proud man.

Almost immediately, the door opened, and there stood a man with long, dirty-blond hair and a thin, ruggedly handsome face. He looked like a lost surfer.

"Sorry to bother you on a Saturday," I said. "I'm a writer from Cleveland. I'm putting together a book on Amy. Amy Mihaljevic?"

"Right," he said, as if expecting me. Then he turned back into the house. "Dale! Dale, there's a kid out here . . . well, come on in."

I followed the man inside a linoleum-appointed kitchen. In sauntered a larger man, round and tall with dark hair and a smile behind his eyes. *I'll be taking that smile away now*, I thought sadly.

"This guy says he's writing a book about Amy," the lost surfer said.

Dale looked at him and then back at me. The smile faltered. It did not disappear. "Did you speak with my mom?" he said.

"Yes. But Kathy said I shouldn't try to anymore. Said she's been sick."

"Yeah," he said. "But I'm glad you stopped by. Hey, want a beer?"

"Sure."

"Mike, grab us a beer, will you?" He motioned to a table. "Here, have a seat."

Mike returned shortly with a couple of Bud Lights. I cracked one open and took a long swig. Yes. That was better.

"We were watching the game," said Dale. "Or about to."

"Do you mind if I run out to the car and grab some paper," I said, "if you're up to talking?"

"Sure," he said.

When I sat down again, it was Dale who asked the first question. He wanted to know what was new with the case, if there was any fresh information. I told him about my recent encounter with Sam Tillerman, the man who looked so much like the composite sketch.

"Does he own a green van?" Dale asked.

"No, I don't think so," I said. "Was the FBI looking for a green van?"

"They were looking for a green van for a while," he said.

Reports of the vehicle Amy got into at the Bay Village plaza are confusing. I had heard everything from a pickup truck to a minivan. I wasn't sure the FBI had a witness to verify that for sure. Dale couldn't tell me where the "green van" info had come.

"What can you tell me about Amy?" I asked.

Dale snorted a small laugh. " 'Uncle Dale, come see,' " he said. "That's what she was always saying to me. 'Uncle Dale, come see, come see.' I remember visiting Margaret one summer. We all went to the park to swim in the pool, and Amy ran up to me and pulled on my arm. 'Come see, Uncle Dale,' she said. She wanted me to watch her jump off the high board. I'd sure love to hear that again.

"She was a very intellectual girl, just like her mom. I remember Amy always wanted to help with the horses. Give her a shovel and she'd go to town. She liked to work. She liked to help. I remember her laying out back in the snow with my sister one winter. They were making snow angels, and the snow was still falling down. I have a picture of that here somewhere.

"But she was very smart. I think once she knew she was in trouble, there was a battle. And maybe he didn't know what to do with her. So he killed her."

Gooseflesh broke out across my arms. This was the same scenario John Dunn had recently described.

"I went to her funeral, I mean the service they had for her in Bay Village. Nobody knew it, but there were six FBI agents there, in plainclothes. Men wearing long coats with machine guns tucked underneath. I bumped into one accidentally and felt the gun. They figured this guy might come to the funeral.

"That guy didn't kill just one person that day," Dale said. "He killed two. Margaret was never the same. Her health got worse. The last time I saw Margaret, I took her to Martin's Tavern—it's a restaurant around here that only opens when the owner feels like opening. I got her to dance to the accordion up there. I was so proud of her. To see her dancing and smiling again. This was right before she died.

"They're both buried up here. They share a plot. Margaret rests on top of Amy's ashes. And Amy's the only girl in the whole cemetery that was allowed to be buried with a personal item. She was buried with her teddy bear. Kathy did that. She convinced the people in charge to make an exception."

I thanked him for the beers and stood up.

"Do me favor," said Dale. "Don't make Margaret out to be . . . well, we all have our hang-ups, you know?"

"Anyone who thinks they can write off Margaret as just some alcoholic is small-minded," I said by way of a response. "Anyone who knows an alcoholic knows better than that. Your sister was a smart, beautiful woman. If Amy hadn't been taken, she would have done well. That's obvious. I am sorry for your loss."

Dale nodded, and I left.

Highland Memorial Park sits on the border of West Allis and West Berlin. It's a sprawling, well-maintained garden full of flat tombstones planted upon a gradual hill. Elm trees and scattered oaks cast such bright color, it was difficult to feel despondent. It's a beautiful place to sleep forever.

Amy's grave is located in the Mihaljevic family subsection of the park. Section 25, twenty-three rows in. While all the markers are placed at regular intervals as far as the eye can see, the symmetry is broken here. Two markers share the ground in this spot. The date of death listed for Amy is February 8, 1990. FOREVER IN OUR HEARTS, the epitaph reads. Margaret's reads: FOREVER AT PEACE.

I placed a single rose upon each tombstone. I said what I wanted to say to each, and then I returned to Ohio.

CHAPTER TWENTY-SEVEN

Sixteen Years

SIXTEEN YEARS AFTER Amy was taken from the Bay Village shopping plaza, I sat in the parking lot and waited for her killer to return.

I took a spot in front of the convenience store, where I could watch both Amy's memorial across the street and the storefront of the video store that was Baskin-Robbins back in 1989. It was early, just before 8 a.m.

Amy's killer visiting her memorial on the anniversary of the crime is a bit of a Hollywood cliché, and so I didn't really place much hope in the stakeout. But I was also waiting for something else.

So far, I had not discovered any further information concerning the perplexing Sam Tillerman of Ashland County. All I knew was that he once ran a plumbing business with some unknown partner. If anyone could tell me about Tillerman, it was this ex-partner. Except I could think of no way to trace their defunct business back to 1990. After spending a few nights thinking this problem over as I fell asleep, an idea occurred to me. I had no way of calling *him*, but maybe I could make him call *me*.

I drafted a letter to the editor of the *Ashland Times Gazette*. I explained my intentions, and they agreed to publish my letter on October 27. It ran as follows:

Sixteen years ago today, ten-year-old Amy Renee Mihaljevic was abducted from a small shopping plaza in Bay Village by a man who claimed to work with her mother. It was a lie, of course. Her decomposed body was found three months later off County Road 1181 in Ashland County.

Amy loved horses. She liked to ride her blue bicycle to Holly Hill Farms where she spent hours with Razzle, learning to jump small obstacles. She loved pizza. She loved to watch *The Monkees* on

Nickelodeon, curled up in a ball at her friend's house after school. When she smiled, Amy tilted her head sideways—a womanly gesture that would have broken hearts had she lived to be a teenager.

After her abduction, her mother, Margaret, worked as a victim's advocate, helping other families cope with kidnappings and murders. She's dead now, too. Her body was ravaged by lupus and she died, alone, in a Las Vegas apartment in 2001. She died without closure.

We still don't know who stabbed Amy to death in 1989. There are suspects. Some of them live in Ashland County. I've spent the last year researching a book on Amy's abduction and like the FBI agents and the Bay Village detectives still working the case, I have my suspicions. But no one has ever been charged.

Recently, the FBI and Bay Village Police Department released new details about the case which they think might be very important. When Amy was taken, she wore green horse-head earrings and black ankle boots with silver studs running down the sides. She carried a black leather binder with "Best in Class" written on a gold snap. These items were not found with her body. Also missing: a white nylon windbreaker and a blue denim book bag with red piping. The killer may have kept them as tokens. Perhaps you have seen one of these things.

FBI profilers suggest that the person who did this would have showed signs of stress leading to or following the abduction on October 27, 1989 or the discovery of her body on February 8, 1990. The profilers suggest this person may have suddenly found religion, hoping to absolve their guilt. They might have started drinking heavily. Their weight might have fluctuated drastically. There might have been a sudden and drastic change in their physical appearance. Did you notice anything like this?

It's also quite possible that over the years, the killer confided in someone. The guilt might have been too much to handle alone.

If that is the case, if that person is reading this letter, the time to come forward is now. We need closure. The fine men and women at the FBI and Bay Village Police Department will be knocking on your door eventually. Why not save yourself that trouble and do a good thing today?

If you have any information concerning Amy's abduction and murder 16 years ago, please contact me [I included my cell phone number]. The FBI at 216-522-1400. Or, the Bay Village Police Department at 440-871-1234.

Thank you.

Sincerely,

James Renner

It was my best attempt at a covert and guarded communiqué to this missing partner.

My cell phone rang at precisely noon.

"This James Renner?" a man asked gruffly on the other end.

I said it was.

"I just read your article in the paper. And there's this thing that's been bothering me all these years. You see, I was in business with a man named Sam Tillerman."

Never in my life has a plan worked out so perfectly. I mistrusted it immediately.

"I've heard of him," I said. "And I was hoping you'd call."

"Sam had a nervous breakdown around the time Amy's body turned up," he said. As he spoke to me, I watched occasional joggers pass the memorial across the street, none giving it a second glance.

"I don't know if you've ever seen him, but he's a dead ringer for that composite sketch. For a while after the body was found, Sam would show up for work saying the FBI was tailing him. He got really upset about it. I didn't believe him, though, so I set at the end of his road one day and watched an FBI car park in front of his house and wait for him to leave again. I didn't know what to think. Scared me so bad, I took my .357 down to the shop with me after that. Sam went into the hospital shortly after that. That's Richland County Hospital out on Route 39.

"Three months later, he came out. He was a zombie. I knew him for twelve years. I gave him half my company. But he wasn't the same when he came out. I had to let him go. He was in Vietnam, you know. Maybe that's all it was. I just couldn't see him doing that to a little girl."

"Let me ask you something," I interjected. "Did Sam have any connection to Bay Village that you know of?"

"At the time Amy come up missing, Sam was driving to Cleveland every day. His wife had a complicated pregnancy and was up at the Cleveland Clinic. Yes, he was making trips to Cleveland at that time in his brown van. That and his resemblance made me very suspicious. Like I said he wasn't the same after all that. His mind just went, *shhhhhooooo!* So I gave him half the equipment and $7,500.

"I talked to him a couple times after that. He said the FBI did finally come up to his house and question him. Said he was cleared by the FBI. And I think he's doing all right. He's a happy guy after he takes his pill."

It was the call I had hoped for, but there were no real answers. The fact that Tillerman made regular trips to the Cleveland area around the time of Amy's abduction was interesting, sure. Still, there was no direct connection to the Mihaljevics. How far was I willing to follow this thread? The last thing I wanted to do was take another trip down the rabbit hole.

I took notes of our conversation and filed them away. Maybe later some connection would present itself.

The phone rang again. True to his promise, Brannon had done his part to mend fences. It was Wrenn.

Though it went unsaid, we both knew what day it was. I was aware, too, that I did not know what this retired agent looked like. For all I knew, he was calling me from inside the coffee shop, watching me watch the memorial. Maybe that's not quite what happened, but I strongly believe he knew where I was at that moment.

"Do you have time to meet with me?" I asked.

"No," he said. "I'm still not interested in that. I'm not mad. I just wanted you to know you got a couple things wrong in that article. No one ever found that horse-head earring. And I wasn't furious with Robert Ressler. We just didn't think at the time what he did was appropriate."

That was about the extent of our conversation. I took two things away from it. One, I detected a small amount of respect in his voice for the first time. Was that because I was in the good graces of his former boss or because he knew I was sitting in a car, trying to wait out the killer? And two, his choice of words with the phrase "We just didn't think at the time . . ." We who? More important, "at the time" implied a change of opinion. What exactly was he telling me?

That sense of being watched only intensified when Lieutenant Spaetzel called a few minutes later.

"I just wanted to tell you to be careful," he said. "Especially if you talk to any of the witnesses."

"All right," I said. "Can you tell me something since we're on the phone? Do you know anything about this Sam Tillerman guy from Ashland County?"

"I'm afraid I can't help you anymore. I don't want to comment on any of the suspects. There are names we don't want out there."

Effectively, Bay Village had washed its hands of my investigation. I felt paranoid and alone.

The eclipse of time between the present and the moment Amy was abducted ended somewhere around 3 p.m. Since eight o'clock, I had seen no one approach the memorial. If her murderer was replaying events, he would no longer be in this area. Where, then? Euclid Mall, perhaps? Mark remembered authorities discovering a call to the house that had originated from the mall in the days leading up to Amy's last. Could that be where he meant to take her to buy a present for Margaret, to win the girl's trust? Seemed like a stretch at best. No, there was one more place that man might visit today.

I drove toward Ashland County. The trip usually takes about an hour. Thanks to construction on the highway, it was closer to an hour and a half before I pulled onto County Road 1181. The delay gave me time to consider an important point: on a Friday, the day on which October 27 fell in 1989, it would have been worse. Rush hour comes early on Fridays, as eager weekenders rush home to their families. It's possible the killer found himself in such a predicament (assuming he drove her directly out to this secluded stretch of road). Forgetting to take Friday traffic into account could have set his timeline behind a little bit. Perhaps he returned home late that night and someone noticed.

About a half mile down the country road, a land bridge crosses the ditch on the eastern side, a service entrance to a field of harvested corn. I wheeled my car into this spot, as it provided a nice position from which to monitor the site where Janet Seabold found Amy's body. The killer, or whoever brought Amy's body there, more than likely came from Route 224, as that is the road most traveled. If he returned the same way this evening, he would not be able to see my vehicle.

It was twilight. As it grew darker, I turned on NPR and listened to an interview with some celebrity's boyfriend, broadcast from another dimension that cared about those things. After an hour, a pickup truck pulled in from the road closest to me and bounded down 1181 toward Route 224. Then I was alone again for quite some time. Even in 2005, this is a desolate section of the Buckeye State. A cold, lonely place. I thought again of the length of time that passed before Amy died of her wounds. She had been hit on the head with a blunt object. Hopefully, it had knocked her out cold, forever. The thought that she knew her death was coming for as long as thirty minutes is too much to take.

I sat there, in that field, in that fucking car listening to humanity on the radio, waiting for a killer who never showed, for another five hours.

"I'm sorry," I said meekly, to no one, as I set out for home at eleven that night.

Naturally, nothing came in the way of a reply.

Looking back on that night, though, I'm not so sure I didn't get the answer I was looking for. After all, no one showed. That says something, too, when you consider certain suspects.

CHAPTER TWENTY-EIGHT

New Job, New Lead

"DO YOU WANT A JOB?" Frank asked.

My old editor thought of me when a staff writer position opened up at the *Free Times* at the end of October. Even though I still felt exhausted every time I thought about *Scene*, I took the gig. Mostly, I did so because I wanted to tell a couple stories that *Scene* had rejected. The one about the old man from Mansfield who found a robot while cleaning out his father's basement, perhaps. Or the one about the prosecutor from Cleveland who disappeared in Pennsylvania under mysterious circumstances. I thought it would be nice to work with Frank again.

Frank and the other editors liked the missing prosecutor story. I was sent out to report on it.

It was a long drive down I-76 into Pennsylvania in search of District Attorney Ray Gricar (who once prosecuted a truck-stop serial killer investigated by Ashland County detective Roger Martin). But I had a lot to occupy my mind. I had recently received a phone call from a woman named Amy P. (She asked that I not use her full name.) If Amy Mihaljevic had not been abducted that day in 1989, she would have gone to this girl's house for a sleepover.

Amy P. was angry, mainly because I dragged Margaret's drinking problem into the article. It didn't matter that the *Plain Dealer* reported in 2001 that Margaret had died from alcoholism.

"You shouldn't have talked about it," she said. "It didn't have anything to do with it. You should have just talked about Amy."

I told her when it came to tracking down Amy's killer, I didn't really care if I upset a few people. I told her if all the information was spread out on the table instead of locked in some closet, maybe the solution would present itself. I may not be the person who solves this case, but if I wrote about everything I discovered, perhaps it would make enough sense to the individual who's holding the missing piece of the puzzle.

"What can you tell me about Amy?" I asked.

"She was a very intelligent girl," Amy P. said. "I don't know that she would have gone with somebody she didn't know."

"Were you there, at Baskin-Robbins, with Amy?" I asked.

"No," she said.

I had the sense she was hedging her answers somehow. First of all, who exactly was she? She was in the Bay Village yearbook, sure, but why had I not heard her name from Amy's other friends? "Did you know Kristy Sabo or Kristen Balas?" I said.

"I played baseball with Balas. Yeah, I knew Sabo. Heard she was a stripper right after high school."

At least Kristy Sabo never hedged her answers when she talked with me. She had more reasons to distrust reporters than this woman did, and she was always open and honest. I was done beating around the bush.

"You weren't in the plaza that day?" I asked. "You sure about that?"

"I wasn't."

Now, ask her to give you a name and she'll do it just to get you off her back, the smarmy voice that lives inside all writers said to me. *She's scared. It couldn't be more obvious. Give it a try.*

"You told me Amy was going to a sleepover at your house that night," I said. "But you weren't walking with Amy to the plaza after school? You weren't just going to spend the day with her?"

"No. She was going to come over later."

"But you also said you didn't know about this meeting she had with this man that picked her up. She told Kristen Balas about it but not you?"

"She never said two words to me about it."

"That doesn't make any sense. What did she tell you she was doing, then?"

"I don't . . ."

"Who was at the plaza that day if you weren't? Who *was* with Amy?"

Without even a pause, without an ounce of hesitation, she dropped the name I had searched all of Bay Village for—the witness to Amy's abduction.

* * *

Just past the Pennsylvania border, my cell phone rang again, rousing me from a daydream of revenge. The caller had a 419 prefix. That meant it was coming from Ashland.

It was a man named Bill Hayes. He lived in Ashland County and had kept my newspaper article from the *Times Gazette* with him for a week before he summoned the nerve to call.

"I knew a gentleman of a shady character," he began. "Though I wasn't the greatest person myself. In my own little cheap way, I was hurting people, too. I never had nothing to do with *physically* harming anyone. But I was into the drugs and booze and all that for a while. I guess I'm one of the misfits of Ashland County.

"Look, when that all went down with the girl being found out there, my wife—she wasn't my wife then, though—I cried to my wife, I knew this guy, name of Al Matlock. Friend of mine. This Al was picked up and questioned by the cops. When they found that girl's body, Al was at the log cabin a couple hundred yards away—his cousin lived there at the time. We got pot in that cabin from Al's cousin one time. If you watch the news footage from that day, they were shooting the field from a helicopter and you can see Al's white Ford Pinto parked at the cabin.

"Anyway, a couple weeks after they found the body, we—me and Al—were out on a drunk. We went out and got some beer or something like that. I was in the passenger's seat of that white Ford Pinto. After a while, I noticed we were stopped. He said, 'This looks like a good place to smoke a joint.' So we started smoking, and then Al says, 'That's where they found that little bitch. That's where they found that little whore, that little tramp.'

"Well, I started to sober up real quick when he says that. And that's when I notice he has us parked next to the place where they found her body. I said, 'What? What the fuck are we doing here? They're watching this spot! Get me the fuck out of here, now! We'll go to jail if we sit here.' 'Ah, she's dead and forgotten about,' he says.

"From that day on, it's bothered me. Why would he even talk about her like that?"

Good question, I thought. "Did Al have any connection to Cleveland?"

"Well, one time we got together, and he said his friends Dave and Sandy had some really good pot. 'Where?' I asked him. 'Cleveland,' he says. It was in Westlake, though. Sandy was a really pretty woman. She offered me a drink and this and that. Meanwhile, Al and Dave, them two were off by themselves. They were whispering. 'Don't worry about it,' I heard Dave say to Al. 'Nobody's going to know nothing.'

"I think all this happened over about two months. And it's been fifteen years now since I had a drink."

"Is there anything else you can tell me about Al Matlock?" I asked.

He thought for a moment. "His aunt, the one he was living with out here, she made the best sausage and biscuits. But she made it out of squirrel. It was absolutely delicious. Man, it was the sweetest meat. I made a pig of myself."

"About Al and his business with the body," I said.

"I was told the cops found his coat by the body," Hayes said. "Fifty or a hundred feet away. His name or initials were sewn into the coat."

Of course that could be a misunderstanding. After all, "A.M." stands for both Al Matlock *and* Amy Mihaljevic. The symmetry gave me goose bumps, though.

"I knew in my heart all these years that Al was involved," he said.

I was beginning to believe him.

CHAPTER TWENTY-NINE

The Cavalry

AL MATLOCK WAS NOWHERE to be found. I was also having trouble finding an address or phone number for the woman who, according to Amy P., was a witness to Amy's abduction—a young woman I'll refer to as "Maddie." So I called in the cavalry.

Without a doubt, the smartest thing I did as a reporter was write an article about a private eye named Mike Lewis. Lewis ran an outfit called Confidential Investigative Services and was kind enough to tell me stories of cheating spouses for a special *Scene* Valentine's Day news piece. The article generated a certain amount of business and made Lewis happy. "Let me know if there's anything I can do for you," he said.

"I need help finding a few people," I told Lewis when I reached him by phone in November. When I started to tell him about Amy's case he stopped me short.

"Can you meet me at the Bob Evans in Willoughby tomorrow night?" he asked. "I'll bring my partner along and you can tell us both about it."

Meeting a pair of private investigators in some public place really puts a different spin on the whole restaurant experience. For one thing, how often does this happen? How many of those couples we sit next to at Longhorn Steakhouse or Applebee's—how many of those couples are actually a detective and his client, some spouse worried about a cheating husband? Secondly, there's this game Lewis and his partner like to play.

"Lookee there," Lewis said. He's a big man, with muscles pushing out of his shirt, under a thick neck. He was smiling, though, looking at a table behind me. As he said this, Lewis nudged his partner, a young man, probably not yet thirty, with short dark hair and not enough stubble at five in the evening to require shaving. I followed their gaze to a middle-aged man sitting across from a middle-aged woman.

Lewis's protégé nodded. "Uh huh," he said.

"What?" I said.

"They're having an affair," Lewis said.

I looked at them again. To me they appeared to be just another couple out for a cheap meal. "How can you tell?"

Lewis shrugged. "It becomes second nature," he said. "It's in their body language. The way she touches his hand whenever it gets close to hers. The way he looks at her and then around at the restaurant. Married couples don't work like that."

God, that depressed me. I looked around the room at all the secret perverts on secret dates. That stuff will make a person paranoid.

"Tell us about Amy," Lewis said.

And so I did.

By the time I was done, they had learned all the major plot points and I had learned the younger man's name was Dan Washington.

"We want to help you in any way we can," Washington said.

Lewis nodded. "No charge. You can just call us consultants or something."

I told them that sounded fine. I said I'd throw in the Bob Evans as a bonus.

Lewis asked me what I needed, and I handed them each a short list of names. Al Matlock was on there. Maddie's real name was too, along with Sam Tillerman and a number of Amy's childhood friends I couldn't track down. "Can you find these people for me?" I said. "And can you tell me if the men on that list have criminal records?"

"Get it to you by tomorrow afternoon," said Lewis. "E-mail fine?"

"E-mail's great," I said.

I noticed Lewis was suddenly distracted by another couple just ordering food. He looked at Dan and smiled. Lewis will never want for business.

Sure enough, the e-mails arrived the next morning. Maddie's profile contained her address and phone number as well as those of her neighbors, going back ten years. Her height and weight were included too, taken, no doubt, from reports through the Department of Motor Vehicles.

Amy's friends—Renee Moran, Elizabeth Jeffers, Cindy Meeks—were located, too.

"I want you to notice that all of these women are still unmarried," Lewis wrote in one e-mail. "That's pretty unusual. That says to me this incident was pretty traumatic to anyone that was close to Amy. So, just watch how you approach them."

Sam Tillerman's background was clean.

Al Matlock's was more interesting. "He's not very integrated with society," Lewis wrote. "So it will take a little bit of detective work to find him. I didn't even find a date of birth on this guy."

What he did find was a number of addresses and post office boxes listed under Matlock's real name—Alvin—in Indiana, Florida, Kentucky, and several hamlets in Northeast Ohio. Alvin Matlock's most current address was somewhere in Savannah, Ohio, a short drive from County Road 1181. It also appeared he had a close relative named Wayne Doyle Matlock. A brother, perhaps, or a cousin.

Not long after I learned of Matlock's nomadic wanderings, I got another tip from Ashland County. "Are you looking into [the Amy Mihaljevic case]?" asked a man named Don Parsons, who'd also seen the article in the *Times Gazette*.

"I am."

"Well, did anyone tell you about the videotape yet?"

"What videotape?"

"The one that shows Amy. The child porn tape?"

"Are you saying you've seen a video of Amy Mihaljevic?"

"Not me," he said. "But I know people who did. If you come out here, I'll give you all the proof you need."

"I wouldn't trust this guy," Lewis said, when I told him about the phone call. "Where did he want to meet?"

"At a farmhouse out on State Route 60."

"No. This might be an ambush for all we know. This guy could be Matlock, himself. If you're going out there, we'll go with you."

"You wouldn't mind taking a few hours out of your day?" I said.

"No," Lewis said. "Sounds fun."

Even though I wasn't a week into my job at the *Free Times*, Frank let me take off for the afternoon to search for evidence of Amy's murder in the Ohio backcountry. My adrenaline already amping up, I drove out to meet Lewis and Dan at a suburban Applebee's. I left my car behind and climbed into Lewis's Lincoln Town Car. It smelled like a vehicle that was lived in. Not bad, but musty. Most of their job consists of late-night stakeouts. With the windows tinted as strongly as they were, it's likely they could go unnoticed for as long as they wanted.

"Ready?" Lewis said. Beside him, Dan looked as excited as I felt. It seemed like a bad omen to me. No way could it be this easy. No way were we driving out to take down Amy's killer today.

"Yeah," I said. "But I don't carry any weapons. Not even a pocket knife."

"Dan, you packin'?" Lewis asked.

"No," he said.

"That's all right," Lewis said. "I am. Let's go."

Don Parsons lived in a trailer set up on blocks behind a farmhouse in New London, Ohio. When Lewis pulled the Town Car into the driveway an hour later, Parsons was outside, waiting. He was a short fellow, rugged looking, like a guy who has worked outdoors his entire life, shaping the land. On his head was a tan army cap. Two other men stood on either side of him. They were older than Parsons and taller, dressed in jeans and long-sleeved flannel shirts. Their lanky bodies framed the smaller fellow nicely. They appeared to be identical twins.

"Looks like they were hoping for a little three-on-one action," Lewis said. Then to Dan: "Keep your eyes open."

We got out of the vehicle. Parsons approached Lewis, with his hand out in greeting. "James? I'm Don Parsons."

Lewis shook his hand and told him he had the wrong guy. I introduced myself and then Parsons introduced Terry and Jerry. Apparently, we both had bodyguards that day.

Parsons led everyone to a semicircle of plastic chairs and wooden rockers. There, the detectives took a seat on either side of me while Parsons and the twins remained standing. Terry and Jerry wouldn't give out their last names, referring to themselves only as "concerned citizens." Terry said he had retired five years earlier from a well-drilling business after an injury. Jerry said he had recently been laid off from a local golf course. Sleuthing was their hobby.

"So, tell us about the tape," I said.

"Chief Deputy Roger Martin knows all about it," Parsons said. "But by the time he got a warrant to search the safe at the restaurant where it was being kept, the tape was gone."

"What else is going on out here?" Lewis asked, sitting up in his rocker a little.

"Well," Parsons began, haltingly.

"Tell him," Terry prompted.

"I used to work as a federal investigator," Parsons said. "I discovered this company out here was making junk life vests, life vests that's wouldn't work when they got wet. But when I turned them in, the sheriff here arrested me and threw me in jail. They tortured me so I wouldn't talk. They brought women to my jail cell and forced me to have sex with minors."

I looked over to Lewis. Lewis looked at Dan. Our eyes all said the same thing. *This is crazy. And the other two believe him.*

We let Parsons talk for a while. He outlined a wild, sweeping conspiracy. It involved paying a kidnapped woman's ransom with his farmhouse and being run down on the street by an FBI informant. Eventually, the ranting became too much for any of us to handle, and I stood up to leave.

"Thanks for your time," I said to the men and walked back to the Town Car. I waited for Lewis and Dan to say their own strained good-byes.

"What was that?" Dan asked, once we were back on the road, heading back toward the land of the sane.

"Guys, I'm sorry I wasted your time," I said. "I should have sensed that man was nuts over the phone. I guess I got a little excited."

"Well, he had Terry and Jerry convinced," Lewis said. "And it seems to make sense to him. Gotta feel sorry for the guy."

I felt awful all the same. And it would be a long time before I asked Lewis for another favor.

CHAPTER THIRTY

Strange Characters in the Firelands

CAPTAIN ROGER MARTIN was amused by the report of my meeting with Don Parsons and the twins from New London. He'd dealt with Parsons before, though he had "never heard *that* story." On the subject of Alvin D. Matlock, he was slightly more interested.

"Few years ago, Alvin come up missing," Martin said over the phone. "We still have a warrant out for him on a theft charge. Last I heard, he was maybe in West Virginia. He was drinker, a small-town punk. I can see him trying to impress someone with a story about killing a girl. I can see him doing that. Doesn't mean he did, though."

Luckily, the phone calls kept coming.

A woman named Paula Varney called me one evening as I sat down to eat supper with Julie, who, thankfully, still found my obsessions endearing. Shutting the door to my home office, I asked Varney to repeat what she'd just said.

"Margaret Mihaljevic was down here, in Ashland, about two years before Amy disappeared," the woman said, her voice a bit harsh, a familiar bluntness I'd encountered in many rural matriarchs while reporting.

"How do you know that?" I asked.

"Well, it's a little complicated. But let me try to explain," she said. "There's a woman here named Pat Stokes. Pat was over at the house of a woman named Joanne Stillion one day, not far from County Road 1181. While Pat was at Joanne's, Margaret Mihaljevic shows up. She's selling raffle tickets. She knew Joanne from when Joanne lived near Bay Village. But Pat thought Margaret also knew Joanne's friend Bud. Bud lived in a log cabin at the corner of County Road 1181 and Township Road 126. He was Alvin Matlock's uncle."

My head spun almost painfully as I tried to digest this information. "One more time," I said.

Varney laid out the scenario again. "A woman named Liz Rush can explain it better," she said. "Liz talked to the FBI about this. You should know there was another Matlock. Doyle Wayne Matlock is the other Matlock. He lived with Bud. And he called himself Alvin sometimes. He told everyone around here his older cousin killed Amy."

I got Liz Rush's phone number from her and hung up. Apparently, Wayne Doyle Matlock was also Doyle Wayne Matlock, who sometimes went by his cousin's name: Alvin. And in a roundabout way, according to Varney, Margaret Mihaljevic was friends with a woman who knew Bud, Alvin Matlock's uncle. Hopefully, Liz Rush could make better sense of it.

"I spoke to Detective Spaetzel about this three years ago," Rush said. Her voice sounded gentler, younger. "Mark said he needed a connection between Amy and Matlock, any connection. And then I read your piece in the *Times Gazette*. You called Amy a ragamuffin. That right there. It reminded me of a comment Al Matlock made. 'No one cared about that kid anyway,' he said. Like she wasn't all made up like a girl, you know?

"A woman I knew, Mary Johnson, thought she had information for the FBI, too, so we called them together. Mark Spaetzel and some other guy—Gary maybe—met us at Mary's house three years ago. Mary told them about this guy she met at a flea market in Marion, Ohio. Told her he had to move. So she decided she would let him come live with them. She had two daughters of her own.

"Then one day this guy took a kitten and hung it on the top part of her bed and then sexually pleasured himself on the sheets. When the police went to get this guy he had taken an overdose of drugs and liquor. So, Mary wanted to tell Spaetzel about this guy, and I wanted to talk about Margaret being down here in Ashland. Mark wanted to know if we knew anything about Matlock."

Only more questions. All I could make of it was that Varney and Rush strongly believed Margaret Mihaljevic had been seen at the house of a woman connected with Matlock's uncle. I called Varney back for further clarification, such as there was.

"The day Joanne Stillion died, she told Pat Stokes that they'll find out it was Bud's boy that killed Amy," she said. "I didn't see Margaret myself, but Pat Stokes did."

I found Stokes's number in the book. An elderly woman answered the phone. I managed to explain why I was calling in a sentence or two before she cut me off.

"I don't think they want anyone to know about that," she snapped. "I talked to the FBI, and they said not to talk about it."

"Are you saying you did see Margaret Mihaljevic at Joanne Stillion's house before Amy disappeared?"

"Yeah, I seen her," Stokes said, and then she hung up.

At this point, names meant little. Wayne Matlock was also Doyle Matlock. But Wayne masqueraded as his cousin for some time, too. It took a concerted effort to keep the cousins separate in my mind. It was obvious they were being confused by a number of people. Easy enough to do after sixteen years, even when one wasn't pretending to be the other. In the end, it came to this: Many people in Ashland County were convinced one or both of the Matlock boys had something to do with Amy's murder. And the Matlocks were only two degrees of separation from the Mihaljevics.

If Margaret came to Ashland, what's the possibility she brought Amy with her? Pretty good, I thought. Friends of the family say Amy was practically Margaret's shadow, especially when she was a little younger. If Margaret was in Ashland, Amy probably was, too.

Frustrated with the lack of bread crumbs leading back to Alvin Matlock, I decided to try finding Wayne. On a whim, I entered his name into Google. What appeared on-screen was shocking, but not exactly surprising. Wayne was in jail, charged with the murder of his girlfriend. Death by stabbing.

According to articles from the *Lorain Morning Journal* and the *Toledo Blade*, Wayne Matlock lived in Polk, Ohio, in February of 2005. His sometime girlfriend, Lori Ann Wright, lived in the nearby nowhere burg of Greenwich. Wright was apparently leaving him for good when Doyle showed up at her apartment on February 28, 2005, and a "domestic squabble" ensued. Doyle stabbed Wright more than twenty times in the head, chest, and right arm. He attacked her with such force, the knife blade broke off in her skull.

Deciding to turn himself in, Doyle specifically sought out Greenwich chief of police Kevin Verberg, whom he had met around town. He was arrested and charged, and ultimately struck a plea deal with prosecutors. He pled guilty in exchange for a recommendation of twenty years to life in prison. Sentencing would be delivered in a matter of weeks in the Huron County Court of Common Pleas.

I immediately placed a call to Chief Verberg at the Greenwich police station.

"When we spoke with him, Doyle was very evasive about his family connections," Verberg said. "I believe he has two sisters. Mother lives in Cleveland, I think. And he has two kids from another lady. From what I understand, he grew up with grandparents. I think Doyle did make a reference to the search for Amy Mihaljevic. He lived nearby where she was found. He was somebody who always wanted to be a police officer, so I think that's why he was interested. Nobody wants to leave this earth without leaving a little bit of a mark. It's strange, though, how things come around sometimes."

Verberg wouldn't arrange for me to meet with Doyle personally but agreed to take a list of questions by e-mail that he would ask Doyle after sentencing. Sensing Verberg was a man of his word, I sent him the list of questions and waited.

I also placed a call to the Huron County Sheriff's Department, where a deputy spoke to me on the condition I not use his name.

"Doyle originally lived not far from where Amy was from, and then moved to a house not far from where her body was found," he said.

"Are you saying Doyle Matlock was from Bay Village?" I asked.

"Amherst."

Indeed, it checked out. Doyle had lived in Amherst, a suburb near Bay Village, when Amy was still alive. I found his father still living in Amherst. "Bud" was apparently not his father—or Alvin's uncle—but a relative of another sort. The father didn't want to talk about Wayne. And he hadn't seen Alvin in many years.

In the weeks leading up to Doyle's sentencing, I made another trip out to Ashland County to visit with Paula Varney, to learn more about the Matlocks' connection to Margaret Mihaljevic. Varney owns a small shop that sits off State Route 224 at a crossroads that sees little traffic. Most days her husband mans the counter, selling "tobacco enhancers" and water pipes and black-light posters while Varney watches TV in the section of the store they have converted into their home.

I sat in their living room, several feet behind the bongs and other merchandise, and spoke to her for a half-hour.

"Six years ago, a guy from Bay Village came in here on his way to visit his aunt, who lives out on one-twenty-six. He saw the poster of Amy and then the composite sketch of her kidnapper that I had hanging behind the cash register. He said, 'Yeah, I know that guy.'"

Varney described the man for me. He was about five feet, nine inches tall, with dark hair under a ball cap. He had a boyish look to him.

"He said a cop was involved in it," Varney explained. "Said Amy was held at his [the cop's] house. Then, he grabs this pad of paper and draws me a map."

I had heard the cop rumor before but didn't lend it much credence. All the cops in the city were accounted for that day. Most of them were in a meeting at the town hall. But I took a copy of the map and filed it away. It sat, forgotten, in the back of a folder for many months.

On the morning of Doyle's sentencing, the streets of New London were empty, the false-fronted business district shadowed by winter clouds, gray as oiled snow. The Huron County courthouse is an old building, marble and concrete, and inside it's kept suffocatingly warm. On a wall on the second floor was a sectioned mural depicting rough-hewn landscapes of surrounding towns, including Greenwich, New London, and the section of Ruggles where Amy's body turned up. It was a giant painted history of Huron County titled *The Survey of the Fire Lands*.

A plaque underneath read as follows:

In the summer of 1808, Almon Ruggles started surveying at the southeast corner of the Connecticut Western Reserve, previously established by Maxfield Ludlow. The survey then continued eastward. The field books of both Ludlow and Ruggles expressed the difficult task that these men performed. One entry that illustrates this was found in Ludlow's notes describing the area in the Willard Marsh . . . "Sat a post in Hell. I have traveled the woods for 7 years, but never before saw so hideous a place as this."

Amen.

As I waited for the courtroom to open, a man in uniform ascended the stairs and walked toward me. He was an older gentleman with narrow eyes and a pleasant just-my-job expression. The gold plate on his shirt read: VERBERG.

"Chief!" I called.

"Ah, yes. Nice to meet you," he said. "They just brought Matlock in. I've got your questions. Should be time afterwards for me to speak with him a bit."

"Is this a rare thing for your town, for Greenwich? Murders, I mean."

"Been busy, lately," Verberg said.

"Something in the water?" I meant it to sound tongue in cheek, but he nodded seriously.

"I've heard that recently," he said. "Beginning to think maybe there's something to it."

Verberg walked into the courtroom then. I followed close behind.

The courtroom had a tall ceiling and white spackled walls over dark wood trim that ended three feet from the floor. Large glass globes hung from the ceiling like dim planets. Seated just in front of us were three men in orange jumpers. Not having seen a picture of Doyle before, I couldn't tell which was him. Doyle was scheduled last, so I was forced to sit through the sentencing of a man who had raped his daughter, and of another man who had been caught with a crack pipe shortly after his release from prison. I can't imagine the spiritual strength it takes to work as a lawyer or judge or policeman. If I had to watch that sort of thing day after day, I'd start to think these people make up the majority of the population. I'd rather continue to believe such people are the exception, not the rule.

Finally, it was Doyle's turn. He stood up, and for the first time I caught a good long look at one of the "Matlock boys." Doyle was diminutive—probably not much more than five feet and a couple inches, 140 pounds dripping wet. He had curly dark hair. His lawyer told the judge that Doyle had been in jail for exactly 313 days since the crime. Doyle had turned forty just the day before.

When it was his turn to say something, Doyle mumbled, "I just want to apologize to the court and everyone who cared about Lori."

From behind me came muffled sobs from Lori's family. No one was there for Doyle.

The judge gave him twenty-five to life with a flick of the gavel, and the room emptied. Doyle was led through a separate door. I left, too.

"I talked to Matlock for about three hours," Verberg said over the phone a few days later. "I tried to get him to talk about Amy Mihaljevic. He said his uncle lived near the intersection where Amy was found [1181 and 126]. His cousin lives in Kentucky. It was a little bit weird. He broke down a couple times toward the end. I think that was just the realization that his life is determined for the next twenty-five years. I don't think he'll survive in prison."

"Did he say anything more about Amy?" I asked.

"He said he heard it on a radio scanner when they found her," Verberg said. "He went to his cousin's house to tell him the road would be blocked by the cops soon. He knows how cops work."

Two questions came to me then. First, why had Doyle been listening to a police scanner at 7:30 in the morning? Second, why did he want his cousin to know the road would be blocked? Did he want his cousin to leave?

Chief Verberg, however, was fresh out of answers.

For a moment, Alvin Matlock seemed like my most promising lead—that is, until I spoke with a woman who had worked as a volunteer inside the Bay Village police station for the duration of the search following Amy's abduction. That woman revealed to me a dark secret she had not shared with the FBI, a secret that returned my attention to Billy Strunak.

CHAPTER THIRTY-ONE

Stephanie's Story

ONE OF THE UNSUNG HEROES of the search for Amy was Howard Kimball. Kimball was the volunteer chairman of the city's youth commission. He ran the children's center behind city hall, where Boy Scout troops and Brownies meetings were hosted. The day after Amy was kidnapped, he spoke to police about organizing citizens to help with searches. They let him set up a room at the police station, where he could photocopy missing posters and serve as a liaison with media and community. His trusted assistant was a woman named Stephanie Sunseri. (She has since remarried and changed her name.)

Stephanie was a longtime Bay resident. Married, one child, a son. She was a housewife who saw the reports of Amy's abduction and became obsessed with helping bring the girl home.

It was actually Dick Wrenn's displeasure with my article for *Scene* that led me to this woman. I had said the FBI command post was on the second floor and the volunteers were set up in the basement. In actuality, it was the reverse—a minor detail, but one that rankled him a bit. I wanted to get a better picture of the command center this time. So I found Stephanie's name among a list of full-time volunteers and tracked her down, a good move for many reasons, not the least of which was that this woman wouldn't stop talking. She, too, had been waiting sixteen years to tell everything she knew.

Stephanie's job as a volunteer had been contacting large corporations throughout the country by mail and phone and asking them to include Amy's missing poster in their mailers.

"I contacted all sorts of trucking lines," Stephanie said, her voice warm and motherly. "I got Bonne Bell, the Westlake cosmetic company, to put flyers in with their orders. We sent over a hundred thousand flyers through different companies."

She recalled that Howard Kimball had driven to the Cleveland airport once to meet up with John Walsh, host of *America's Most Wanted*. After much coaxing from Kimball, Walsh agreed to air Amy's photo and a description of her abductor on his program.

"Howard just thought John Walsh was the greatest person on earth, and then Walsh gave him fifteen minutes," Stephanie said. "I think he was kind of hurt."

I had known Billy Strunak helped in the volunteer center, supplying them with paper stolen from BJ's Wholesale Club, where he worked. I knew he was asked to leave for some reason, that he had sent Margaret Mihaljevic trinkets in the mail—necklaces pilfered from his employer. Stephanie remembered him well.

"He was my worst nightmare," she said. "He came in out of the blue one day and said that he could bring us paper. Then he kind of hung out. I had a desk in the corner and he would just sit and stare at me.

"Bill always wore long-sleeve shirts, because of his psoriasis. He had reddish patches on his face and hands. He was small, too. About five-seven. Medium build, not slight. And he had blondish hair. He would sit and pick at his fingers until they bled. Kind of a twitchy guy.

"Bill told me he liked to go to college campuses and walk around, looking at women. He liked to go and have lunch out at Lorain Community College. Then he started going out to Ashland University.

"He just had too much interest in Amy. He would ask me, 'What do you think her last hours were like?' I mean, this is when we were still looking for her. He would sit in the office, there, and look at her picture and run his fingers over her face. It just didn't feel right. He asked a lot of questions about Margaret. He was real interested in Margaret's emotions. Margaret would come in once a week to see the new posters and talk with Howard. She came in one time and Billy hugged her and wouldn't let go. He asked Margaret if he could come over and clean her house. And another day, he asked to babysit my son.

"Then, he started bringing me presents.

"First, he just brought me doughnuts and coffee. Then he brought me a book. Then a stuffed animal. I would come in, in the mornings, and there would be things propped up against the door from him. Then he brought me a nightgown. I was married at the time. I told him, 'I can't accept something this personal.'

"He seemed hurt. It was pretty and everything, but that wasn't the point. You really had to explain the hell out of things to make him understand.

"I told Howard Kimball, and Howard sent Billy away. About three days after he was banned from the Amy Center, I found a dead cat placed on the hood of my car. I also got a lot of hang-up phone calls at home. There was something really wrong there. Then we learned he had a conviction for sending porn in the mail.

"He sent me letters that I gave to the police and never got back. They said stuff like 'I'd rather die than hurt you.' The guy was obsessed with me. The dead cat, though—that was the last straw. It was my cat. Its neck was snapped, and it was left for me. And around that time, someone pooped on my porch."

"This whole thing obsessed me. When they found Amy, I couldn't go to her funeral. I couldn't do it. To me, it was the wrong ending. It wasn't the way it was supposed to end. I felt like I let Margaret down. It pretty much ended my marriage, too. My husband didn't understand."

Eventually, I interrupted Stephanie. I felt I had enough information to portray the volunteer center in detail. She'd given me the names of other people with whom I could speak. It seemed like she would go on for hours, circling around the same information, if I didn't pry myself away from the line. Admittedly, this was a bit of a rookie reporter mistake. If someone keeps talking, sometimes it means they're leading you along to something more important, something you'd never guess they knew. I should have let her go on, but I cut her off and said I had to go.

Five minutes later, as I arranged my notes for the evening, Stephanie called my cell phone. I almost didn't answer when I saw her number. *She's probably remembered what she was wearing the first time she met Billy*, I thought. But as soon as I heard her voice again, I knew this would not be a boring conversation. Stephanie had been crying. Her voice was shaky.

"What's wrong?" I asked.

"I want to tell you something," she said. "This has been eating me up inside, and I guess I was waiting for someone to call, but they never did, and so I've had this on my conscience for sixteen years. I don't know why I didn't tell anyone. Or yes I do. I saw what the Mihaljevics went through with the media, and I didn't want that to happen to me. And I don't know if this proves anything, anyway. But it's important. I should have said something by now, I just . . ."

"What is it?' I said. "What happened?"

"Bill Strunak raped me."

"What?"

"The night we had the party at Margaret's, Bill Strunak raped me." My mind tried to process this information. All I could think was that it's pretty easy to implicate someone in a crime who's been dead for sixteen years. Today, it's no longer a "he said, she said" situation. It's just a "she said." If she never reported the rape, what could possibly be done now? Any evidence was long gone. Turned out I was wrong about that, too.

"Nine months later," Stephanie said, her voice just a rough whisper now, "I gave birth to his son."

We met at a Burger King in Elyria so she could tell me, in detail, what she remembered of the night she was raped. I was sitting at a booth overlooking the parking lot when she arrived in an SUV. She climbed out, pulled a large black binder from the passenger seat, and walked inside with deliberate steps. Middle-aged now, she still looked trim and well maintained, like a den mother who works out on the weekends. Her hair was bleached blond by a professional—and regularly enough to not reveal many dark roots. She wore a blue sweater that looked like it cost more than my car.

As she passed through the door, I waved. We introduced ourselves, and I offered to buy her a soda. She accepted: Diet Coke. When I returned, she pushed the black binder toward me.

"Here," she said. "You might find this helpful."

Feeling like an archaeologist uncovering the door to some abandoned treasure, I opened the book. The first thing I noticed was two photos tucked into the inside pocket. One was Amy's fifth-grade picture. The other was the composite sketch. But these weren't copies.

"Are these . . ."

"Originals," she said, nodding. "Or official reproductions of the originals. We used them to make flyers. I think they were made by Bay Village police."

I noticed the composite sketch was dated 10/30/89.

The bulk of the material inside the binder was newspaper clippings pasted to colorful construction paper, clippings from a variety of newspapers across Ohio. The first was dated 10/29/89. The last, 12/31/89. At least a hundred pages.

"This is invaluable," I said.

Stephanie smiled. "You're welcome."

It was hard for her to pinpoint the exact date of her rape, an event she did not want to set in her binder—she knew only that it was sometime between Thanksgiving and Christmas.

"Margaret had a get-together," Stephanie said. "A thank-you. It was at her home on Lindford Drive. I made her a wooden horse, one that mounted on the wall. It galloped. On the back, I wrote, 'For the love of Amy.'

"The party was kind of surreal. Margaret sat in a corner by the fireplace. I don't think she moved out of that chair the whole night. It was too much of a party atmosphere for her, I think. There were probably fifteen or twenty people there. It was very dark inside. And Jason was there, too, but stayed upstairs. Mark stopped by, but he stayed mostly in the kitchen. Margaret was drinking, but she always drank. I left about a quarter to midnight. I had a son who was five or six at the time. So I wanted to get home. There were lots of cars there. So many, you had to park on the street . . .

Stephanie is fishing for her keys when she notices the white van parked behind her car. It's unfamiliar to her and looks like some kind of delivery van. Someone sits behind the steering wheel, watching her draw closer. The shadowy figure leans out the driver's side window. It's Billy Strunak.

"Will you talk to me for a little bit?" Strunak asks.

Annoyed but not yet afraid, Stephanie says, "No" and starts to get into her own vehicle.

"Hey, I'm sorry if I caused any trouble at the Amy Center," he says. "I still want to be involved with the search."

"You'll have to talk to Howard or Lieutenant Wilson," Stephanie says. "It's late, Billy. I have to go home."

"Why don't you come inside the van and talk to me for a little bit?" Strunak leans out the window even more, one hand dangling outside. A set of keys reflects the light of the streetlamps along Lindford Drive.

"I said I can't, I have to . . ."

Stephanie watches the keys fall to the pavement, ringing loudly in the night as they land. Her first thought is that this is an excuse for him to get out of the van, so she moves for the keys to retrieve them instead.

"Stay there," she says. "I'll get them."

Stephanie bends down toward the keys. When she does, the driver's side door shoots open. The mirror hits her face with enough force to knock her to the ground. Blood shoots out of a nose she can only assume is broken.

Strunak steps out quickly and grabs the woman, rushing her toward the back door of his van, murmuring apologies. "I'm sorry," he says. "I didn't mean to hit you with the door." He opens the latch on the back and sits Stephanie down inside. "Stay here. I'll get help."

Strunak turns to leave, then spins around and punches Stephanie in the nose with a balled-up fist. Stephanie feels her head connect with the interior of the van before she passes out.

As she comes to, she can feel the movement of the van and knows Strunak is driving them away from the Mihaljevic house. There are no seats in the back of the van. The floor is metal. Stephanie reaches out for a door handle but finds none. No latch. Nothing to open the doors from within.

She turns, crawling toward the man with his eyes on the road. "Billy, you have to stop the van and let me out!"

He doesn't even look at her.

"Be quiet," he says. "Do what I need you to do and you can go home."

The van stops. He climbs out and, after several full minutes, opens the back doors again. Then Strunak climbs on top of her. He disrobes. She can feel rough patches of skin on his back. It reminds her of the way her father's skin felt when she put lotion on his back as a little girl. For the next several minutes, he rapes her. "Please let me go home," she whispers. "Please let me go home."

*   *   *

"I think he got mad because it didn't last very long," Stephanie said. "And when he was done, he took me home. I lived on Lake Forest, off Columbia Road, and we didn't go far, so I think we were in Bay Village the whole time. When we got to my house, he went around to the back and opened the door. He even said, 'Good night.' He was crying.

"My husband was up, waiting for me to get back. He hated the Amy Center, hated the time I spent there. He liked having me home.

"'Who dropped you off?' he asked me. 'Where's your car?' He probably thought I was having an affair. All I wanted to do was take a shower. All I wanted to do was scrub my skin raw."

When she discovered she was pregnant, her Catholic upbringing wouldn't allow her to consider an abortion. Besides, she had been adopted herself. She decided to give the baby to Catholic Charities instead.

Five months after Billy Strunak succumbed to methanol poisoning there, Stephanie gave birth to his son at the same hospital in Fairview Park. She never saw the baby, except as it was carried from the room.

CHAPTER THIRTY-TWO

Gollums

SOMEONE ELSE WAS DIGGING into Amy's case, my sources informed me. For a while, I couldn't track it to any specific journalist. Then, during November sweeps, Channel 19 Action News reporter Denise Strzelczyk (pronounced "*Strell*-zick") contacted Lieutenant Spaetzel about the status of his investigation.

I pounded my fist against the steering wheel as I headed home, having just confirmed this bit of treachery with Spaetzel himself.

On the forty-minute drive from Cleveland to Akron, I imagined the ways Action News might screw up this story. I wondered why they were doing a story at all. Who had contacted them? Was there something new? Did she know about Billy Strunak's alleged rape?

And what if Strzelczyk's story didn't suck? What if this woman aired the story and received the call that would finally solve the case? Would the months of investigation on my part be rendered meaningless by some tug-at-the-heartstrings ratings stunt?

A couple days later, I sat at the TV with Julie, fuming as Channel 19's news anchor teased Amy's story, touting "new developments."

"What's wrong with you?" Julie said, shooting me a half-concerned, half-annoyed look.

"They're going to screw it up." I was shaking with anxiety. "And what if this woman who just picked up the story because it landed on her desk or something—what if this woman solves it when somebody calls in a tip after it airs?"

"Wouldn't that be a good thing?" Julie said, her tone shifting fully to concern. "Isn't that what you want?"

"No," I said. "It's . . ." I caught myself before I could finish. What I had started to say was *It's mine.*

Oh my God. It had finally happened. I was one of *them*. One of those people who coveted what they knew of Amy's case and didn't share it unless it was on *their* terms. People like Karen Emery, wife of the Ashland County coroner. Gollums, I called them. It was an assumption of power, twisted and dangerous.

It's mine. My precious.

"You're right," I said after a moment. I felt my heart kicking against my chest. I felt dirty, guilty, shamed. "You're right. That *is* what I want. You're right. I'm sorry."

Julie took my hand in hers and slowly looked back at the television as Strzelczyk's clip came on. "Don't be that person."

"I won't," I said. "Promise."

The report mainly showcased a new interview with Mark Mihaljevic inside his Avon home. He looked older, somehow weaker. But there was also a renewed fire in his eyes. He talked about Amy with more passion. This was a man still searching for his daughter's killer.

Mark showed the viewers Amy's ceramic pig.

Strzelczyk herself did a beautiful job of summarizing the case history in three minutes. It was not over the top. It was not saccharine. I calmed down a little more.

A few days later, I spoke to Strzelczyk over the phone and thanked her for keeping Amy's name in the news. More than a professional courtesy, it was my attempt to salvage a piece of my soul.

When you're surrounded by Gollums, it's hard not to become one yourself.

The fight with Ashland County over access to Amy's autopsy file grew mind-numbingly intense around the beginning of December 2005. Mostly, I wanted to know what Amy's last meal was. There are persistent rumors in Bay Village that imply Amy ate a meal after her abduction. Some hinted that she was kept alive until late January. I wanted to confirm or deny this. Ashland County, however, wanted to continue their bullish interference.

Karen Emery, the Ashland County coroner's wife, kept me from directly contacting her husband, Dr. William Emery. Calls to Cuyahoga County coroner Elizabeth Balraj also became mired in bureaucracy. She'd hand the file over if it was Cuyahoga's case, Balraj said, but she needed permission from Ashland first.

I sent another round of letters to Dr. Emery, explaining these files were public records. I left more phone messages. Finally, Emery himself called my cell. The message was brief: "Mr. Renner, you will never see what's in those files."

Mine. My precious.

Taking the good doctor up on his dare, I discussed my dilemma with Kenneth Zirm, a First Amendment attorney in Cleveland who works as a consultant for the *Free Times*. He agreed to send some letters on my behalf pro bono. In brilliant legalese, his letter told Dr. Emery and Ashland County prosecuting attorney Ramona Rogers to give me what I wanted and I'd go away.

Instead of yielding, Rogers hid her client behind a technicality. According to Dr. Emery, she stated, he had already let me see all public records in the possession of the Ashland County's coroner's office. In a particularly childish jab, she also informed Zirm that Ashland County had included my *Times Gazette* piece as well as the *Scene* article in Amy's permanent file.

Subtext translation: *Careful there, bucko. We're keeping an eye on you, too.*

I now found myself in a macabre catch-22. Ashland County couldn't release public records they did not have. And Amy's original file is kept in Cuyahoga County, which won't release the file without Ashland County's approval. The autopsy report was stuck in limbo.

Luckily, I was able to gain access to some of this information through other sources.

The Department of Vital Statistics keeps copies of death certificates. While it wasn't the full autopsy report, Amy's death certificate, at last, revealed some of the tidbits Dr. Emery and his wife were so eager to keep secret.

Cause of death was listed as "cardiovascular shock due to exsanguinating hemorrhage due to laceration of carotid artery due to stab wounds of the neck;" she bled out, slowly. The interval between being stabbed and time of death was thirty minutes.

Most interesting, however, was what was not included in the original certificate of death. Initially, Dr. Emery listed "unknown" for date of injury, date of death, and county of death. In an amendment to the certificate, dated May 30, 1991—more than a year after Amy's body was recovered—Dr. Emery states the date of injury as October 1989; date of death as October 1989; and county of death as Ashland. Karen Emery's signature is also on this correction, as notary public, showing at best a lackadaisical system of checks and balances in Ashland, at worst a deliberate bid by the Emerys to keep specific details of Amy's murder away from the prying eyes of reporters while the case was still fresh.

If I were to take Dr. Emery at his word, I could infer that Amy was stabbed to death inside the boundaries of Ashland County sometime between October 27 and October 31, 1989. This, in turn, suggests some forensic evidence must link Amy's murder to the site of her recovery.

CHAPTER THIRTY-THREE

The Gift Giver

A FEW WEEKS INTO my job at the *Free Times*, I found myself on the phone with a public relations official for the Cuyahoga County Sheriff's Office. I needed a mug shot of an Olmsted Falls city supervisor who was busted for drugs. On a whim, I asked him to search the county database for Billy Strunak's missing mug shot from his 1983 arrest for disseminating material harmful to juveniles. "Yeah, it's here," he said.

I rushed to the Justice Center for a copy of the original photograph. Though it was taken six years prior to Amy's abduction, Billy looked exactly as Stephanie had described. He was handsome. His hair was parted to the side, draping down in front. I couldn't help but see a similarity to the first composite sketch.

The reason I had been unable to obtain further records from Parma Heights or Fairview Park was simply because his case was tried in Cuyahoga County Common Pleas. I should have figured that out sooner. Charges of such magnitude don't end up in municipal courts.

The rest of Strunak's files were in the courthouse archives. Though they didn't spell out the specifics of the offense, the name of the victim appeared on the top page. Her first name is Mary; I promised to withhold her last name at her request. She was sixteen at the time of the incident.

Mary had grown up, moved, and married. It took considerable time and another favor from Mike Lewis to track down her phone number.

"Hi, Mary," I said. "I wondered if I could ask you about Billy Strunak."

She laughed sarcastically. "That's a name I haven't thought about in a while. The FBI asked me about him after that girl went missing. Long time ago."

"Because of the conviction on disseminating material," I said.

"Yes."

"Well, 'dissemination of material' can mean all sorts of things. Can you tell me what happened back in 1983?"

"Sure," she said. "He started buying me presents."

"What kinds of presents?"

"Well, I was waitressing at the time. He used to come in and just stare at me while I worked. Really obsessed over me. He always made sure he sat in my section. And I was only sixteen at the time. He was twenty-eight. He asked me a few times to go out and have coffee with him. And then he started leaving presents with the tip. One was a key chain with my name on it. Shortly after I got my first car, he left me an air freshener.

"One night after my shift, I went out to the parking lot to get in my car. Bill's car was parked next to mine, and he was leaning against his car, waiting for me. He was pissed off that I wouldn't go out with him. When I got closer, he grabbed my shoulders and pushed me to his car. He had his back passenger's door open and was trying to push me inside. I pulled away and ran to my car and then hit him with my driver's side door, hard.

"A little while after that, I came home and there was an envelope addressed to me sitting on the porch. Inside was a porno magazine. He had clipped out letters from a newspaper, like a ransom note, and had used them to write my name over the women in the pictures and his name over the men. That's when my father called the police. When they got into his apartment, they found a whole section devoted to me, a kind of shrine." I thought back to the pictures taken of Strunak's apartment, specifically the picture of a bottle of lubricant called Act of Love and winced.

Mary ran into Strunak years later, when she stopped by BJ's Wholesale Club to do some shopping. He was working the register for the line beside hers. For a moment they locked eyes and Mary froze. That chance reunion still gave her chills.

Again, it came back to gifts. Strunak loved giving gifts, even if the people for whom the presents were intended didn't delight in his generosity. It was a familiar motif. The man who called Amy lured her into his vehicle with the promise of presents: one for Margaret and one for her.

Strunak seldom received gifts himself.

I noticed one more thing amidst Strunak's files. His birthday was October 24.

I wondered what sort of present Strunak wanted for his birthday in 1989. Was there something he wanted more than anything in the whole world? Did he finally treat himself? And, was it possible he made a phone call on his birthday to set the whole thing up?

CHAPTER THIRTY-FOUR

The Man Next Door

A MAN NAMED JIM LONDON lived in the apartment beside Billy Strunak's in the months leading up to his suicide. He'd been e-mailing me for some time, asking that I meet with him, and once Strunak became interesting to me once more, I took him up on that invitation. We met at a McDonald's near the Aberdeen Commons apartment complex in Fairview Park, a suburb situated between Cleveland and Bay Village, one with easy access to Interstate 71.

London was kind of a twitchy man himself. He had thin dark hair over eyes that darted about in a slightly paranoid manner. I offered him a milk shake, but he declined. Instead, he passed a hardcover book across the table at me. It was Robert Ressler's *Whoever Fights Monsters*. I had only ever seen the paperback edition.

"He changed some stuff between the hardback and paperback," London said. "Take a look."

In the hardback, Ressler had mentioned Strunak by name—though it was misspelled as "Strunack." For some reason, this name had been removed from the paperback edition. Why? Pressure from the family? Pressure from Dick Wrenn, perhaps? I found it slightly troubling.

Reading the short chapter again, I noted the passage about Amy's clothes. Ressler said they had been removed and then put back on after death. How did they know this? One possible solution was that there had not been blood on her clothes, suggesting she had been naked, then cleaned and dressed again. If so, that certainly painted the murderer as a more calculating man. Why dress her back up if she was already dead? That seemed like an odd token of respect to show toward a person you had just killed.

London remembers being awakened the night before Strunak committed suicide by the sounds of someone vomiting. It was an awful, violent sound. It concerned him enough that he almost went to Strunak's door to see what was wrong, but eventually the noise died down. And it wasn't like this was the first time he'd lost sleep because of his neighbor. Around that time, there had been a lot of shouting between Strunak and his girlfriend, Lori. That night, however, she was not around.

"He would gun the engine on that Maverick every morning, too," London said. "About six, six-thirty in the morning."

I asked if he had met any of the family after Strunak's death.

"Billy Strunak's brother left a message on my answering machine the day after Billy killed himself," London said. "I can't remember what his name was, Gary maybe, but he said something like, 'This is Strunak. Give me call. We have some things to talk about.'"

"Were the FBI there, looking at the place?" I asked.

London flipped Ressler's book opened and pointed to a business card stapled to the front page. It was Special Agent Barry Gummow's. John Dunn's name was written above it.

"They were asking about Billy's car," he said. "They looked in the apartment, too, but the family had tossed everything into trashcans and who knows where. The FBI went through the trash, though."

As we continued to talk, I followed London to Aberdeen Commons, to the townhouse where he once lived beside Strunak. The doors were locked. London walked me over to the maintenance man's back door, a few hundred yards away, located in a ranch-style complex. The man was home and was luckily still the same guy London remembered from his brief stay there.

Harry the maintenance man was tanned from long summer hours working outside. A tattoo of a panther stretched across one toned bicep. He had a couple of steaks on a grill out back for him and his wife, and he tended to these as we discussed Strunak.

At one point his wife came out, because she had a memory of her own she wanted to share. She remembered Strunak peering out his window at the swimming pool with a pair of binoculars. He liked to watch the young girls sunning themselves. The pool was gone by the time of our meeting, but she pointed to his window and then the patch of yard where the pool once was. Apparently, he stopped this after some parent complained.

London walked me back to my car, looking relieved to have shared his story, unburdened of some weight. I couldn't help but think that if more people were like Jim London, this case might have been solved before it became entangled in myth.

CHAPTER THIRTY-FIVE

Last Round

EVEN THOUGH I HAD Maddie's address, I could not seem to contact her. Maddie, I knew, was the young girl who provided the description of Amy's abductor to police. She lived on the third floor of an apartment complex that was locked up tight, and the doorbell out front didn't work. I had her phone number but decided to keep trying the apartment instead of calling. It's much easier to say "Get lost" over the phone.

After one failed attempt to meet Maddie at her door, I drove over to O'Donnell's pub. Kristy Sabo was bartending. Months had passed since I had last seen her, and she looked healthier, happier. There was a nice glow to her cheeks, which seemed fuller now. She smiled her dimpled smile as I took a seat at the bar.

I ordered a Labatt's, which I sipped while she served a man at the other end of the bar. When she was done, Kristy came back to me.

"Just stopping in for a beer?" she asked.

"Well, I was trying to meet up with a girl that was at the plaza the day of Amy's abduction. But she's not home. I was in the neighborhood, so I thought I'd say hi."

"Good."

"So what's new?" I said. "How are you?"

Her smile grew wider. "I'm pregnant," she said.

That explained the glow. "Congratulations," I said. "You'll be a great mom."

"Thanks. I hope so."

"Who's the lucky guy?"

"Ex-boyfriend. He came around. Said he was sorry. He even talked to my mother. So that scored him a lot of points. We're living together. It's good."

"Good," I said.

Kristy stepped away to tend to a new group of early-evening revelers. By the time she returned, my pint was nearly empty.

"Want another?" she asked.

"No, thanks. Hey, would you know of anyone else that was in the plaza that day Amy was taken? If I can't meet up with this girl, I'd like to talk to someone who was there. Nobody else seems to know, and the cops aren't telling."

"My friend Dan Monnett," she said. "Here, I'll give you his number."

She went one better. She called Monnett on the bar's phone and set up a meeting for me. I thanked her again for her help and wished her well.

Kristy was probably unaware that she had broken the spell that hung over Amy's old friends. She was the first to start a family of her own, the first who dared to bring another child into a world where the Boogeyman is sometimes real. It felt to me like a good omen, a promise that things might change, that closure was still possible.

Monnett had a Boogeyman story of his own.

We sat at a North Olmsted bar, next to a Golden Tee arcade game, drinking Miller Lite. He was good-looking in a scruffy bad-boy way with his goatee and black button-down short-sleeve shirt. A Grateful Dead ball cap finished off his persona nicely.

Monnett was writing a memoir, he informed me, one with all the drama of a bestseller. Shortly after graduating Bay High, he was busted for intent to sell LSD. He was incarcerated for nine years for ten hits of blotter acid. Since his release, Monnett had made a lucrative career selling DJ software online, the kind of stuff used at weddings and house parties. During the day, he managed tchotchke pagodas in malls from Cleveland to Pittsburgh.

He took a longer sentence for the LSD, he said, instead of snitching on his pals. "One officer offered to pay me as an informant," Monnett said. "I told him, 'Go fuck yourself.' I'm sure a lot of kids took his twenty dollars, though. You wouldn't believe what goes on at Bay High."

Before we got down to business, Monnett wanted to tell me about another Bay Village nightmare. "This goes back much further than Amy Mihaljevic," he began. "But I think it might be directly related. I would have been six or seven when this happened. Okay, there were these two sisters, Pam and Tricia Gogol.

"Pam was in my class. But this is about her sister, Tricia, who would have been four at the time. You have to understand that Mr. Gogol is this big, tough guy. Well, Tricia would go to bed, and one night she came down and told her father there was a man in her room. Little kids always say there's a monster in their closet. So he told her to just go back to bed.

"Well, this went on for three or four nights, and eventually he went upstairs to check it out. And there really was a man in her room, hiding in her closet, watching her. He beat the shit out of the guy. I mean, he *totaled* the guy. They arrested the pervert and took him to jail.

"Then this guy got out a month before Amy's abduction. He was a big-time suspect."

Another lead, another suspect. I was reminded of the back page of *Highlights for Children* magazine, where those puzzles test you to follow a tangle of strings back to where each begins. That's what it felt like investigating Amy's case sometimes. Chasing strings that bisected others, occasionally turning onto the wrong one.

I found Monnett's bedtime story terrifying but doubted the connection. A guy who simply walked into a girl's house and waited in her closet didn't seem like the type of guy who took the effort to call a girl and win her trust before snatching her away in a very public place. If he had been released from jail the week before, he would have done well to pick a better rendezvous spot than across from the Bay Village P.D.

Still, I spoke to the Gogols. The gist of Monnett's tale was true. But it happened over the course of one evening, not several. Mrs. Gogol remembered walking into her daughter's room and opening the closet door, only to have it closed by some unseen hand. She called the cops while her husband subdued the intruder. The intruder's name was James D. Sullivan, and at the time he happened to live in the same Rocky River apartment complex in which my mother once resided. He was sent to prison in 1982 and did not get out until 2002. In 2005, he skipped probation and, at time of publication, was still at large.

I asked Monnett to tell me everything he remembered about October 27, 1989.

"Every day of my life, we were at that bowling alley at the corner of the plaza, me and my friends," he said. "That's where we hung out, just outside the bowling alley. We were a little older than Amy and had cut school early to hang out there that Friday. Only the fifth-graders got out early. That's why they stopped us. We looked too old."

"Who stopped you?"

"The cops," he said.

"There was a police car there while this was happening?"

Monnett nodded. "Can't remember who it was for sure," he said. "He was mad at us because we skipped school and because we were loitering. I wasn't looking the cop in the eye, though. I was looking down the way at a girl swinging on a pole in front of Baskin-Robbins. I didn't know it would be a pivotal moment in Bay Village history. You don't know what you're seeing sometimes. I just didn't want to look the cop in the eye. I distinctly remember the guy that walked up to her and took her away. I wish I could print the image I have in my head."

On the table in front of him, I placed three pictures. One was Harold Bound, one was Richard Folbert, one was Billy Strunak. Without hesitation, Monnett picked up Strunak's photo.

"This looks like him," Monnett said. "Put a green jacket on that guy. His face was *reddish*."

According to Monnett, this was information he gave to authorities years ago.

"Me and my friends were walking home from school when the FBI stopped us in this big van," he said. "It wasn't quite as big as a box truck. Kind of like a UPS truck. This was on Wolf Road, just past the bridge.

"They took us in this truck. It was more sophisticated than you'd expect. It wasn't like you see in the movies, but there was electronic equipment in there. And two or three agents. They wanted to know if we saw the guy. They wanted descriptions. I was scared, I remember that."

Monnett and his friends offered up what they remembered. Then they were allowed to go.

(A law enforcement official denied that Monnett and friends were questioned inside an FBI van and said he doubts Monnett witnessed the abduction. He said he considers Monnett unreliable, pointing to his history with drugs and a felony conviction at age nineteen.)

"I have a brick from Sam Sheppard's house," Monnett said before I left. "A lot of people think nothing happened in Bay Village since Sam Sheppard. They're wrong."

"Who do you think killed Sam Sheppard's wife?" I asked, because that was the polite thing to ask a Bay Village native.

"Well, it wasn't Sam Sheppard," he said. "My grandparents were at a party in Bay Village that night, near where the Sheppards lived. My grandmother says she saw this bushy-haired guy running down the road, away from the Sheppard house. It wasn't the doctor."

Monnett's story about the secret FBI van is hard to believe. It's possible it never happened. I would later learn that Monnett was not the most reliable witness. The circumstances of his imprisonment were more complicated than a LSD bust, too. According to court records, Monnett served time for gross sexual imposition. The crime involved a young woman from a neighboring city and the details are too sordid to recount here. Suffice it to say, like many Bay Villagers, Monnett had secrets of his own.

How long does it take a crime to become legend? Does it vary based on circumstances, on affluence? If the Bay Village police charged someone in Amy's death after sixteen years, would anyone really believe it? Or has so much time passed that the residents of this quiet suburb will stick to their own conspiracy theories, as they have with Sheppard's case, no matter what evidence comes to light? Does it really matter anymore, if the man responsible is long dead himself? When Amy and her mother are only ashes under the earth?

I thought of Amy's fifth-grade picture, the image I had fallen in love with when I was eleven. I thought of how much her death affected my own life, even though I was so far removed, even though we had never met. I thought of Kristy Sabo and the effect it must have had on her, on all of Amy's friends.

Yes, it still mattered. But for how much longer?

CHAPTER THIRTY-SIX

The Witness

I WAS TIRED OF WAITING to talk to Maddie. I knew I had to get into that apartment complex. I also knew that if a strange man showed up on her doorstep, Maddie was likely to be quite upset. The only way I saw around this involved taking Julie with me.

Hesitantly, Julie agreed to come along, to put this woman more at ease by her very presence. God bless her. I'm a lucky sonofabitch.

"No leaving me," she said as I parked the car in front of the tall brick building.

"I won't."

As we approached the front door, which led to the common area of the apartment complex, we reached a young couple standing there, the man fishing in his pockets for the door key.

"Can you help us out?" I said. "I'm trying to visit a friend, and her buzzer is busted, I think."

"Sure," the man said. And then we were in.

"Is this the sort of thing you do every day?" Julie asked as we climbed a steep set of stairs.

"Not *every* day."

At the top was Maddie's door. I could hear the television inside. Muffled voices, somehow familiar. I knocked. The fish-eye grew dark as someone peered out at us from the other side. If Julie had not come with me, I'm quite sure the door would have never opened.

But it did.

Maddie stood there, her jet-black hair pulled into a ponytail. She was a short woman with a cute round face. Her nose was red and shiny from an apparent cold. Her voice was congested. "Can I help you?" she asked.

Julie introduced herself first, then I told her my name and reason for the visit. The woman's eyes grew wide. She seemed more than surprised—more like scared.

"How did you find me?" she said.

"Private detectives," I said, opting for the truth.

"I don't know how. I've been very careful about giving out my address to people."

"They're very good at what they do," I said.

"I'm sorry," Julie interjected. "I know this is awkward. But he's trying to do a good thing. Really, he is. He's taken this case to heart. I know this is creepy, us just showing up at your door, but he's a good guy."

Maddie regarded me with half-closed eyes. "Well, you should probably come inside," she said. We followed her in.

Everything, save for some bric-a-brac, was white. It was a theme of innocence repeated in the carpet, couch, and candles throughout the living room and what I could see of the kitchen and bedroom. Maddie kept things immaculately clean, ordered, minimal. And although she was under the weather, there were no tissues or teacups or lozenges strewn about the room. This wasn't the home of a carefree twenty-seven-year-old in between cities and careers. This was the domicile of one who has set up for the long haul.

In a way, this place also served as a prison, keeping Maddie safe, hidden. Why shouldn't she make it nice?

As we sat on a white love seat, I noticed what was on TV: *The Wizard of Oz*. I had that disjointed feeling again, that sensation of finding myself inside some other writer's horror novel. I had followed the yellow brick road, literally beginning with the one mounted on the shelf in Lieutenant Spaetzel's office, and now here I was at the end of my journey, finally meeting the man behind the curtain. Or woman, as it were.

"So, what happened?" I said. "What happened in the plaza?"

"I don't want to ever see my name in print," she said. "I already have to tell the FBI that I met with you. I look for that man's face in the crowds and on the streets every day. My name can never be printed."

I promised, and Julie promised to make sure I kept my word.

"I had this free coupon for a Baskin-Robbins ice cream," Maddie said. "I was walking toward Baskin-Robbins, but there was this bully hanging out over by the bowling alley."

I thought of Dan Monnett.

"This boy was in the fifth grade, but I won't tell you his name," she said, as if reading my mind.

So, no, not Monnett, but maybe someone nearby.

"Amy was hanging on the pole, circling with her head down. She was halfway between the bowling alley and Baskin-Robbins. I heard the bully say, 'Hey, Amy!' I stopped to watch them in case they tried to pick on Amy or something. Then, I watched a man walk up to Amy. I thought it was her dad, but that's just because I had never seen her dad, you know? I just assumed. He was skinny. He wore front-pressed khakis with a beige jacket with plaid lining. Some button-up colored shirt. An Izod shirt, maybe. Not Izod for sure, but it looked like it could have been. I didn't see glasses. He was clean-cut.

"He went up to Amy, put a hand on her. They talked for a second. Then he put an arm around her shoulders and they walked away. This was before the 3 p.m. classes let out, a little after 2:30 p.m., I think."

Maddie said the police had used a different sketch artist for her than they did for a second eyewitness, the bully, who claimed the abductor had been wearing glasses. While she wouldn't reveal his name, she did tell me that the police requested she and the other witness sit at the memorial service for Amy held at Bay Presbyterian and scan the crowd for the man. But Maddie did not see the abductor in the crowd.

"It was hard to see Jason in the halls at school," she said. "He had no idea I had anything to do with the investigation. I felt a bond to him, but he never knew."

For the first three years following Amy's disappearance, Maddie was asked repeatedly to view series of pictures, possible suspects. A year ago, the police called again, but Maddie felt there wasn't anything more she could do to help.

The image of Amy's last moments as a child are burned into her memory, sometimes replaying in an endless loop against her wishes. "I still remember him as he looked sixteen years ago. Not a day goes by I don't think of this. I shouldn't remember these details. I don't know why I do. I was there for a reason, I think. It was like God said, 'You have to remember all this later, so pay attention.'"

"So you think you'd recognize him if you saw a picture?" I asked.

"I think so, yeah."

I met with Stephanie again shortly after my meeting with Maddie. I asked a simple question. How did Billy Strunak dress? She had sat beside Strunak for weeks inside the Amy Center and remembered only too well.

"He never wore jeans," she said. "He wore dickies, work pants. Always a shirt with a button-up collar, never a T-shirt. He wore this jacket. It could have been a Members Only jacket, a windbreaker. It made this sound when he walked." She made a swishing sound of cheap fabric rubbing against itself. "Oh, and his button-up shirts were always plaid. Usually blue plaid of some kind."

Is it possible Maddie thought the liner was plaid when it was actually the design of the shirt the man wore?

As soon as Julie and I returned home from Maddie's, I scanned Billy Strunak's mug shot into my computer. I e-mailed it to the address Maddie had given me. She replied the next day.

"I have to be honest," she wrote. "I cannot be certain about anything after sixteen years but, as soon as I looked at him, I actually got tears in my eyes and had a vibe that this is the guy I saw meet Amy. I cannot say if I for sure viewed this photo before or not. I don't ever remember seeing this one. Again, I was ten years old at the time and I was very fearful of pointing out someone that may have had *nothing* to do with it. I had a lot of pressure on me for being so young."

"I'm real sorry to drop in on you like this. Hey, is that a rottweiler?"

I was at Jeffrey Strunak's front door, facing a large dog drooling at me like I was a T-bone in a Kent State T-shirt. Jeff was on the other side of the glass. He was a rotund man, easily more than three hundred pounds. Though we had never met face to face, I got the impression he already knew who I was. Maybe he just wasn't the type who received visitors after dark.

"It's a Heinz 57 variety, I think," Jeff said, referring to the mutt, and its mixed pedigree.

He stepped outside and closed the door behind him.

"Here's what's going on," I said. "Over the last couple weeks, I came across some information I had to turn over to the police. I don't really know where to begin."

I told Jeff about Stephanie. I told him two witnesses had identified his brother as the man who took Amy. The whole time, he seemed unimpressed. Occasionally, the sound of a train cutting through Fairview Park overpowered my voice, and I had to stand there silently, awkwardly, while it passed.

When I finished, Jeff said simply that Billy was at the bank with their mother at 3 p.m. "He couldn't have been in both places, and he stayed at my parents' until supper. And, I don't even know if he could father a child with the medication he was taking. Nobody can defend themselves. We talked to the FBI. They said it was all just a coincidence. They said they didn't have anything, and that's why they kept coming back to the same people. It seems like a cockamamie story to me. The whole family has been tortured by this. And even if he had done anything, nobody could do anything about it now.

"Billy had a heart of gold. He was just always trying to please."

Minute by Minute

THE DAY AMY WAS TAKEN, Bay Village was enjoying an Indian summer. Though it was late October, a balmy breeze cut off Lake Erie. It was the last breath of summer warmth before the world fell cold again until spring.

A little after 6 a.m., Amy awoke and dressed herself. Sweats again. She picked out green pants and a pale green sweatshirt with lavender trim. She brushed her hair and slipped on her favorite earrings, silhouettes of horse heads rendered in turquoise, mounted on gold studs.

On the way out the door, Amy put on a white windbreaker; it was still a little chilly first thing in the morning. She slipped on a pair of black riding boots, laced up the front. She slung a blue denim book bag with red piping around her shoulders, having recently grown too old for that silly koala backpack.

Outside, she climbed onto her blue antique bike and met up with Kristen Balas and Katy from down the road. Together, they pedaled to the middle school.

Amy sat at her desk in Ms. Stewart's classroom before the 7:50 a.m. bell.

The students' schedules were abbreviated that day thanks to an assembly at the nearby high school. Amy and her friends climbed onto buses for the short ride. Olivia Masiak, who was new to Bay Village but had become fast friends with Amy, sat alone as the other students stepped inside.

"I remember you, you're Liv! I haven't seen you in such a long time!" Amy shouted, pretending that they had just been reunited after twenty years. Amy was always play-acting with her friends. She slid into the empty seat next to Olivia. They sat next to each other at the assembly and listened to officer Mark Spaetzel talk about the dangers of strangers. (Masiak and several other students remembered the talk taking place at the high school assembly; Spaetzel, though, recalls giving it in Amy's classroom at the middle school.)

Later, Amy ate spaghetti for lunch in the school cafeteria.

For many of her classmates, the school day was nothing special. Events meshed together with the days and years that came before. It's hard for most of them to recall when they last saw Amy alive.

Renee Moran later told a reporter that she thought Amy had been oddly quiet the whole week. Elizabeth Jeffers remembers talking to Amy near her locker sometime on Friday, though she cannot pinpoint a specific time. Kristy Sabo recalls passing the door to Amy's classroom and seeing her friend scribbling on a piece of paper.

Classes let out that day at 2:10 p.m. for the fifth-graders. Normally, Amy would reclaim her bike from the rack, but this day she left it behind.

"Can I walk with you?" she asked Olivia Masiak, as she jogged up beside her.

"You never walk this way," said Olivia. (Amy would normally have been on her bike.)

"I'm meeting someone," Amy answered. "I'm meeting a friend."

A few minutes later, they crossed in front of the shopping plaza.

"This is where I'm at," Amy said.

A classmate named Haley Pritchard, walking a few steps behind them, watched Amy dart over to a black van. It looked like Amy knew the owner of the vehicle. But then, Amy stepped away and walked toward Baskin-Robbins. She did not go into the ice cream shop. She stood outside, swinging around a pole, keeping her head down, apparently lost in thought.

Across the street, almost every cop in Bay Village was assembled for a weekly staff meeting called by Chief William Gareau. A few patrol cars remained on duty. Around 2:30 p.m., one of those cruisers pulled into the plaza.

Outside Bay Lanes, a group of older kids nervously watched the officer approach. Dan Monnett, Nicky Kline, Jill Prochaska, and Dave Kotinsley were skipping last period, enjoying the last perfect afternoon of the year. The cruiser stopped in front of the gang, and the officer stepped out to give them a stern talking-to. Avoiding the cop's eyes, Dan looked over to the girl in front of the ice cream shop and watched her swing around in lazy circles.

Less than twenty feet from Amy, Jim Kapucinski loitered outside his barbershop, surveying the parking lot. Not that there was much to see. His business was empty, as was everyone else's, practically. There were only five vehicles parked there, and those probably belonged to the employees of the other various shops. He casually monitored the teens standing by Bay Lanes.

A fifth-grader named Julius Holinek was in the plaza, too. He was the second eyewitness that Maddie did not want to name. And he also watched Amy twirl around. However, it's hard to say exactly where he was standing. Though he witnessed Amy's abduction, he has remained silent about the crime. As of this writing, he was living in Florida, having graduated college as a star football player. He did not respond to repeated interview requests. His parents said the experience was too troubling for him to remember. But he was, after all, able to live his life.

It was around 2:45 p.m. when Maddie approached Baskin-Robbins.

"Amy!" Holinek called out. It sounded like a taunt to Maddie, so she watched him to see if he might bother Amy. And she watched as a well-dressed man in a beige jacket walked up to her instead. He leaned forward and whispered something in Amy's ear. He put his arm around her and led Amy away.

Must be her dad, Maddie thought.

Ten minutes after 3 p.m., Amy's brother Jason arrived home. He called Margaret's desk at *Tradin' Times* and told her Amy was not there.

A few minutes later, Margaret's phone rang again. It was Amy. Margaret assumed Amy was calling from home. Amy told her mother she had stayed after school for choir auditions. But she seemed odd, as if she was rushing the conversation along. It so unnerved Margaret that she packed up her things for the weekend and left work early.

Margaret pulled into the driveway on Lindford Drive at around 4 p.m. Jason was there. She soon realized Amy had never been home. She also realized Amy must have lied to her, though she couldn't understand why. It wasn't like her. Maternal instinct kicking in, she rushed to the middle school. Amy's bike was still in the rack. It was a detail that terrified Margaret. It seemed to suggest something terrible. Things were off-kilter. This was not routine, not normal. She had never known Amy to lie.

Later, Margaret would learn it was only the promise of surprising her with a present that caused Amy to make a series of poor choices that day.

From school, Margaret drove to the police station and relayed her feelings to Officer Barbara Slepecky. Slepecky did not waste time treating Amy as a runaway, which is standard protocol. She believed in Margaret's instincts. Somehow she knew this was the real deal.

A call went out to officers in surrounding towns at 5:58 p.m. The call included an incomplete description of Amy.

Mark Mihaljevic, unaware of the growing storm that would batter his life, arrived home from work at 6:30 to find his family fractured. He spent the rest of the evening scouring Bay Village with a friend. He drove his car down every street between his house and Holly Hill Farms, between the school and Huntington Park. He trampled through ravines and woods, calling his daughter's name in all directions.

At 11 p.m., thanks to the efforts of Jeanne Silver—then Jeanne Sabo— Amy's face was broadcast on the local news channels. Ohio was introduced to Amy Mihaljevic for the first time.

CHAPTER THIRTY-SEVEN

A Return to Bay Village

"IT'S LIEUTENANT SPAETZEL OF the Bay Village police department."

"Oh, hi," I said. "What's going on?" I glanced at the clock on the wall. It was exactly 9 a.m.

"I need to talk to you," he said. His voice sounded gruff, and possibly a little excited. "Can you come down to the station?"

"Sure. Today?"

"No. Next week. How's Monday at 9 a.m.?"

"Fine. Is something happening with the case?" I asked.

"Oh, I'll tell you all about it when you come down to the station."

"Well, I can come down today, if it's important."

"No need," he said. "Monday's fine."

Next Monday was December 12, a day after Amy would have turned 27. I slept on the couch the previous night, getting maybe thirty minutes of shut-eye. Different scenarios ran through my head, endlessly repeating: *He's solved the case and wants me to be the first to know. He wants to leak some new bit of information. He plans to arrest me for interfering in the investigation.*

"If I'm not back by five this evening, check the county jail," I told Julie as she went to work. I was only half joking.

The hour drive from my house to Bay Village was exhausting. I went through about three CDs of eighties music, skipping past the power ballads. It was a little before nine when I arrived. I pulled into the Bay shopping plaza and picked up a mocha. I emptied the notes concerning Amy's case from my satchel and weighted it down with a couple of books. Then I left my car parked at the plaza and walked across to the police station. If I was going to be arrested, I didn't want all my notes confiscated. I figured it would be difficult for Spaetzel to get a search warrant to break into my car if it was parked in a private lot.

I still hoped for good news, but I wasn't taking any chances.

I waited by the display case again, the one with the logbook notating Dr. Sheppard's arrest.

Spaetzel called my name from the doorway to his office. He gestured for me to join him.

It had been a while since I'd seen the detective, but he looked the same. His hair did not look grayer. There were no new wrinkles around his eyes. If anything was different, he looked less happy. I took that as a very bad sign.

Spaetzel shut the door behind him. That was new. He'd left it open for our earlier interviews. Then again, this was the first interview *he* was leading.

I sat in the chair against the wall facing Amy's poster. Spaetzel sat behind his desk. "So how are things going for your book?" he asked.

"Good." I filled him in on Alvin Matlock and his cousin Doyle, because this was a suspect we had not spoken about before and also because I wanted to burn some time. I felt that if I stopped talking, he would have to start. After a few minutes, I noticed him relax a little bit, even smiling occasionally.

"Maddie says you stopped by her place the other day," Spaetzel said as soon as I stopped yammering.

"I did."

"Says you showed her a picture of Billy Strunak."

"Yes," I said. "She said she hadn't seen the picture before."

"As detectives, we have to follow certain rules that citizens don't think about," Spaetzel said. Boy, he was revving up. I could tell he was pretty angry. "When we show pictures to witnesses, we have to line up a bunch of similar pictures for them to choose from. That's how we don't show bias. You understand?"

I nodded.

"You tainted my witness by showing her that photo," he said. "That might be considered obstruction of justice. That's a felony."

I am getting arrested, I thought.

"I'm sorry," I said. "I just got excited when she was describing the man to me. I told her I had a picture. She said she'd look at it. I didn't think about it."

"Did you tell her you were going to name Billy Strunak as the killer in your book?" he asked.

"I'm not going to name anyone that you don't confirm for me first," I said.

Spaetzel looked at his screen and read an e-mail I had sent to Maddie. I had told her I thought she could rest easy.

"Everything she described sounded like Strunak," I said.

"Do you have any evidence? If you do, I'd like to know about it."

"No," I said. "It's all circumstantial. I mean, is it a coincidence that Billy fits the description? That this woman says he raped her outside the Mihaljevics'? That he stalked this waitress back in 1983? And all the stuff with the presents. It always comes back to presents with Strunak. The gifts he gave Mary, the presents he gave Stephanie, the trinkets he sent to Margaret, and the fact that whoever took Amy did so because he wanted to buy a present for her mother and then one for Amy herself. You're right, though, it's all circumstantial."

"But it still could have been someone else," Spaetzel said.

"I know," I said. "And that's what keeps me up at night. Because if whoever *did* take Amy had decided not to, someone else *would have*. She was surrounded by creeps who noticed her. I hope that's rare. I'd like to think when I have a daughter of my own one day, she isn't being watched by a dozen would-be abductors. I'd like to think Amy was a rare case."

"Me too," he said.

We sat there for a while, measuring the time. I looked out his window. From my seat I could see the pole Amy had twirled on.

"Did you find Stephanie's story to be credible?" I asked, finally.

Spaetzel nodded. "I found her to be very credible. It was helpful that you asked her to come in here. That was something we didn't know about."

"Do I have to worry about being arrested here?"

"No," he said. "Just don't do it again. Don't show my witnesses any more pictures."

"All right."

"You could work on this case your whole life, you know?"

"No," I said. "I don't think I could do that. I don't envy your job anymore."

Back at the car, I slipped the notes into my satchel. I took a last look at where Baskin-Robbins used to be. I listened to the air for a whisper of a sound. Nothing.

I thought that was the end of it. Once again, I was wrong.

CHAPTER THIRTY-EIGHT

As Far As I Can Go

THERE ARE TWO GREAT TRAGEDIES in the history of Bay Village. The first is the murder of Marilyn Sheppard, wife of Dr. Sam Sheppard, the playboy osteopath. Someone bludgeoned Marilyn to death in her bedroom in the early morning hours of July 4, 1954. Dr. Sam stood trial for that murder and was found guilty. Later, he was vindicated when the case was overturned on appeal, but his name was tarnished forever. The second is the abduction and murder of ten-year-old Amy Mihaljevic on October 27, 1989. For whatever reason, the two cases whirl around each other in unexpected ways, like the DNA double helix extracted from a drop of human blood.

The Mihaljevics moved to Bay Village exactly thirty years to the day after Marilyn's murder.

Marilyn and Sam's only child, Sam Reese Sheppard, left Bay Village in 1971. He did not come home again until October 27, 1989. He returned to give a speech at the City Club in Cleveland at noon the day Amy was taken. He wanted Bay Village to reopen his father's case and hunt for the real killer. Few people noticed that bit of news in the papers the next day. Amy's story was the lead, and the police focused on searching for her instead.

One of the two Cleveland homicide detectives who first responded to the Sheppard crime scene was a man named Pat Gareau. His nephew, William Gareau, was the chief of police for Bay Village in 1989. It was Gareau who finally revealed to me the secret hidden for years inside Amy's sealed autopsy report.

I found him in plain sight, working as the clerk of courts for Rocky River. One February day I stopped by the Rocky River municipal building, uninvited. Gareau was just back from vacation, refreshed and willing to talk about Amy's case. He led me into his office and spoke candidly with the door open.

His light-gray hair sat high atop his forehead, combed back neatly. He wore a sharp polo shirt and slacks. During idle conversation he motioned to a plaque on the wall that he had received after completing the same intensive training at Quantico that Spaetzel had endured.) One of his instructors was Robert Ressler. But I saw no yellow brick.

Gareau sees the odd symmetry that surrounds Amy's story. When they discovered Amy's body in Ashland County, he felt very disconcerted about the name of that country road. At the time, the number assigned to Gareau's cruiser was 1181.

"Nobody saw a vehicle," he said, when asked about witness statements. That was something I had already suspected. All the different descriptions—a white van, a green truck, and so forth—probably came from rumors and hearsay. No one I had spoken to remembered a vehicle of any kind. Could that mean there was no vehicle?

"Would it be fair to say there was no blood on her clothes?" I asked. "Is that how we know her clothes had been taken off and put back on?"

He shook his head. "I wouldn't say that. There was blood on the clothes—plenty."

"Was Amy kept for any length of time before she was killed?"

Gareau looked out to the room beyond his door. "When we found her, she was still wearing the same clothes she had on that day. Same panties. So, no, not long."

"So what was in her stomach? What did the autopsy show?"

"Soy," he said. "A soy meal. She had soy in her stomach."

"Like a soy burger from school?"

He shook his head again. "No. Only soy."

I don't know what I had expected, but this wasn't it. This was odd. In 1989, consumer products made mostly from soy weren't so common on ordinary grocery store shelves.

"So, nothing from her school lunch that day?"

"No, just the soy," he said. "It leads you to believe she was kept alive for several days." Long enough to digest everything else.

"What does that mean to you?" I asked.

"Well, I went down to Grandpa's Cheesebarn in Ashland. That big barn off I-71. There was a health food store attached to it back then, called LaRue's. And I found a backpacker's protein bar that had a similar makeup. Could have been a protein bar."

This man wanted to share. So many questions swirled in my mind. I thought maybe he would answer them all.

"Why were so many FBI agents involved?" I asked.

"They owed us," Gareau said. "We held some prisoners for them."

He let that statement hang in the air, and I didn't fish. I wanted more about Amy.

"Spaetzel once mentioned a fiber was found during the investigation that was important in some way." I said.

"We found a yellow, gold fiber at the recovery site. Possibly from a '79 Ford or a camper."

"What did you think about Billy Strunak?"

Gareau shrugged. "We looked at a lot of people."

I started to tell him about Stephanie's rape, but he held up his hand. "We knew about that," he said.

Until then, it had not occurred to me that Spaetzel was manipulating me much as I had manipulated others. If Gareau knew about Stephanie, then Spaetzel must have known, too. Why would he hold that back? What would be gained by letting me believe I had discovered new information against Strunak? Nothing—unless he wanted my attention focused on Strunak instead of someone else.

I quickly summarized my research over the past year for Gareau, making sure to mention each potential suspect. He didn't seem too interested in Harold Bound or that unnamed suspect mentioned in newspaper articles who worked for the Westlake manufacturing plant. When I told him about interrupting Brad Harvey's shower, he laughed and asked what Harvey said to me. Then I continued and filled him in on Sam Tillerman and Alvin Matlock.

When I was through, he told me about another suspect he had found particularly interesting for a short time.

On October 27, 1992, an eleven-year-old girl named Shauna Howe was abducted from Oil City, Pennsylvania, as she walked home from a Halloween party. Her body was found three days later, near a fishing hole, not far from her house. She had died from multiple lacerations and blunt force trauma.

The date of the abduction and age of the victim were enough to grab the attention of Bay Village detectives and local FBI. But the location of Oil City was even more intriguing. If you were to drive all the way down County Road 1181 in Ashland County and turn left, you could stay on State Route 224 until it dead-ended in Oil City.

"So, we find this guy from Bay who owns a camper like the one we're looking for," said Gareau. "And he keeps the camper in *Oil City, Pennsylvania*. I thought for sure this was our guy. I even made a bet with Jim Tompkins during dinner. This guy had just sold the camper and his cars. But we tracked them down and scoured them down. Nothing. We couldn't get a search warrant for his house. Out of sheer frustration, we knocked on his front door. He lives on Lake Road, near the Sheppard house. We asked him, 'Could we take a look inside?' And he says, 'Sure.' But nothing matched that fiber."

Gareau was certain this man had nothing to do with the case. Should he ever see Tompkins again, he said, he planned to pay on the wager, without interest hopefully.

The Oil City case has since been solved, but only recently. In August 2004, three Oil City men were arrested for the young girl's murder.

For a time, Gareau believed Amy's killer might have worked with Margaret at the *Tradin' Times*. That lead didn't pan out either.

"So, who do you think did it?" I asked.

Gareau leaned back in his chair and squeezed his eyes together.

"Do you have a hunch?" I persisted.

Gareau nodded. "It's someone you've already mentioned."

Even though Gareau concluded that the two cases were not linked, I wanted to follow up on the Oil City connection. It felt like a loose end. So I tracked down the name of the Bay Village man who had once been a suspect in both Shauna's and Amy's murder.

Raymond Brahlers' home was less than a quarter mile from the Sheppard house on Lake Road. From the driveway, I could see the town hall and the plaza beyond. It was Judy Brahler who answered the door when I showed up early one weekend morning.

"Ray passed away," the woman said. She was older, perhaps sixty-five, with thin hair dyed red and pushed back a bit over her eyes. She wore a nightgown and, opening the door, motioned for me to step inside the house. At my heel, her white long-haired terrier sniffed at my pants cuffs and licked at my hand as I bent to it.

"You'll have to excuse me," Judy said, clutching her cheek with one liver-spotted hand. "I just had new inserts put in." She motioned for me to sit at a table with her.

Ray had been an air-traffic controller for fifteen years before the job became too stressful. He was diagnosed with an anxiety disorder in the late seventies and lived off disability until his death from cancer five years earlier.

On a whim, during their honeymoon, the Brahlers had purchased a plot of land in Oil City, where they had often vacationed. On one trip to Oil City, in 1982, Ray was on a cable car that took tourists over the Allegheny River when a wheel came loose. The car slipped off the track and dropped sixty feet to the rocky ground. Ray barely survived the ordeal; doctors found part of his shoulder inside his chest. He lay in a hospital for weeks.

When they returned to Bay Village, Ray could no longer lift his right arm very far and could not grasp things in that hand. As he was right-handed, this made any number of routine tasks very difficult.

On October 27, 1989, Ray was at the Bay Village shopping center at the time of Amy's abduction, shopping at Avelone's market. After hearing the news reports later that weekend, he recalled seeing a strange black van in the parking lot that day. He called the police and gave them the information.

"That was the beginning of our troubles," Judy said.

After the girl from Oil City disappeared on the anniversary of Amy's abduction, Ray was called in to the station for questioning. It didn't help his case that he happened to have been in Oil City the day Shauna disappeared. He was interrogated for hours in the presence of Bay Village detectives, FBI agents, and Oil City state troopers. FBI agents followed Judy to a hair appointment and escorted her back to the house so she could let them in. She let the FBI agents take carpet samples from their bedroom and the hallway by the door.

"They were nasty," Judy said. "The FBI were so mean to us. We had to hire a defense attorney. It cost us six thousand dollars before it was over. Our lawyer told us not to talk on the phone because it was bugged. And he said not to talk in the house because they probably put a listening device in the bedroom while they were here. So we didn't really talk about Amy for a year in our own home. They never even called us to say he wasn't a suspect anymore."

I told her that Gareau had told me her husband had been ruled out as a suspect years ago. At first, she seemed angry. Then she just seemed relieved.

"He never could have done something like that," she said. "Not with his arm the way it was. And the guy they saw at the plaza was shorter. Ray was six foot three. And he had a mustache."

As I got up, I asked her what she thought about the Sheppard case. Her eyes widened, and suddenly she looked ten years younger. A typical Bay Village resident, she loved to talk about that crime.

"I was returning with my family that day from Catawba Island," she said. "There were no highways then, so we took Lake Road all the way home. When we passed the Sheppard place, there were all sorts of people milling about. We didn't know what had happened until we heard the news."

"Who do you think did it?" I said.

"Richard Eberling, the window washer," she answered without missing a beat.

I started for the door, but she had something else to say.

"It's strange," Judy said. "But when you knocked on the door, I was sleeping. And I was dreaming about that black van."

When I thought back on my conversation with William Gareau, he hadn't seemed interested in any of the suspects I had met along the way. He hadn't said a single word during my summary.

No, that wasn't exactly true.

He had asked for a little more information about just one man.

I ran a records check on Brad Harvey, a simple task I should have performed months before. His offenses, though minor, were prolific. They were mostly mundane traffic violations, peppered with a disorderly conduct, a DUI, and a theft charge, but they occurred with such regularity, it's clear that this man has been watched closely by the local police.

I decided to drive out to his house once more.

"Who is it?" I could hear Brad Harvey through the door, muffled a little. His windows were covered from the outside with sheets of rough-cut plastic that fluttered in the brisk air.

"James Renner," I said.

"No, thanks."

"Can I buy you a drink? I just want to talk to you."

"No, thanks."

"It's about Amy Mihaljevic."

"I said, No, thanks."

I thought about knocking again, just to work him up a bit, see if I could draw him out. Instead, I walked over to his neighbor's house and spoke to a guy who said his name was Tom.

"I'll tell you about Harvey," said Tom. "I can hear him watching pornography really loud during the summer, when his windows are open. We almost went at it one night. He was picking on my kids. We were going to fight. He's not always here anymore, though. His mother just passed away. She lived near the Bay Village shopping plaza when he was growing up."

Hoping Harvey could see me through the plastic, I crossed the street and walked to the house directly across from his own. An attractive middle-aged woman answered the door but did not open it. She asked what I wanted.

"I'm a writer," I told her and said I wanted to ask her some questions about Brad Harvey.

At that moment, her sixteen-year-old daughter appeared in the doorway. "Is it about Amy Mihaljevic?" she asked.

"Yes," I said. "How did you know that?"

"Let him in, Mom," the girl said.

The woman opened the door and introduced herself. Her daughter sat on the couch and picked up a copy of *To Kill a Mockingbird*, which she said she was reading for a school project. She took notes as I asked questions.

"How did you know he was connected to Amy's case?" I asked.

The teen told me a friend's mother dropped her off once and had said to watch out for him because he was a suspect in the murder.

"He's mean," the girl said. "When I'm outside sometimes, he stands at the window, naked."

The woman turned to her daughter, shocked. Then she looked at me. "He's done that to me a couple times, too."

I no longer believe it was an accident that Brad Harvey happened to be naked when we first met.

"I wish people would tell us these things," Spaetzel said when I told him the story. "We'd love to pay Brad Harvey another visit."

However, he cautioned against giving too much weight to his old chief's hunches. Spaetzel had recently had a detective thoroughly investigate Harvey.

"He just doesn't fit. Everyone knows who he is. You'd think someone would have recognized him in the plaza that day, if he was there. But I never like to rule anyone out 100 percent."

Of course. Nothing in this case seemed 100 percent certain.

I did eventually manage to get answers to some nagging riddles, though, from two other law enforcement sources.

Retired FBI spokesman Bob Hawk, the face of the bureau in Cleveland for so many years, agreed to meet me in March 2006. I asked him how the police knew that Amy's clothes had been taken off and put back on.

"Her underwear were inside out when we found her," Hawk said. To my surprise, he also revealed that not one, but "a bunch" of fibers was found on her body. Enough for multiple forensic tests. "This guy kept her alive for several days. Two or three days, or two or three weeks. We don't know."

I later spoke with another former law enforcement official who worked the case and is very familiar with the FBI's investigation. He met with me on the condition that I not reveal his identity. He told me Amy had been naked at the time of her murder, but she had not been raped. The soy in her stomach, he said, came from Asian food; perhaps her last meal was Chinese takeout. And her body, he said, was in that wheat field for a week at most, possibly no more than twenty-four hours—an estimate based on the condition of bugs found on the body. He said he believed Amy's body had been stored in a fishing cabin or hunting lodge.

He also told me that "six or seven" other girls from Bay Village and neighboring suburbs North Olmsted and Westlake had received similar phone calls inviting them out, but they had not taken the bait.

It's hard to believe none of those girls ever made that fact public. But so much that I'd heard about this case was hard to believe.

Bob Hawk had offered one last bit of frustrating speculation in our interview.

"There's some thought out there that the reason this case was so hard is because the killer was not the man who called her on the phone," Hawk told me. "It may have been an unrelated opportunity. Maybe the killer happened to be passing through Bay Village that day and Amy comes up to him and says, 'Are you the guy who is supposed to take me to buy a present for my mom?' and he says, 'Sure. Sure I am' and takes her away. Maybe the guy who was originally involved with setting her up heard she was abducted and said, 'Oh shit! See you later.' And then he went into hiding and never talked about it."

As random as that seems, it's as good a guess as any I've heard.

That's all I had left, it seemed. Guesses. Too many of them, and all leading . . . nowhere. Or anywhere.

And yet, while sifting through my notes . . . one last possibility.

I happened upon the map given to me by Paula Varney, the Ashland County shop owner. The one drawn by the man who said he was from Bay Village and who claimed to know the house where the killer lived at the time of Amy's abduction. I hadn't thought about it much at the time. So it came as quite a shock when, looking at it again, I realized the map pointed to the house in which Brad Harvey had grown up, located near the shopping plaza where Amy was last seen. I remembered that Varney had also warned me that a cop was involved. Before he died, I knew, Brad Harvey's father had worked for the Cleveland police.

The house near the shopping plaza had a rustic, matronly feel. But no one lived there. Harvey's mother had died the year before, and it had been cleaned out, perhaps being readied for sale.

No one was there when I dropped by.

What I found curious was the garage that sat behind the house. Attached to this garage was a two-room apartment. Several open windows offered a view inside. The rooms appeared long-abandoned, cluttered with ceiling panels that had fallen sometime in the past. The gold-colored carpeting was caked with dirt and dust. In the middle of the carpet in the farthest room I noticed a dark crimson stain.

I considered opening the window further, so that I could climb in and get a better look. It would have been easy. I was hidden from the road, and no one would see me.

I stood there for several minutes, thinking. This would be trespassing. No way around it. If I got caught, Spaetzel would be forced to arrest me. Whatever I found inside would not be admissible in court. Still, I thought about it.

Then, I turned away.

I realized I couldn't risk it. This was as far as I was willing to push, for my own safety and sanity. It seems there are some things I'm not willing to do to solve this case. Apparently, committing misdemeanors is one of them. It's nice to have boundaries, I guess. More than likely, that patch of crimson was just some spilled cabernet or spaghetti sauce, anyhow.

So I turned away.

And with that, I was done, because there was nothing left to do.

After almost two years, all those hours of interviews and research and driving around, all those notebooks filled. Every lead followed, but none leading where I had hoped.

Now I suppose I'll just have to wait, like everyone else.

Wait to see if the killer will give himself up.

Or if someone he's confided in contacts police.

Or if the small amount of forensic evidence finally makes sense to someone.

Wait for my answer.

Where is the boundary between interest and obsession? One day I simply became aware that I was on the other side of the tide pulling me out to sea, too far from shore to swim home. I have to hope for a solution, the only rescue from the open waters of obsession. I'm too far in now. And the current is much too strong.

Epilogue

Frustrating isn't the word.

It's disheartening. Amy's case is that rare mystery that becomes more complex as time rolls onward, swallowing witnesses, friends, and suspects like some spiritual black hole. At some point, you have to start moving away from it before it pulls you in.

I often wonder what sort of person Amy would have become. How would the lives of her friends and family have been different? What would Bay Village be like? And if she hadn't disappeared on the day Sam Sheppard Jr. returned to town to clear his father's name, would Bay Village have heard his pleas and reopened the case to find his mother's real killer?

Shakespeare believed that if the chain of destiny is broken, we must all pay the price: the more influential the murdered soul, the more serious the repercussions for humanity.

So, who was Amy supposed to become?

I called my father late one night not too long ago. "You know, the more I look into this story, the more patterns I see," I said. "It's strangely tangled up with the Sheppard murder and in some ways my own life. It's like, if you look close enough, you can see a kind of blueprint connecting everything."

"I think that's there in everyone's life," he said. "God has an order to things and a plan for us all."

God doesn't play dice, Einstein once said.

I wanted to agree, but if you become too obsessed with those patterns, you could end up like Richard Alan Folbert. You could end up walking into a church on October 13, thirteen years after Amy's abduction, shouting to heaven that you know the truth.

"You were right, though," I told my father. "I think it's going to come down to what they found in her stomach. Soy is a strange little detail. That's going to make sense to someone."

I think about Margaret sometimes, too. And my own mother. That fearful symmetry might finally be diverging. My mom has made it through a winter without getting sick. Her immune system is recovering. The lupus, for now, remains dormant. She seems happy and healthy and strong. I visit her and my sisters as much as I can, but it's probably not often enough.

It is such a dangerous world in which women live.

Natalee Holloway, Elizabeth Smart, JonBenét Ramsey . . . to name a few of the thousands of other cases of abducted young girls that have sent ripples across the consciousness of America.

Just let me solve this one, a selfish part of me thinks sometimes. *I don't really care about those other cases. Just let me figure this one out. This one affected me. I deserve an answer.*

So many lives were affected by the death of this one little girl from Bay Village, Amy Mihaljevic, so many more affected by all those others.

Eventually, we learn to move on. Some manage better than others. Jason Mihaljevic seeks comfort by placing his faith in religion and Team Destiny. Mark Mihaljevic keeps his memories in storage, choosing to remember his daughter not through photographs but through a small gift she made for him in art class.

The two eyewitnesses to Amy's abduction remain in seclusion, fearing the man will return for them one day. Amy's friends have chosen to step out of that man's shadow, slowly. Kristen Balas returned to Bay Village to teach. Kristy Sabo is a mother, responsible for protecting new innocence.

Special Agent Laura Henry has been reassigned. Special Agent Philip Torsney is now the lead agent involved in the investigation.

Lieutenant Detective Mark Spaetzel's office is no longer located in the town hall, across from the Bay Village shopping plaza. In the spring of 2006, he organized his department's move to the newly constructed police department complex beside the fire station on Wolf Road. Spaetzel is still actively investigating, though. And he cautions that Amy's killer may be someone still unknown to investigators. He said there are "around fifty other people as compelling" as any mentioned in this book. A frightening thought.

*   *   *

I've tried to move on, too. I try not to talk about the case with Julie anymore. But in bed at the end of the evening, when my mind is somewhere between awake and dreaming, the details of Amy's case resurface like the corpses of dead animals in a raging river. I try to make sense of everything. My subconscious wants to solve the mystery even if I consciously avoid it. Part of me still believes it can be solved. That it's really as easy as some Sherlock Holmes story and if I were only smart enough, I might see the solution before the end. I'm afraid I can never let it go.

I know that we live in fear, all of us. We fear the Boogeyman, not in our closets, but in the man next door. The one you wave to as you pass each other on the sidewalk.

Perhaps that is a penance well deserved. Because sometimes we forget to watch after each other. And then another soul is taken away from us all.

The Investigation Continues

A NOTE FROM THE PUBLISHER: This memoir stands as a record of a specific period of time in James Renner's investigation of the abduction and murder of Amy Mihaljevic. Since the book's publication, James has continued to search for Amy's killer. Follow the rest of the story at:

www.amymihaljevic.blogspot.com

Acknowledgments

IN MEMORY OF AMY MIHALJEVIC, I will be donating ten percent of my earnings from sales of this book to the Lake Erie Nature and Science Center. Amy enjoyed many happy days there, befriending the creatures that live inside. If you would like to personally contribute, you can do so by visiting their website at www.lensc.org or by calling 440-871-2900.

I want to thank everyone who was interviewed for this book for giving up some of their time to talk about Amy and for trying their best to remember how things played out nearly seventeen years ago.

Thanks also to my string of editors at both *Cleveland Scene* magazine and *Free Times*, who helped teach a film nerd from Kent State the basics of reporting. Thanks Frank, Pete, Kevin, and Erich.

The Lorain *Morning Journal* and the Ashland *Times Gazette* graciously granted permission to reprint several photos in this book, as did my friend Walter Novak; Jim Mravec kindly allowed me to use his illustrations of Amy's missing earrings and shoes, which were originally published in *Cleveland Magazine*.

Mike Lewis and the employees of Confidential Investigative Services were very helpful to me, particularly in locating some hard-to-find characters.

Thank you to all the McNultys as well as Mark and Jason Mihaljevic. I hope this helps in some small way.

Special thanks to Detective Lieutenant Mark Spaetzel of the Bay Village Police Department, who spent something like ten hours being interviewed for this book. I tried to do my best to describe how passionately the Bay Village police department and the FBI pursued this case. I imagine, though, that I only touched the surface.

I'm grateful to my first-draft readers: Jenna Bates, David Claytor, Brandy Marks, Amanda Moore, David Thomas, and Julie Strebler; to Erik Esckilsen, who took the time to give this book a very detailed and helpful edit from his home in Vermont; and to Rosalie Wieder for her careful attention to detail.

David Marburger, Terry Gilbert, and Kenneth Zirm provided much-appreciated legal expertise.

Thanks to all the folks at Gray & Company, specifically Chris Andrikanich, Jane Lassar, Frank Lavallo, Rob Lucas, and Jane Wipper. And finally, thanks to David Gray, for taking a chance on this strange memoir.

If you have any information that might be helpful in this case, please call the Bay Village detectives: 440-871-0773 or the FBI: 216-522-1400.

I will update an account of the investigation as it continues on my blog at amymihaljevic.blogspot.com. I can be contacted there.

This case is solvable.

About the Author

Christopher Yohn

James Renner is freelance writer and author. His film adaptation of a Stephen King story was an official selection at the 2005 Montreal World Film Festival. He is also author of the true-crime collection *The Serial Killer's Apprentice* and a novel, *The Man from Primrose Lane*. A graduate of Kent State University, Renner lives in Akron, Ohio.

www.jamesrenner.com

OTHER BOOKS OF INTEREST . . .

The Serial Killer's Apprentice
And 12 Other True Stories of Cleveland's Most Intriguing Unsolved Crimes
James Renner

The author of *Amy: My Search for Her Killer* cracks open 13 cold cases, including the 1964 murder of Garfield Heights teen Beverly Jarosz; the mysterious suicide (or murder?) of Joseph Kupchik; and eleven other equally haunting tales. These stories venture into dark alleys and seedy strip clubs, as well as comfortable suburbs and cozy small towns, where some of the region's most horrendous crimes have occurred. Renner's unblinking eye for detail and unwavering search for the truth make this book a gripping read.

"James Renner is genuine. He cares about these victims . . . When it comes to true crime, this is the kind of writer we need." – Crime Shadow News

It Came From Ohio
True Tales of the Weird, Wild, and Unexplained
James Renner

An investigative reporter looks into 13 tales of mysterious, creepy, and unexplained events in the Buckeye State. Includes the giant, spark-emitting Loveland Frog; the bloodthirsty Melon Heads of Kirtland; the lumber-wielding Werewolf of Defiance; the Mothman of the Ohio River; the UFO that inspired "Close Encounters of the Third Kind"; and more.

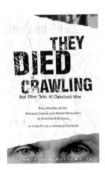

They Died Crawling
And Other Tales of Cleveland Woe
John Stark Bellamy II

The foulest crimes and worst disasters in Cleveland history are recounted in 15 incredible-but-true tales. Delves into the city's most notorious moments, from the 1916 waterworks collapse to the Cleveland Clinic fire to the sensational Sam Sheppard murder trial. These gripping narratives deliver high drama and dark comedy, heroes and villains.

"A rollicking, no-holds-barred account of the facts (and continued speculation) about some of the darkest events and weirdest people in Cleveland's history." – Youngstown Vindicator

Read samples at **www.grayco.com**

Made in the USA
Coppell, TX
20 January 2021